# LEAVING IRAN

## OUR LIVES: DIARY, MEMOIR, AND LETTERS

Social history contests the construction of the past as the story of elites —
a grand narrative dedicated to the actions of those in power. Our Lives
seeks instead to make available voices from the past that might otherwise
remain unheard. By foregrounding the experience of ordinary individuals,
the series aims to demonstrate that history is ultimately the story of our
lives, lives constituted in part by our response to the issues and events of
the era into which we are born. Many of the voices in the series thus speak
in the context of political and social events of the sort about which histor-
ians have traditionally written. What they have to say fills in the details,
creating a richly varied portrait that celebrates the concrete, allowing
broader historical settings to emerge between the lines. The series invites
materials that are engagingly written and that contribute in some way
to our understanding of the relationship between the individual and the
collective.

## SERIES TITLES

*A Very Capable Life: The Autobiography of Zarah Petri*
John Leigh Walters

*Letters from the Lost: A Memoir of Discovery*
Helen Waldstein Wilkes

*A Woman of Valour: The Biography of Marie-Louise Bouchard Labelle*
Claire Trépanier

*Man Proposes, God Disposes: Recollections of a French Pioneer*
Pierre Maturié, translated by Vivien Bosley

*Xwelíqwiya: The Life of a Stó:lō Matriarch*
Rena Point Bolton and Richard Daly

*Mission Life in Cree-Ojibwe Country: Memories of a Mother and Son*
Elizabeth Bingham Young and E. Ryerson Young, edited and with intro-
ductions by Jennifer S.H. Brown

*Rocks in the Water, Rocks in the Sun*
Vilmond Joegodson Déralciné and Paul Jackson

*The Teacher and the Superintendent: Native Schooling in the Alaskan Interior,
1904–1918*
Compiled and annotated by George E. Boulter II and Barbara Grigor-Taylor

*Leaving Iran: Between Migration and Exile*
Farideh Goldin

# LEAVING

## BETWEEN MIGRATION *and* EXILE

# IRAN

**FARIDEH GOLDIN**

**AU** PRESS

Copyright © 2015 Farideh Goldin

Published by AU Press, Athabasca University

1200, 10011 — 109 Street, Edmonton, AB T5J 3S8

doi: 10.15215/aupress/9781771991377.01

ISBN 978-1-77199-137-7 (pbk.) 978-1-77199-138-4 (pdf) 978-1-77199-137-1 (epub)

Cover and interior design by Natalie Olsen, kisscutdesign.com

Printed and bound in Canada by Friesens

Library and Archives Canada Cataloguing in Publication

Goldin, Farideh, 1953–, author

    Leaving Iran : between migration and exile / Farideh Goldin.

1. Goldin, Farideh, 1953–.   2. Goldin, Farideh, 1953– — Family.   3. Jews, Iranian — United States — Biography.   4. Iranian American women — Biography.   5. Iranians — United States — Biography.   6. Refugees — United States — Biography.   I. Title.   II. Series: Our lives (Edmonton, Alta.)

DS135.I653G654 2015        305.891'55073092        C2015-906546-1

                                                            C2015-906547-X

Assistance provided by the Government of Alberta, Alberta Media Fund.

Government

*For Norman,*
*who always believed in me.*

*For Lena, Yael, and Rachel*

# CONTENTS

## PREFATORY NOTE
*and*
## ACKNOWLEDGMENTS

This book is a work of creative non-fiction. In writing it, I have drawn from the memoir of my father, Esghel Dayanim. Portions of his memoir have been translated from Persian, shaped, and integrated into this narrative.

I would like to thank my family, friends, mentors, and editors who have guided me with their wisdom and encouraging words as I wrote this book: Alisa Dayanim, Farzad Dayanim, Freydoun Dayanim, Neli Dayanim, Rouhi Dayanim, Anita Clair Fellman, Nahid Gerstein, Megan Hall, Pamela Holway, Connor Houlihan, Carol Laibstain, Manijeh Mannani, Lesléa Newman, Princess Perry, Carolyn Rhodes, Annabel Sacks, Hal Sacks, Joyce Winslet, and Karyn Wisselink.

The distant, muffled sounds of bumping coal containers at Lambert's Point by the Elizabeth River, the freight trains rolling on their tracks on Granby Street, conjure memories of a happy childhood for my husband Norman, fun times with his father, Milton. I imagine Norman at age twelve in his father's light-green Dodge Dart waiting at a train crossing, its bells ringing.

"Son, what do the initials NS stand for?"

Putting his head outside the car window to feel the wind off the cars, screaming, "Wooo ... woo-wooooo," Norman plays along: "Norfolk-Southern." The longer the string of initials, the more fun the game.

I, too, have learned to enjoy these familiar reverberations during the twenty-some years we have lived close to downtown Norfolk. They don't take me back in time to my hometown of Shiraz, a valley in southern Iran, where there were no rivers or railroad tracks, no coal mines or coal dust. Some nights, when these muted whooshing, clanging, thumping noises sing a lullaby to Norman, I keep awake, vigilant. In my mind's eye I see the dark stains on the windowsills and imagine the invisible coal particles coating our lungs black.

A foghorn wakes me up at 4:00 a.m. just before the phone rings, or maybe I wake up from the phone call and then hear the ship announce itself. Such early phone calls often beckon Norman, a physician, to the emergency room, but he is not on call.

Maybe it is my father, who has the habit of calling in the early hours. He ignored the nine-hour time difference when he lived in Iran and Norman and I were in Stamford, Connecticut, and later the seven-hour time difference when he sought refuge in Israel and Norman and I had moved to New Orleans — but Baba has not called in a very long time.

I grab the phone.

The flat voice of Niloufar, my Israeli sister, buzzes through the receiver from across the Atlantic. She rarely makes these expensive phone calls to the United States.

"Allo, Farideh. Baba is in the hospital. Maybe one of you can come to Israel." She pauses. Then in a subdued voice she adds, "I can't manage it all by myself anymore."

MY SISTER IS a child of the Iranian Revolution; she was a refugee in Israel at age four. My family escaped Iran on one of the last El Al planes that evacuated Iranian Jews from Mehrabad airport in Tehran to Ben Gurion airport in Tel Aviv on February 4, 1979. Niloufar is my only sibling still living in Israel with our parents.

I left Iran for the United States on July 4, 1975, four years prior to the Islamic Revolution. My mother, six months pregnant with Niloufar, said goodbye to me with the longing eyes of an entrapped woman, having never had the opportunity to escape a fate planned for her by others. Maman was given away in marriage at age thirteen to a man neither she nor her parents knew and sent on a bus over the mountains to my father's hometown, Shiraz, more than a day's drive from her home in Hamedan in northwestern Iran.

I am the oldest of five siblings; Niloufar, the youngest, is twenty-two years my junior. I was finishing my senior year at Old Dominion University in 1975 and had already met Norman, my future husband, on a blind date, when Niloufar was born on September 16, 1975. We have never been together longer than a month, yet I am the one she calls.

≈

THE NIGHT BEFORE, Norman and I had had a Shabbat dinner of brisket, latkes, and homemade applesauce with friends who lived just a few blocks away. We had had a few drinks to celebrate the seventh night of Hanukah, the festival of lights that had coincided with the regular festivities of Friday night, Shabbat.

As we walked home late that night, I shivered in the cold December air. I am a desert woman. I hate cold. Norman felt exhilarated. His grandparents came to America to escape pogroms and anti-Semitism in Russia and Poland, places much colder than southern Iran. Norman's face has traces of his paternal grandmother's Russian features: defined cheekbones, fair skin, hazel eyes.

We had hoped to sleep in late.

"ALLO, FARIDEH? Are you still there?" Niloufar asks.

Awake now, my head buzzes. "When did it happen?" Whispering so as not to awaken Norman, I try to figure out the tone of my sister's voice. Exasperated? Worried? Not knowing what else to say, I ask, "Is it pneumonia?"

"How am I to know? They never tell me anything. Work has been so demanding. I just wanted to relax today. I called to excuse myself from Shabbat lunch. They weren't at home even though services were finished at the synagogue. I called Maman on her cell phone. They were already at the hospital. I'm heading there now."

MY SISTER SPEAKS in Hebrew-accented English, our common language. My first language is Persian, hers Hebrew.

A computer engineer with expertise in software design, Niloufar keeps our parents up to date with modern technology such as cell phones and Skype to contact the rest of us, the four children and eleven grandchildren who live in the United States. She taught our mother how to use e-mail and, later, Facebook. But the more gadgets and technological know-how my parents acquire, the less they keep in touch. They could have called Niloufar, but Baba, an old-fashioned Iranian patriarch, believes that his children should be the ones calling him. He often breaks his own rule when he is happy but enforces silence and demands our mother to do the same whenever he suffers from a deep depression.

Niloufar complains about this lack of communication. She lives in Tel Aviv, a short distance from our parents' apartment in Holon. After the Intifada, the Palestinian uprising in 1987, and the constant bombing of public buses, many Israelis bought cars, clogging roadways, sometimes increasing the fifteen-minute drive to our parents' apartment into an hour of nerve-racking stop-and-go traffic and impatient horn-honking. Niloufar no longer stops by Baba and Maman's apartment after work for a cup of tea and a slice of watermelon, or even for her favourite dinner of herb stew over basmati rice, *qormeh-sabzi*. Baba told Niloufar repeatedly, "If you cared, if you wanted to know what is going on with us, to know if we're living or dead, you'd call regularly, you'd stop by more often." Baba never accepted the fact that Niloufar, a young single woman, chose to to move out of their apartment to a place of her own. In my father's mind, this would have never happened in *his* Iran, where his little girl would have lived with them until they found her a suitable man to marry.

THE CURTAINS TO my bedroom balcony are open, revealing the crescent moon, *rosh khodesh*, a new month already, Tevet. My grandmother believed that upon seeing the crescent we must think of something good, look at a happy face, say something pleasant; otherwise, the entire month would be ruined.

Sobered now by my sister's news, I pull myself up and lean against the pillow.

Norman rolls over and faces me. With his eyes still closed, he asks, "What's wrong?"

"It's Neli." I use my sister's nickname. "Baba is in the hospital."

"I'M SORRY. Go back to sleep," he says. "She'll call you back." He pulls the covers over his head. "You *are* a good daughter," his voice muffled from underneath the quilt. He knows that I feel guilty about my parents' unhappiness, sense of alienation, loneliness.

THE PHONE RINGS again thirty minutes later. Norman pushes the covers aside and searches blindly for his glasses on the side table. I grab the phone.

"Baba *mord*," Niloufar says in her halting Farsi.

"What do you mean?" And she has to say it again in Farsi, and one more time in English, and that's when I believe her.

NORMAN LOST HIS father two years earlier to throat cancer. We were all by Milton's bedside during his last days, even as he said *vidui* with the rabbi and the cantor. Each one of us, his children and grandchildren, spent time alone with him as he lay on his hospital bed, knowing that the angel of death was perched by his side, watching, waiting. I kissed his hand, his forehead, and whispered in his ear, "I love you; you've been like a father to me." The cancer and a pre-op stroke

5

had paralyzed his vocal cords. He couldn't speak but nodded, tightening his grip on my hand. Courageous in the face of death, he welcomed his grandchildren to his bedside, where they put the occasional ice chip on his cracked lips. With his functioning left hand, he scribbled words of encouragement for them. "RN," he wrote to my oldest daughter Lena, who had spent the night with him at the hospital. "STOP SMOKING," he scrawled for another grandchild. "See what it did to me?" he wrote, pointing at the hole the doctors had cut in his throat to enable him to breathe.

Norman and his brother took a bottle of Glenfiddich, Milton's favourite Scotch whisky, to Norfolk General Hospital and said "*le'chaim*," to life, even though their father lay half paralyzed from a stroke and dying. On the last Friday night of his life, Milton's five children gathered around him, put their heads close to his, and asked him to bless them as he had when they were children, as he had when they were together for Shabbat.

"Bless us. Say it in your head, Dad. We can feel it."

For his funeral, members of the various organizations he belonged to, the Jewish Federation, synagogues, Hadassah, his colleagues in the medical field and his many devoted patients, filled the expansive sanctuary at Congregation Beth El. At his grave, his grandchildren helped to bury him by adding shovelfuls of dirt so that he wouldn't be buried by strangers or by a bulldozer heaping dirt on top of him.


AND NOW MY father is dead. He died without saying goodbye to any of his children, even Niloufar. He died with no one by his side but my mother.

"You've been a good daughter," Norman whispers in my ear as he hugs me. Still in bed, my shoulders shake. "I'm sorry," he adds.

"ALLO, FARIDEH?" I hear Niloufar's voice again.

"Let me talk to Maman."

"Allo?"

"Maman *joon*," I stop for a minute, crying aloud. "I'm so sorry."

"*Aay...che gerye-ee mikone*; how she cries! Don't cry."

"I'm so sorry." I repeat, the only words I can summon up in Farsi.

"So is life," she says, her voice toneless, without a trace of emotion. "Don't cry so much."

I speak to Niloufar again. "We'll be there," I say, accepting the role of the first-born child. "I'll contact everyone. Just take care of yourself and Maman." Then, worried about the two women alone at home, I add, "Let Shemuel know." Along with his bright blue eyes and perpetually tanned skin, Maman's younger brother is her only sibling with curly black hair like hers. Still single, he devotes his time to the extended family, always eager to help.

I make the first phone call to my sister Nahid in Maryland. Her family observes the rules of Shabbat, not driving or answering the phone from sunset on Friday until sunset on Saturday. Sensing an emergency, her husband picks up the phone immediately.

"May I talk with my sister?" I ask, and without the usual Iranian roundabout evasive speech, I tell Nahid, "Baba *mord*."

She says something like, "What happened?" I hear her crying.

"I don't know," I think I tell her. "Neli called me from the hospital."

"What are we going to do?"

"I would like for all of us to go to Israel together if possible. Let me call a few airlines. Let me call our brothers." I think this is what I tell her, in Persian.

STILL IN BED, Norman asks, "What can I do to help?"

"Nothing." I am my father's daughter, not accepting help readily.

"I'll look for flights," he volunteers. He is his father's son — a practical, involved man, a doer.

I CALL FARZAD even though he is the younger of my two brothers, and by custom, I should give Freydoun priority. My brothers live in the suburbs of Philadelphia, my only siblings living in adjacent neighbourhoods. My father, who never envisioned his family living anywhere but in Shiraz, preferably within walking distance of one another, was often appalled that we were scattered like sinners from the Tower of Babel, living in different countries, different states, speaking different languages.

Farzad says, "I'll walk over to Freydoun's house and let him know." His subdued voice cracks just a bit, betraying his emotions. "Did Neli call?" he asks.

"Neli called. I don't know much."

NORMAN, in the adjoining room, is on his cell phone trying to find tickets to Israel for that night. He raises his voice, "Are you telling me that you don't have any bereavement rates? The deceased is to be buried in Israel. How are we to get a death certificate?" He keeps arguing with the airline representative in a loud voice as he walks downstairs. "No, they have to leave tonight. Next week isn't acceptable." The coffee grinder muffles Norman's voice. Then the front door opens and shuts as he picks up the newspaper, all along arguing with the airline representative, multi-tasking as usual. The aroma of coffee fills the house. French roast. My stomach growls. I am disgusted with myself for feeling hunger, for craving a good cup of coffee at a time like this.

I throw the quilt aside, but before stepping out of bed I decide to call Freydoun myself, Shabbat or not. His wife picks up the phone immediately, just the way Nahid's husband had. They both have sick fathers; they are expecting the worst. We are all at that age, all waiting for the phone call.

"Baba *mord*," I tell Freydoun. There is a long silence on the other side of the wire. "Norman's trying to find tickets for all of us, but it's probably easier for you and Farzad to find tickets since you don't need a local connection. You could drive to New York and catch a direct flight. I'll have to do something else since there are no direct flights out of Norfolk," I babble in response to my brother's silence.

"Okay." I think he says without a trace of emotion. Suddenly I am worried about him and glad that Farzad is on his way.

I DON'T KNOW why I keep using the Farsi words just the way Niloufar had. We rarely speak Farsi to each other even when our American spouses are not around to be used as an excuse to forsake our mother tongue. Norman finds this habit very curious. We have tried so hard to put the past behind us, doing our best to cut off the strong arm of our Iranian culture that tightly wraps itself around us even when we feel betrayed by it. But now, in pain, we revert to our beginning, to our first language.

WHEREAS MY IRANIAN-born family often takes solace in inaction, Norman thrives on finding solutions. Disappointed by one airline, he calls another. No one has seats for four. He laughs nervously. "You're joking, right?"

Still holding the cell phone to his ear, on hold with another airline on our land line, Norman brings me a cup of coffee and explains that the airline has one seat in economy class and one in business class for $5,000. He talks to the representative. "But the sisters would like to sit next to each other." They reassure him that someone would be happy to exchange the seat in economy for the first class accommodation. Norman repeats the words to me, shaking his head. Finally, he calls the office of El-Al airlines not in New York, which he discovered is closed on Shabbat, but in Israel; seven hours ahead of us where Shabbat had already ended. He speaks in Hebrew. I understand maybe one out of five words. Sympathetic, they know — no explanation necessary — that Jews bury their dead quickly and they agree to bump other passengers for us. Norman thanks them profusely, "*toda raba*." He tells me, "What a difference!"

COMING HOME FOR the weekend, for the last day of Hanukah, my middle daughter Yael opens the door and throws her arms around me. Her long flowing curls caress my face.

"Home!" she screams. Then she notices my pajamas, unkempt hair, puffy eyes, a half-packed suitcase in the foyer.

"Baba-bozorg died." I sit on the stairs, shaking. "I don't know what to pack," pointing to the suitcase. "Sorry you've come home to this."

"I'll pack for you." She puts her arms around me. "Don't worry, Maman; I'll pack for you." My three daughters sometimes call me by the Persian word for "mother" to show extra love, but it sounds strange now since I have just used the word to speak to my own mother.

Yael kneels in front of me. "I want to go with you. I'll call work."

"No, you've got your own life. It isn't necessary." My father's lessons again. "I told Daddy not to come either. I'll be back in a week, ten days. It's going to be okay."

Norman runs downstairs to give Yael a hug. "Your mother's so stubborn," he says, turning to me, "Why don't you want us to go?"

"Please don't argue with me now — no need to interrupt your life."

They both nod; a certain look is exchanged as Norman winks at Yael. I am annoyed, jealous of this father-daughter bonding. (They both travel to Israel a few days later and accompany us to the cemetery for the customary recitation of *kaddish* following a week of sitting *shiva*.) We decide not to share the news with Rachel, our youngest daughter, who is on her honeymoon in New Zealand. Norman calls Lena, who is attending nursing school in Northern Virginia, but I don't remember my conversation with her nor the one later on with Rachel. I do remember a sense of gratitude that all my daughters had been given a last chance to see their grandfather in August at Rachel's wedding, that they had received those very last hugs and kisses, taken the very last pictures with Baba.

DURING THE ELEVEN-hour flight, the four of us sit squashed in the middle row at the back of the plane. Nahid and I whimper. Farzad takes turns holding our hands; Freydoun recites *tehillim*, once in a while pointing out a line or two, "See? This was his life. So true."

> *Wicked people rise up against me, O God, and question me of things I do not know. Instead of kindness, they curse me; they want to destroy my life. When they were sick; when they were needy; I treated them like a brother, like a mother who bends over to care for her children. But when I was in need, they turned against me; they gathered around me with joy; and they laughed at my miseries.... O God, how long are you going to watch this? Save me from these lions, save my life and my soul from their sharp teeth.*

No one awaits us at Ben Gurion Airport. Although we don't expect to be picked up, I scan the cheerful faces. When I arrived at the airport last June, Niloufar and Baba had been waiting for me, waving, screaming my name from behind the water fountain that separated the welcoming parties from the arriving passengers. Maman was at home cooking a feast.

I have always loved going to Israel in spring or early summer, when flowering trees shower the streets and the passersby with their petals — red, orange, yellow, white — the air smelling of life. This time a wintery chill swirls around us with every turn of the revolving door; the country feels cold and barren; the smell of death hangs in the air.

We can't remember our parents' new address. After much begging and cajoling, they had finally left their dingy fourth-floor apartment on Golomb Street, a poor subdivision of Holon, and moved to a sunny apartment with an elevator. At the old apartment building, returning from the market one day, my father had fallen on the third floor staircase as he carried a large watermelon. The red fleshy melon exploded, scattering its slippery seeds on the steps. My mother rushed to clean it up before the neighbours complained.

It had been the juiciest watermelon yet; my father knew how to pick the good ones. "Hear this?" he asked me once as he knocked on a watermelon with the back of his index knuckle. "Tap your chest; tap your head." He watched me as I mimicked his actions. "The sound should be somewhere between those two for the watermelon to be perfect."

Soon after, my mother fell down those same stairs while carrying a large bottle of water; a vertebrae shifted. She had been stocking up the old apartment with basic commodities. They were preparing for the possibility of a missile attack from Lebanon by Iranian-backed Hezbollah. "Iran always follows us," Baba said once, "not letting us rest."

After returning from Rachel's wedding, Maman and Baba moved to the new apartment. Worried that he would run out of money to live independently, and too proud to accept financial help from his children, Baba refused to install heating and air-conditioning. He didn't buy a satellite dish to watch his favorite Iranian channels nor did he purchase special filters for the safe room to ensure they would have more than a day's air in case of biological or chemical attacks. Instead, Baba kept the family's gas masks like trophies of an exotic trip on a shelf of the wall unit next to the pictures of his children and grandchildren.

AT THE AIRPORT, Nahid asks an agent in the money exchange kiosk for permission to use the phone to call Niloufar for our parents' address. A taxi drops us off at the unfamiliar building. Maman opens the door. In the cold apartment, Niloufar is huddled underneath a blanket, the way we had kept warm during my childhood in the *mahaleh*.

We hug our mother. She pushes me away, saying, "I was by his side at the hospital, helping him walk when he fell on top of me. We both went down. I hit my head and screamed."

Maman's first words surprise us — her adult children still in need of comfort from their mother. Why is she so defensive? What is she afraid of?

Soon the phone starts ringing. The news of Baba's death has reached family members. They call from Shiraz, from Los Angeles, from Baltimore, from New York. They speak to my mother, to my siblings. They often do not ask for me, a pariah, who has written and published a memoir about private family matters, about their mistreatment of my mother.

The phone rings again. My mother picks up, saying little, then the receiver hits the ground. Maman leans against the hallway wall; looking pale, her body shakes. We run to her. "What happened? Are you okay? Who was that?"

"It was your father's sister, your *ameh*" she finally says after we force her to drink a cup of tea with a lump of sugar, thinking that, a diabetic, her blood sugar has dropped. Maman continues in a low voice, "She asked where I was when your father died, when he was sick. She asked me what I'm going to do now that I'm all alone."

A woman alone is a woman unwatched, a woman in charge of herself, a woman unleashed. Maman trembles. A year earlier another *ameh* and this same aunt had accused my dead uncle's wife of negligence in his sickness and death.

"You don't care as much as we do," the sisters told my

uncle's heartbroken wife. "You'll find a new husband; where are we going to find another brother?"

Maman assumes that my aunts are blaming her for Baba's death.

"They think," she encompasses all my father's siblings in one voice, one call, "that I didn't take care of him. They don't know that I had to bend over to put his shoes on for him; they don't know I cleaned up after him all day. They don't know that in anger he would cough up his infection in tissue papers and throw them at me."

"Baba was angry at death, Maman," I tell her. "He was scared. Maman, he cared about your health. Why do you think he moved to this apartment, knowing that he was sick? He was thinking of you."

"And now his sisters think that I killed him." Maman's voice trails off.

"Maman, no one has said that," I try to reassure her.

Another *ameh* asked my mother, "What did my brother die of?" And then she'd repeated Maman's reply, "Lung disease? I have to lose two brothers in two years to lung disease? How can that be?" Maman is certain that a comparison was already being made between the deaths of the two brothers, and that a comparison of the two wives is soon to follow.

"Maman," I tell her, "they are not here. They can't do anything to you. They can't demand that Baba punish you. He is gone. Your children are here now. We love you. We know you did your best."

Maman doesn't cry. She lowers herself to the ground, folds her arms over her knees, and cradles her head in her arms. She hides her face, which has turned pale with fear, fear of her in-laws who live an ocean away. But in her fragile state, Maman imagines Baba's family still holding the same authority over her as they had when they inhabited the same ghetto, the same house in Shiraz. As an unwilling stranger who had arrived as a child bride to her in-laws home, my mother never had the protection of her parents who lived far away; she rarely had the support of her husband, who adored his own mother and siblings above all. She had once been at the mercy of her in-laws and although she was no longer under their control she continued to feel vulnerable and unprotected.

To justify her actions, Maman repeats the story of Baba's final day over and over. She called a taxi, leaned Baba's feverish body against hers, ignored her own back pain, and took him to the hospital. She didn't call Niloufar. "Why bother a child?" she reasoned. She didn't call me; she didn't know how to dial an overseas phone number. Baba had always been in charge of those rare phone calls.

But she didn't Skype me either. Living so far away, what could I have done?

Used to suffering alone, Maman doesn't display her grief. Baba's loyalty had always been with his mother and siblings, he had rarely protected Maman. Alone and far away from her family, my mother had learned that her tears never brought sympathy, only annoyance. She learned to swallow her hurt and grief, her tears.

I sob intermittently. My mother's eyes remain dry and vacant.


IF MY FATHER had died in Iran, his funeral would have been a community event. He often told me how members of the Jewish community had shut down their businesses and, candles in hand, marched to the cemetery behind the coffin of his father, Mola Meir Moshe Dayanim, the judge and leader of the Jewish community.

The Iranian Revolution took away more than just Baba's livelihood. He lost his good name and community position as well. Few in Israel knew that he had once been an active and generous leader.

UNCLE SHEMUEL FRIES FISH; chops parsley, tomatoes, cucumbers, and onions for a Shirazi salad; steams basmati rice and brown lentils; fries herb omelets; buys golden raisins and roasted chickpeas: all foods associated with the house of mourning. He arranges rides for us to the cemetery and volunteers to walk over to the gurney to identify the mummy-like body that had once been our father.

Holon's cemetery, where my mother's parents rest, is full. My father is not to join the immigrants and refugees from his part of the world: Iranians with curvy letters of Persian poetry on their tombstones, Russians with black slabs of marble engraved with their images, a *babushka* with a scarf around her head, a man in Russian army uniform. My father's permanent home will be a newly built distant cemetery, Ha-Yarkon, which, despite the meaning of its name, isn't so green, but looks desolate and empty. The neat rows of cemetery plots await among newly planted leafless shrubs, too young to provide shade, to hang over the graves, to hide the severity of the end. *Do the dead need company? Can we leave our father alone in such a vast empty space?*

Not sure of religious burial rules in Israel, I prepare myself emotionally for an argument if someone tells me that because of my gender I can't be present at the gravesite to bury Baba with a fistful of dirt, but I am not prepared for what follows.

None of Baba's six living siblings comes to the funeral. From his side of the family two elderly cousins, who live in Israel, attend. One, lanky and languid, his long white beard blowing in the wind, takes charge of the funeral protocol.

He walks over to my brothers and orders in Persian, "You two stay here."

When he is told about the decision, the cemetery attendant asks in Hebrew, "Why? Are they *Kohanim*?"

I understand that. Traditional Jewish law forbids the descendants of the Temple priests, who had to remain pure in order to perform the Temple rituals, to be in the presence of the dead.

The old man dismisses him curtly, "Sons may not be present at their father's grave."

The cemetery attendant shrugs his shoulders and shakes his head in disapproval and bewilderment, "*be'seder*. Okay. Whatever."

*What? Why*? I ask. Freydoun, forever a scholar of Jewish trivia, knows the reason, which he shows me later in a Jewish prayer book. Baba's cousin follows a little-known and archaic custom.

At a father's grave, the sons not born of his wasted seed appear before him. *Why didn't you give* us *a chance to be born? Why couldn't* we *be here like those to whom you gave life?* And in order not to embarrass the dead father's spirit in front of these unborn sons, my brothers are ordered to remain behind.

I did not expect my father's siblings to attend the funeral, but my own brothers? Feeling powerless and dejected, I scream at Freydoun in English, "How can you do this? How can you abandon us as we bury our father? What is wrong with you?" I am mad at Freydoun for following the rules of the elders and at Farzad for following his older brother in order not to embarrass him even though he doesn't know the reason behind the edict. I must be a strange sight, screaming like a madwoman not in my own language, not in Persian, but in English, a language few of those at the cemetery understand. *How would Baba have reacted to this archaic custom that bars his sons from burying their own father? I want my brothers to be with me, my sisters, and Maman. I want us to act like a family. Why are we allowing these distant cousins, these strangers, to make decisions for us?*

"*Che khabareh*?" my mother who doesn't speak English asks in Persian, "What's going on?"

No one answers.

"Freydoun? Farzad?" She reaches her arms towards them. "Not coming?"

Nahid puts her arm around Maman and leads her away. My mother is silent after that. She's used to others making decisions for her; she doesn't protest. Sometimes my mother accepts life's punches without wincing.

The women — my mother, my sisters, and I — follow the four elderly men carrying the stiff body of our emaciated father on the gurney, chanting in Hebrew:

> *The Lord is my shepherd, I shall not want. . . . He leads me beside the still waters to revive my spirit. . . . And I shall dwell in the House of the Lord forever.*

According to Israeli Jewish tradition, there are no coffins to hide the cruelty of death. I avoid looking at the contour of Baba's body, visible underneath a white cotton *talit* with three wide blue stripes. It cradles him like a hooded towel put on backward. It is customary for a Jewish man, especially a religious man like my father, to be buried in his own *talit*, in the garment he had wrapped himself in to pray at the synagogue. As the proprietor of the cemetery gently lays Baba's body in the grave I realize Baba is wrapped in a borrowed burial garment — we were so distraught that we had forgotten to bring Baba's *talit*. My father, skin and bones, is easy to lay down to rest like a baby.

The grave is much shallower than those I have seen in America. "Six feet under" must be an American term. The cemetery caretaker places large square pieces of stone (or are they

19

cement blocks?) on Baba's head first, then the rest of his body, slowly removing the *talit* before laying each one down, without these stones the sandy ground collapses easily in flashfloods and the bodies wash away. The unfamiliar sight appalls me. *Why does he have to remove the talit? We would have paid for it.* Nahid says that she has seen bodies of the dead dumped into graves unceremoniously. "This isn't so bad, really."

IN MY MOTHER's apartment, Freydoun covers the mirrors with wrinkled sheets; no vanity is allowed during the first seven days of *shiva*. We sit on the hard floor and do not bathe; we wear torn shirts as a sign of mourning. Baba's cousin from B'nai Barak returns to the apartment to lead *shiva*. He doesn't eat our food — not kosher enough. He orders the women to sit, only men stand to say *kaddish*. I, too, want to stand up to say *kaddish* for my father — but, obediently, I sit crossed-legged on the floor with my mother and sisters, listening to the men chant Hebrew prayers and sing sections of the *tehillim* in Persian. Women, family and friends, gossip in a mix of Persian and Hebrew as they prepare a *shiva* meal in the kitchen. Niloufar's Ashkenazi friends and co-workers watch with compassion, bewilderment and, a few secular ones, with uneasiness.

Afterwards, running his hand down his long white beard, my father's cousin puts his head close to Freydoun's, the new male head of the family, and tells him in Shirazi-accented Farsi, "These next few weeks, you've got to be very careful. The *neshoma*, the spirit of your blessed father, hovers over you." He adds, "Some say that it's beneficial to make a *kaporah*, to sacrifice a rooster, cut his head and bury it next to the grave." He rubs his long white beard like worry beads. "Just to be safe — you know — just to be safe."

It has never crossed my mind that my father's spirit would be anything but protective, the way we have all viewed our grandfather's *neshoma* to be benevolent. I want to laugh at the absurdity of the situation but cry instead because I am angry, because I am forced to bend to someone else's will.

My head hurts from the whip of three languages lashing at me, each vying to be the first spoken. I retreat to the soothing, cold, dark place of silence.

≈

THREE YEARS LATER, early June 2009, we return to Israel for Niloufar's wedding. We visit the cemetery to pay our respects to my father. I stand by Baba's grave with Norman, our daughters and son-in-law, my brothers and their families, and Nahid and her family. Niloufar is getting married a few days later so she doesn't join us; it would not be a good omen for her.

Baba had dreamt about his youngest daughter having *saro-saman*, not so much white lace and flowers, but a place of her own — even though she had already bought herself an apartment without the help of a man. Although Neli, a computer engineer, had plenty of her own *shekalim*, my father wanted her to be taken care of financially. He had also wanted his youngest daughter to have children, something Neli would never have done outside marriage even though many Israeli women have chosen to because so many men have died in the wars.

Baba would have loved seeing his five children and eleven grandchildren, together in Israel, a country he had finally accepted as his own. The last time we had all been together was on our turf, in America, for Rachel's wedding in Virginia. At no time in my father's life did we gather around him, in his home. I hope that Baba feels our presence as he lies beneath the slab of marble we had ordered, choosing the words so carefully, "A FATHER TO ALL," a painful truth for his children. We tried to keep his grave simple but dignified, the way he had lived, but eventually we added an extra piece of pillow-shaped marble to mark the spot where his head rests.

FOR MONTHS BEFORE the trip, I envisioned standing beside my father's grave, uttering the ancient words *yitgadal ve yitkadash*, honouring him with my prayers, with the words of *kaddish* that were denied to me at the time of his death.

By the time we find Baba's grave, my young nieces and nephews have already put pebbles on the headstone. Freydoun chants *tehillim* in a low voice. He has our mother's round face but our father's date-coloured, almond-shaped eyes and straight black hair. I wait for him to finish.

"Aren't we going to say *kaddish*?" I ask.

I had deferred to Freydoun during the *shiva* period because he is more observant, but really, although I hate to admit it, because he is the oldest son. Even though I am the first child, religious duties often fall on sons rather than daughters.

"We can't say *kaddish*; we don't have enough men," Freydoun says.

Including the two taxi drivers, who wait impatiently underneath the shade of a tree nearby to take my family back to Tel Aviv, and my young nephew, who has recently had his bar-mitzvah, we are short two men to make a *minyan*, the quorum of at least ten men required to say *kaddish*.

I ask my brothers to search for other mourners around the cemetery grounds. I would do it myself, but I fear that it might be inappropriate for a woman to walk around alone, asking strange men to follow me to my father's grave.

"There's no need," Freydoun says. "I already read what I could."

Turning to Farzad, I insist. "Please go. For me. Please."

Farzad's Hebrew is excellent. After escaping from Iran, he attended high school in Israel. Outgoing, he is not afraid of these strangers, they are from a land he knows well, to him they are a part of an extended family. He looks at me with our mother's hazel eyes and nods. He and Freydoun disappear behind the tall trees, which had been just small sticks when we buried our father.

The cemetery has expanded and filled rapidly since our last visit. Where do all the dead come from in such a tiny country? Israel has become a permanent motel for dead Jews from around the world, although I doubt that anyone from abroad would consider the Yarkon to be a desired resting place, worthy of an expensive and long journey. Jerusalem is the preferred choice – really, the only choice.

I wait, hot, sweating, dazed, and I wonder why strange men can say *kaddish* for my father just because of their gender and not me, his oldest child. A religious man, what would Baba say? Why do we need a gathering of ten men for God to hear our voices? Freydoun goes by the rules; I tend to break them. His wife, the wisest among us, asks the men to leave. We have a *minyan* of ten women, still breaking the rules according to some traditions, but it gives me the chance to say the mourners' prayers, and when I stumble over the tongue twisting Aramaic words, my daughters whisper them in my ears.

Nahid sits quietly on the edge of an adjacent empty grave, her long skirt draped over her legs, her big black eyes full of tears. Although she is fluent in Hebrew, Nahid doesn't utter the difficult words that she knows better than me. She doesn't break the rules. She hides her anger and hurt in long-held, devastating silences – a learned family trait – mine, too.

WE DON'T HAVE a *minyan* of ten men because we didn't invite my father's cousins to join us. What would my father say? Is it too much to expect that *kaddish* be recited at my father's graveside once a year? He had said *kaddish* for so many, among them his younger brother who died a year before him but had only daughters.

In his little Iranian/Afghani synagogue in Holon, Baba had marked and studied the *parshot*, the assigned weekly readings of the Bible, for his mother's, father's, and brother's *yahrzeits*, the anniversary of their deaths; but twenty family members do not make a *minyan* for him because we are mostly women.

Observing a loved one's *yahrzeit* is about mourning the loss anew, but more importantly, it is about remembering the dead. Baba had tried to set the example for us through his devotion to the departed members of our family. Surely, he expected us to do the same for him, to keep his memory alive. What would Baba say about this? Have we failed him? Are we going to forget his life, his achievements and his failures? Are we going to forget his story as well?

BABA GAVE ME his memoir on his last visit to the United States. I had begged him to write to keep himself busy, to keep his mind off his great loss — the loss of his Iranian life. I asked him to write about his childhood, about his father, about Jewish life during World War II in Iran, but the notebook he entrusted to me the year before his death recorded his last years in Iran. Reading it, I realized that we, both father and daughter, butted heads because we are so much alike, both stubborn, both dreamers, both humbled by our mistakes.

MY FATHER NEVER imagined that we would live far away from one another. In the summer of 1976, I struggled to convince him to let me go and start a new life in America with Norman.

Baba's filled with tears: "I'd imagined that you and your husband and your future children would come over for Shabbat, that we would have the holidays together, that your in-laws would be my family, too." He sat down in a chair, put his balding head between his callused hands, farmer's hands, and sobbed. "Where will your siblings go if you, the oldest, abandon us? Africa? Australia?" He looked at me with pleading eyes, "Iran is our home — not perfect, but it's home. We're together."

I ignored my father then. Suffocating under the patriarchal rules imposed on me by both the government (in the name of the king) and by my father (in the name of religion), I didn't wish to replace my father's control with that of a husband's authority. Even during the Shah's reign, a woman couldn't apply for a passport and an exit visa without the permission of her father or husband. Back then, I held the utopian vision of America tightly to my chest. In America I could start anew, forsake my heritage, and leave my family problems behind. In America, I imagined, I could be an independent woman. I could read uncensored books and listen to uncensored news, be an individual, a free thinker. I could choose my own spouse, be adventurous and unafraid to travel, to experience life.

ALONG WITH THE handwritten memoirs Baba gave me, I inherit his black briefcase filled with documents. After the funeral and the *shiva* period, when the visitors stop coming, the six of us, my siblings and my mother, try to clean up the apartment. We go through Baba's belongings. There isn't much. We pack his clothes to be given to charity. He wore few of the American items I gave him. My spiritual father had accumulated many *siddurim*, including a few from Iran. We each take one and leave one for our mother. I find a notebook filled with my uneven handwriting from my high school years when I attended the Iran-America Society in Shiraz. Trying to learn English, Baba made meticulous notes on its borders. My brothers and Nahid each choose a *talit* for their sons. Freydoun finds Baba's briefcase in a drawer underneath my parents' bed. We break the lock to find seemingly random collection of letters, old passports, visas, bits and pieces of papers. Freydoun adds the briefcase and its contents to the pile of old books and junk to be taken to the dumpster.

"That's mine," I grab the briefcase.

"It's of no value. What do you want this for?"

"It's the record of Baba's life. I want it — *my* inheritance."

Freydoun shrugs. He must feel the same way as I had just the previous year when I had tried to discard my father's rickety stools that he refused to let go of.

"Are you sure?" my brother asks. "You should let him rest in peace."

"I'm sure. He would have wanted me to have this briefcase and all its contents."

MY FATHER'S HANDWRITTEN notebook only covers his perilous trip from Iran to Israel and his disastrous return to Iran.

I will start the retelling of our lives with my own story, beginning with the ominous years leading up to the Iranian Revolution. We are our memory, our history, without which the present would be devoid of its rudder. I will try to portray our earlier lives in Iran, acknowledging that they are coloured by my own biased lens. Baba's story is uniquely his. I have tried to remain true to his words when translating his memoir, deleting little. I wish he had written a longer memoir, so that I wouldn't have to insert myself as the narrator, but our lives were intertwined. When I tried to sever our bond by moving to the United States, he didn't let go; when he turned away from me, I pulled him back, even if in death.

## FARIDEH

### *1975, Portsmouth, Virginia*

During my first few months in America, I refused to answer
the phone at Uncle Shapour's house. Not being able to see the
speaker's mouth, I rarely understood the caller.

One day while working in the yard with my aunt, my uncle's
American wife, the doorbell rang.

"It must be the gardener," she said. "Ask him how much we
owe him."

At the back door there stood a middle-aged black man, his
hands in front of him clasping a worn and faded brown hat.
His back is slightly hunched, making him look smaller than
he was. His posture reminded me of pictures I had seen of
Iranian peasants in the presence of the Shah, bowing to kiss
his hands, kneeling to kiss his feet. I felt uncomfortable that
this gardener, a man much older than me, was paying *me* an
elder's respect.

He spoke so humbly and without making eye contact. I didn't understand a word he said.

I asked, "Sorry, what?"

With his head still bowed, he repeated his words, but again I understood none of them.

Such a terrible situation. If I asked him one more time, the implication would be that he did not speak clearly, and who was I to suggest such an insult? He, too, probably struggled to understand my broken English. Even after years of studying English, choosing its literature as my major, reading Hemingway and Twain, *The Scarlet Letter* and *Uncle Tom's Cabin*, I had not yet trained my ears sufficiently to the nuances of America's many accents.

I went back to my aunt, who, covered in sweat and dirt, was pulling weeds and cleaning up flower beds.

"What?"

"I don't understand him."

"Go back; ask him again."

I didn't move.

"How are you going to survive college, studying English for that matter?" Sighing and shaking her head, she took off her gardening gloves and walked away. When she returned a few minutes later, I didn't ask what the gardener wanted. We both went back to gardening in silence.

Worried about surviving as a senior transfer student, I pulled the weeds out furiously, not caring about ruining my long nails that I had so meticulously polished with sparkling pink in preparation to meet America.

I RENTED A room on 49th street in Norfolk from an elderly woman, just a few blocks away from the university, so I could walk to classes at the College of Arts and Letters and to Gray's Pharmacy, which was across from the library on Hampton Boulevard. At the pharmacy I bought tuna sandwiches on white toast (drenched in a newly discovered flavour: creamy mayonnaise), mailed letters, or purchased necessities: shampoo, makeup.

I looked at hair conditioner for days, not quite knowing which one would be right for me. In Iran, there might have been two brands to choose from; in this little pharmacy, there were numerous options. I chose the cheapest one, the one that looked different from the rest and applied it to my hair that night, not knowing that it was made for afro-textured hair. Having never had any African-American friends or classmates, I had assumed that they used the same kind of hair products. That night, after washing my hair over and over to remove the greasy conditioner to no avail, I called my friend Susan with a trembling voice.

She had a hard time understanding me. "You did what?" She finally stopped laughing, apologized, and asked her mother for advice. She visited me the following day with a large box of baking soda and an old flowery kerchief that I wore for weeks.

Norman called from Charlottesville to let me know he was coming for a visit. To his surprise, I begged him not to. I didn't want to tell him what had happened to my shiny hair.

BEFORE WE WERE MARRIED, Norman took me to meet his sister during Hanukah, a minor holiday with little celebration during my years in Iran. For Hanukah, my father lit candles stuck to tiles and mumbled a few prayers. Norman's sister and her family, on the other hand, owned beautiful *chanukiahs*, one for each member of the family. They recited the prayers together with a beautiful melody that was unfamiliar to me. They sang *maoz tzur* by heart. They laughed; they ate latkes; they exchanged gifts. Hanukah was an important holiday for them.

For me, as for most Iranian Jews, Purim had much greater significance. After attending services on Purim, Baba would bring home sparklers and tell us about the fun and merry-making at his father's synagogue in the old section of the Jewish Quarter. Sometimes he would share bits and pieces of the story of Queen Esther, the heroine of Purim, who had prevented the massacre and extinction of Iranian Jewry with her courage. Both holidays share the theme of survival for the Jewish people; both celebrate heroes who endangered their lives to save their Jewish communities and to ensure the continuation of Jewish life and rituals, but, whereas, the setting for the story of Hanukah is Jerusalem, Purim happened in Iran.

I WAS STILL ASSESSING the American way of celebrating Hanukah when my sister-in-law gave me a piece of cardboard and asked, "Do you mind making a sword?"

Norman's young nephew was going to a holiday party dressed as one of the Maccabee brothers, the heroes of the holiday.

I knelt on the floor and drew an outline of the sword on the cardboard. "Not wide enough," I said.

"What do you mean?" my sister-in-law asked. "That's a big piece of cardboard."

With my index finger I drew the shape of a scimitar in the air. "Not enough room for the curve."

Norman and his sister threw themselves on the sofa and laughed hysterically. She had a King Arthur-type sword in mind, a straight blade with a cross-like handle. I stood there not knowing what to say or what was so funny.

Norman has always loved my foreignness, believing it to be spicy, fun. Smiling, he showed me how to create a "regular" sword for his nephew.

Norman and his siblings would have yelled at each other right then. They would have set the record straight, demanded an apology for the insensitive comments and forgotten about the whole affair. But Baba had instilled in me the virtues of a woman's modesty. *Don't answer back; be deferential to family members; don't raise your voice; don't argue; don't contradict people.* Most of Baba's words remain locked in my heart; although time softens their impact. These lessons have never left me. *Think before you talk; silence is golden.*

I didn't know how to tell Norman and his sister how they had hurt me so I dropped the subject and remained silent. This reticence annoys Norman. "Lighten up," he says when I brood over such incidents, often years after they have occurred. "Why do you keep things inside? Answer back. Get angry. Yelling might feel good. You don't have to be even-tempered all the time." Then he puts his arm around me. "Where is your sense of humour? You've got to learn to laugh at yourself. Life isn't always so serious."

NORMAN'S FATHER AND my uncle Shapour were colleagues, physicians in the same hospital. His youngest sister and I had been pen pals for many years. Norman and I met on a blind date shortly after I arrived in Virginia and married two years later. As soon as Norman graduated from medical school, we moved to Connecticut for his first-year internship at Stamford Hospital. Having abandoned my graduate degree in English in order to get married, I worked as an outpatient receptionist at the hospital, which catered to many famous celebrities living in Greenwich and New Haven.

I didn't regret leaving the world of books behind. In America, I had studied mostly the classics, Shakespeare and Chaucer, *Faust* and *Tess of the D'Urbervilles*. Now that reading was no longer forbidden, I couldn't connect with most of them. In Iran, literature had provided me with a badly needed escape from a claustrophobic existence. In my small world, where I rarely socialized and almost never travelled, literature helped me to paint a picture of the rest of the world, even if it was the world of Homer and Sophocles. In the United States, I needed life lessons, to know, to understand myself. Western books didn't give me a glimpse into anyone's life that was similar to mine, a foreigner struggling to fit in. I wondered what my father, who had confiscated and burned my Western novels, would have said about this lack of enthusiasm. I had left Iran to have the freedom to explore and to read. Instead, I stopped reading altogether.

THROUGHOUT THAT FIRST year of marriage in Stamford, my father called weekly, usually at three or four in the morning, to chat. It must have been the only time he could get a line to America, or maybe it was the only free time he had. Baba left for the poultry farm very early in the morning, often before five. He returned home to eat lunch, the biggest meal of the day, and to rest for a few hours around 11:00 a.m. He called me then. We didn't have a phone in our bedroom on the second floor so when it rang I would rush downstairs to pick it up. If I ignored the ring, Baba would hang up and call again.

"Wake up, Farideh. Are you awake?"

I would sit on the steps, yawning. "Yes, Baba. What's going on? Is everything okay?"

I don't remember the details of most of these phone calls. He was just keeping in touch, but every call ended with the same question, "Do you have any news for me?"

Groggily, I would answer, "*Naa*, Baba. Nothing's new." I wanted to tell him, *I have to be at work by 7:00 a.m. and I need my sleep.* I needed to be alert for my work as a receptionist. I had already received a note from the lab that read: "The word is Planned Parenthood, NOT Plant Parenthood."

Baba said, "Wake up. I know you'd like to go back to bed. I've been young, too. There's a saying that 'The heat in a newly-weds' bed can hard-boil an egg.' Wake up. I need to talk to you."

Sexuality wasn't a topic of discussion in our home in Iran. During those phone calls, when I squirmed and, embarrassed, didn't give him a straight answer, he became serious and asked: "When are you going to have a child?" As time went by the question changed, "Are you seeing a doctor for this problem?"

Those were questions that a mother asked her newly married daughter but Baba didn't believe my mother was capable of giving me adequate guidance.

ON THE DAY of my wedding, Maman gave me a heart-shaped baby-blue quilted pillowcase with a satin ribbon handle of the same colour. It took me a few minutes to figure out that it was a holder for the blood-stained virginal napkin to be hung outside the door on the wedding night.

"I didn't know what to get you," Maman said, giggling. "People said this was a nice thing."

I threw it in the garbage can in front of her. What I really wanted was the traditional wedding lace made with interwoven silk and gold threads similar to those my grandmother had given to my female cousins.

After our wedding, Norman and I took a very short honeymoon at the Tides Inn in Yorktown, returning after just two days to spend time with my parents, who were still in the United States. On our first day back, Baba whispered a bit too loudly in my mother's ear, "Ask her if she's okay. Go, ask her."

My mother walked over and asked me the question. Not quite sure what she was talking about, I said, "Yes. I'm okay." Then I realized that she was asking about my first sexual experience. A rivulet of sweat dripped down my back; I couldn't make eye contact with Baba.

Later, we were gathered in my uncle's kitchen, where there wasn't enough room for everyone to sit. I sat on Norman's lap. My father squinted his eyes, and threw his chin up, indicating that I had to get up. He thought I was being impolite, vulgar. I turned red and jumped up. Norman, who had had his arms around my waist, was clueless. "What? What happened? Are you okay?" I stood against the wall. "I'll tell you later," I hushed him.

I DIDN'T KNOW what had changed in the space of just three or four months that suddenly gave Baba the courage to discuss previously unspoken topics with me. For those persistent questions about my fertility, I always had the same answer: "There *is* no problem, Baba. We aren't ready yet."

"It isn't a good thing to use birth control for such a long time," he would advise over the phone. "You might not be able to conceive if you keep this up."

My mother rarely got on the phone to say hello. I would learn later that she was too exhausted to talk. My mother suffered from high blood pressure and her doctor had warned her that another pregnancy could be fatal. But, just as I became engaged to marry Norman she became pregnant with Niloufar. As my father pestered me about having a baby, he had a little child of his own. Running after a toddler, cooking, cleaning, and doing the laundry by hand for the extended family drained Maman.

Maybe Baba didn't think of asking Maman to pick up the phone while the expensive minutes ticked away. However, my assertive grandmother, who always demanded respect and recognition, took the black receiver to chat. I never spoke with my siblings. Maybe they were at school. I did correspond with Nahid, the only family member who wrote to me.

NORMAN BECAME RESTLESS and unhappy in his new position at Stamford Hospital. He had limited access to his wealthy patients, who did not desire to be under the care of a resident.

He decided on a residency at Charity Hospital in New Orleans. In July of 1978, we packed our brown Volkswagen Rabbit tightly with belongings we had not entrusted to movers: our Persian carpets (my dowry), the china still in gift-wrapped boxes (a wedding gift), and a few plants that we abandoned along the way.

After travelling for three days, we arrived in New Orleans in the sweltering heat. During the trip we had argued for the first time in our married lives, partly because we were exhausted from the long drive and partly because without air-conditioning the heat and humidity became more unbearable each day. Norman drove, and it was my job to read the map and point him in the right direction as we entered the city of New Orleans. Norman's father taught him how to read a map and how to carefully refold it across its creases, but I had never seen a map other than those in my geography textbooks. The numbers and letters on its borders meant nothing to me. I refolded the map by bringing two corners together, smoothing the page, then bringing the other two corners together and folding again — treating the map like the bedsheets my grandmother taught me how to fold. Norman didn't know how to fold the laundry. If I asked him for help, he rolled the sheets around his arm and threw them in the closet. "What's the point of spending so much time on them?" he would say if I complained. But he was meticulous with maps.

"Fold it correctly," he said, agitated. He stopped by the side of the road. "Let me show you."

We entered New Orleans by the Carrollton exit late at night and were shocked and alarmed to see the decaying neighbourhood around us.

"Oh, my God! Where are we?" I said.

"You are the one reading the map. Figure it out. I'm driving."

"I don't know. That's what the map said. It's so dark here.

Just keep going. Don't stop. Run the red light. Maybe we can find a gas station."

We finally found a hotel, only to discover that the National Jehovah's Witness Convention had taken over every single room in town.

"Nothing's available from Metairie to Baton Rouge," the hotel receptionist drawled his words. "Some colleges are housing people."

"What did he say?" I asked.

Norman repeated the words, eliminating the accent.

"Baton Rouge? Metairie? Where are these places?" I wanted to know. "You said we didn't need reservations."

"You could've made the reservation yourself. Why do you always expect me to take care of stuff?"

"I trusted you. You're American. I figured you'd know these things." I replied sharply out of frustration and exhaustion, mixing English words with Farsi, but with no one around to translate for him.

After hours of going from one dingy hotel to another and hearing the same explanation, Norman remembered that some friends he had made as a teenager at Camp Judea were from New Orleans. He thought they might be able to help us find a place to stay. We parked outside a phone booth on a deserted street and left the car running, Norman ready to jump in and drive away if a strange person approached us. I looked around, vigilant. Miraculously, Norman reached Susie and Avi, and they graciously invited us to their home. Norman was excited, another adventure. I was annoyed.

That night Norman chatted with our hosts about their experience at Camp Judea. Reminiscing, they laughed out loud.

"Do you remember the kitchen?" Norman had been a busboy at the camp. "The staff fried those bacon strips and shared them with us. That salty fatty taste was so fabulous; we were always hungry."

"Wasn't that a kosher kitchen?" I asked.

"Shhhhh!" Norman said.

"We had a romantic night under the stars; didn't we?" Susie said.

*What the heck!* I wanted to say. *How can you talk like this in front of me and your husband?*

But the conversation went on. This open and playful talk about sexuality was new and strange to me. Living in a place and a country where I had no history, I felt left out of the conversation about the adventures of Norman's past.

THE FOLLOWING DAY our hosts left for work; Norman reported to Charity Hospital; and I studied the ads for apartments in *The Times Picayune* that day, and the day after, and the day after that. "Sorry, it's been rented," I heard over and over, most of the time without the word "sorry." The weekend arrived and we were still staying with friends.

Every day Norman came home tired but excited about his new work and his new colleagues. Charity Hospital, a dump, a mammoth archaic building serving the poorest of the poor, needed him. *I wish I could be so enthusiastic about my day,* I thought, *meeting no one, staring at the walls and the newspaper all day long, making these fruitless phone calls.*

When Norman inquired about my day, I told him, "The same. There are no apartments for rent."

"That's impossible."

"I am telling you *it is* possible. Why didn't we rent that place we found in the paper before coming here?"

"Because that 'nice' place was right in the middle of the Carrollton neighbourhood, where you were so frightened that first night we arrived."

"Really?"

"Yes, really. Nice glossy brochures don't always tell the truth. I'm sure there are many other apartments."

To prove him wrong, I dialed the number of a rental. Rented. Norman called back and got an appointment to see that place and then another. Soon, we had back to back appointments to see places all weekend long. I should have been fuming. I should have called the anti-discrimination centre and screamed, but instead, I met with the same landlords who had rejected me. Smiling, I kept my mouth shut, allowing Norman to speak for both of us.

Norman had a good laugh about the incident, repeating it to others without being outraged. Or so I thought. My husband, the storyteller, conveyed the culture of New Orleans to his friends and family through these tidbits of our everyday life, his world filled with fun moments; his cup half full, mine half empty.

AMUSED BY MY mispronunciations, misspellings, incorrect sentences, Norman, wouldn't correct me when I said, "Thanks God," or wrote, "Thirsdays." He told me playfully how I reminded him of his Russian grandmother Fannie, who grew up without TV, listening to radio shows; who spoke English with a thick Yiddish accent, saying "vater" instead of "water." I say "tander" instead of "thunder," "kote" instead of "quote." At the time, Norman's carefree way of dismissing my fury over the overt discrimination, of teasing me about my Persian accent and my Iranian ways, irritated me. Although I loved him dearly, I resented his perfect American English that had no trace of the *shtetl* accent of his Polish and Russian immigrant grandparents. I did not realize then that his love of diversity had led him to me.

ON OUR VERY first date, Norman stood outside my uncle's door, refusing to enter until he could pronounce my name correctly.

"Fa ... Say it again." Putting his hands in his jeans pockets after shaking hands with me. "Oh, the stress is in the middle, on the second syllable, right?"

Noticing my stare, he ran his fingers through his long bangs.

"I need a haircut. I've been at the library the entire month, studying. Fa-ri-deh? Right?"

Before going out to dinner, he took me home to meet his parents, who entertained us in their library filled with books. Obviously well-read, they asked educated questions about Iran. Milton wanted to know about Iranian "howses" and how they differed from those in Virginia. Lost in his Charleston accent, I thought he was asking about "water hoses."

"Well, the 'hoses' are similar to the ones here," I replied.

With a mischievous twinkle in his eyes, the same one I would soon find in Norman's eyes, he smiled and didn't pursue the question. I learned later that as we were about to leave, he whispered to Norman, "This one is a keeper. Don't mess it up, son."

WE SETTLED INTO an old New Orleans-style row house, known as a "shotgun house" because "if one fired a bullet from the front door, it could potentially exit through the back door," as a friend explained to us. *If no one is in the way of the bullet*, I thought — an analogy that befit a crime-ridden society. I suppose, one hoped that the open back door meant that the occupant had had enough time to escape the bullet. Despite their ominous name, shotgun buildings facilitated airflow in the hot, humid summers of New Orleans, creating a natural air conditioner. Our first-floor apartment had tall ceilings and a gas heating system underneath the hardwood floors.

Having given up on my education (what can a foreigner do with a BA in English anyway?), I found a job downtown at Le Sac, selling leather goods and gifts for an Argentinean Jewish family at the Hyatt Hotel, across the street from the

Convention Center. Each morning, I rode the streetcar downtown. Sitting next to the window, I listened to the sound of its wheels rolling on the tracks. I studied the Uptown mansions with white columns against the pastel colours of the trim and stucco walls; large magnolias, their waxy leaves from fairytale books, their saucer-faced white blooms, fragrant and exotic, all rolling by like film reels in an old-fashioned movie theater, languorous and ethereal.

At 5:00, I rushed to catch the streetcar, knowing that the busy, bustling downtown would soon empty of the men in suits, ties, and black polished shoes and the women in business attire and high heels. I had experienced this transformation before, standing alone at the streetcar stop in the deserted downtown, my heart pounding, wary of anyone coming toward me, fearful of black passersby. I, too, had absorbed racism. Gucci bags and designer clothes were replaced with plastic bags and dirty rags, martinis with moonshine, Parisian perfume with the smell of unwashed bodies, stale cigarettes, and cheap liquor.

SLOWLY, NORMAN AND I came to know and love New Orleans: the music played at each corner of the French Quarter, the young African-American boys tap-dancing on Charter Street, the reverberation of the ferryboat's horn on the Charles River, the Jazz Festival and Mardi Gras, the good friends and good food, and the soulful music of the one-handed Sweet Emma, who played piano at Preservation Hall — such exotic and fabulous experiences I could never have imagined.

Keeping kosher proved to be almost impossible. Used to the large selection of kosher meats and groceries in Stamford, I was shocked to discover that kosher meats were only available at one tiny, unreasonably expensive store that required everything be preordered. We found it surprisingly easy to abandon keeping kosher in order to discover the taste of shrimp remoulade, crawfish étouffée, oyster po'boys, red beans and rice made with ham hocks, chicken jambalaya, stuffed mirliton, café-au-lait and beignets. Life was good.

Norman and I had little money even though we both worked full time. Our free time was scarce. I worked six days a week and Norman was on call every third night and every third weekend, getting little rest, sometimes working a thirty-six hour shift.

Still, we did have fun. The fabric of the city was woven by its poor, those living in the lowlands, in the 9th Ward. Its famous food and music were accessible to most people since those who created it did not fit into the upper echelon of New Orleans society. We found small neighbourhood eateries, like Bright Star and Petrosi's, and feasted on food more scrumptious than that served at the fancy restaurants we visited as tourists in later years. We soon learned how to delve into a large pile of spicy crab, splitting it with nutcrackers, lifting the meat out by hand, and depositing the shells on a copy of *The Times Picayune* that was used as tablecloth. We washed down the burning spiciness with icy longneck Dixie beer. We made great friends, including the couple who had sheltered us when we first arrived, and a few Israelis who had been attracted to the city's unique culture.

BUT AFTER THE initial period of fun and discovery in New Orleans, the intense solitude and loneliness filled me with fear. When Norman was on call, I found coming home to empty rooms unnerving. A neighbour, whose apartment we had decided not to rent, gave me the tally of crimes committed in the area, telling me that her second floor apartment would have been safer for a woman at home alone. I tried to shut her out of my mind, but her words seeped through and bits and pieces repeated in my head. The young college woman ... just down the street ... raped ... they broke in ... the window ... breasts twisted ... bruised ... down there ... torn ... hard to look at ....

During my nights alone, I left the TV on to break the silence, but the news consisted of that day's gruesome murders. Reports of female Jewish victims had a greater impact on me. I remember the story of young woman who had returned home after Shabbat dinner and was raped and killed, her body hidden underneath the bushes on a street nearby. Another woman, a Jewish medical student, was abducted soon after her friends left her at the door to her Carrollton apartment, a place we had considered renting before arriving in New Orleans. She had been raped repeatedly, then killed. The list went on.

I would eventually add familiar faces to the list of people who had been victimized: co-workers, friends. Marsha had opened her back door to put the trash out to find someone waiting for her. Hillary had left a bar to grab a pack of cigarettes from her car's glove compartment; a man attacked her, raping her in the back seat of her own car. I was shocked to find out that there were so many sexual assaults in a sexually open society — I didn't know then that rape was about power and not sex. My morbid curiosity about such awful news kept me up half the night.

Similar to other first-floor buildings in the area, our apartment had all the necessary safety features: double deadbolt locks on the front door and the back door, which opened to a private backyard. Because we had bars on all the windows, I kept a key to the back door next to our bed so that we could escape in case of fire. Still, the grills did not extend to the top of the windows, and I worried about that small space that could be reached with a ladder even though only a child's small frame could enter it. We had chosen this place because of its traditional New Orleans architecture, high ceilings and tall windows, but our charming one-bedroom apartment turned into a prison during those long lonely nights.

The uptown neighbourhoods of New Orleans were often referred to as a checkerboard, a mixture of beautiful mansions and shacks, remnants of the city's history of slavery. And although these houses stood next to one another, there was a clear division between the poverty of the black community and the wealth and privilege of the white community in New Orleans. When I turned on the TV to watch the news, there were always lurid stories of black men charged with robbery and theft and mugshots of black men accused of rape and murder. The hard, blank expressions in those pictures stared out at me from the TV screen. The newspaper reported on random shootings of whites by black people; cases where whites were shot while standing in line at a restaurant, or sitting on their porches on a hot summer day.

I became strangely conscious of my whiteness even though I was a foreigner. There seemed to be only two kinds of people in New Orleans, two colours: black and white. I was white on the outside, and when I spoke with heavily accented English, very black to those who hated minorities and outsiders. At the time, I didn't know that much of the violence in the city was also victimizing African-Americans. I didn't know that the media was racist and that it chose to report only some of the race-related violence in the city. *Was this indeed the reality of New Orleans?* I internalized both the fear and the racist messages.

I found it difficult to accept that criminals would just break into homes, abduct people off the street, rape and kill women. Not in my America. How could there be such lawlessness in a country I had struggled so hard to escape to? I had been incensed by sexual remarks and molestation on the streets of Shiraz, but the shocking crimes in New Orleans compelled me to reassess my utopian vision of America, the land of equality and justice for all.

I COULDN'T HELP but compare New Orleans to Shiraz. The Iranian government had "protected" the public by censoring the news, "shielding" us from reports on criminal activities. I was in my early teens when I heard about the existence of crime for the first time. One of my father's employees in the poultry farm hit another man on the head with a hammer, killing him instantly. Yet, this did not appear in the newspaper. I overheard my father discussing the situation with his brother Morad, the fear apparent in their hushed voices: "... criminal, unbelievable. Who could have imagined that? What should we do? Do we have to testify, to account for this since it was on our property?"

Once I overheard my father speak of his disgust after witnessing a public execution. Baba described passing by Karim Khan Prison, once the palace of a just king, when he saw a large group of people assembling for a public hanging. The bodies, lined up on scaffolds, fell thrashing like hooked fish pulled from water. A few spectators jeered, a few looked aroused, euphoric, but others, probably family members, cried.

That story certainly alerted me to violence in my city, but whatever their crimes, I convinced myself that violence was something that happened in faraway neighborhoods, places my parents had forbidden me to venture. Violence was a demon lurking among those who were less ethical, those without a religious upbringing. Maybe these criminals were hashish dealers, I speculated; maybe they were political mutineers that our teachers had warned us to avoid. My family did not discuss political or social issues, and I was discouraged from examining such things, so I looked for a rationale for these crimes that fit what I understood about the world. I was comforted by my conclusions; they helped to push away my fears.

Perhaps the authorities in Iran didn't report criminal activities because they feared people would panic, as I was about to in New Orleans. In Iran, although my family shielded me from the terrible news, they could not help but communicate their feelings of insecurity.

In a way the fears that controlled parts of my life in New Orleans had been transmitted to and embedded in my consciousness by my grandmother, my mother, and my aunts during my childhood in the *mahaleh*. I had seen and felt the fear in these jumpy, anxious women when at home alone at night, their body language a testimonial to their inability to protect themselves or their offspring.

IN 1958, my mother, age twenty, had two daughters. I was five, my sister, Nahid, was one. My grandmother, two aunts, and Uncle Morad lived with us. My father and his brother, like many other Jewish men, had a *zargari*, working with gold and silver. If luck brought them a commission for a gold and baby pearl bracelet, a necklace, or other jewellery for an upcoming wedding, they worked late into the night.

Our house, just a block inside the gate to the *mahaleh*, the Jewish quarter of Shiraz, had a long corridor that connected the front door to what we called the *matpach*, a kitchen with mud stoves, a deep well, and no windows. The bathroom, a small dark room with a hole in the floor, stood adjacent to the kitchen. A large orchard of orange trees, a side business, separated that part of the house from the main building, a small house with two ground floor rooms used mostly for storage and housework (cleaning rice, herbs, and washing clothes) and two rooms on top of the stairs, our living and sleeping space. The garden, a soothing place during the day, where I played, fed the sparrows breadcrumbs, and watered the flowers, was transformed at night into an ominous black void. During gloomy long winter nights, the household sat in darkness; a lonely light bulb dangling from the ceiling of our common living area cast an amber glow. While the men worked, the women, who felt vulnerable without their protection, broke the silence with hushed exchange of just necessary words. The crackling of charcoal in the brazier, the whoosh of a knife slicing vegetables, the gentle click of knitting needles were loud, intrusive sounds. We feared going into the kitchen at night, but my mother worked in there by herself some nights, cooking and transporting food and water across the yard, up the stairs, and into the living area. Maman left a portable potty on the landing at top of the steps for me because I refused to cross the yard to the bathroom. Some nights, carrying an oil-burning lantern to find her way to the outhouse, Maman was a dot of light in the darkness, disappearing for a short heart-wrenching time behind a branch, then slowly making her way back. Sometimes on colder nights, my grandmother filled a pot with hot water from the samovar, set it on a coal-burning brazier, threw in a fish, caramelized onions, and as soon as our men arrived, a beaten egg. Underneath the coals she hid a few little potatoes, burnt crisp on the outside, steamy and fleshy inside. During Ashura, mourning the martyrdom of Imam Hussein and Imam Hassan, Muslim men paraded through the streets just outside the gates of the *mahaleh*, beating themselves with a cluster of chains tied to wooden handles to express their sorrow at the murder of the Shia Imams. We sealed ourselves in the upstairs room on those nights, waiting for our men, fearing for their lives and ours. What if the mourning frenzy got out of hand? What if a gang of zealots somehow blamed the Jews for crimes we had not committed? What if they roused other troublemakers and attacked the *mahaleh,* as they had once done when my father was a child? Baba told me the story of that attack, as had my grandmother. What if?

Unidentified sounds, maybe the wind whistling through the bare branches of orange trees, maybe a neighbourhood woman screaming at a child, jolted everyone. Could it be robbers stealing our kitchen utensils? Were they going to hurt us as well? We were so afraid that my father and uncle trained a ferocious dog to roam the yard at night. One night, in its boredom, the dog attacked the pillows in the basement. The pillows were stuffed with feathers that my mother had painstakingly cleaned, washed, and dried in the sun. In the morning, the orange trees appeared to have grown feathers: white, orange, and black. After that, fearful of the dog who responded obediently only to our men, we begged them to take it away.

IN NEW ORLEANS, more than two decades after I left the *mahaleh*, I didn't have to worry about an attack by fundamentalists on the Jewish quarter, something my father and grandparents had experienced and still so feared its reoccurrence that they warned us to be vigilant. But I was a woman alone at home without a man's protection, experiencing the same helplessness of my fear-filled childhood. In Iran, my family had tried to keep me within the walls of our house; in America, I voluntarily limited my mobility. Double-bolting the front and back doors, setting a piece of furniture behind the door to the bedroom, I slept fitfully in the living room with a kitchen knife underneath my pillow.

DURING THE TWENTY-three years of my life in Iran, I had never been alone. When we moved out of the *mahaleh* to a "nice" neighbourhood, my many aunts, uncles, and cousins visited often, filling the house with noise and drama. Because my grandmother, the elder of the family, lived with us, our house was a regular meeting place. My male cousins chased one another in the backyard during the late afternoons of summer days; my female cousins joined the gossip circle with their mothers and grandmother. My mother ran in and out of the kitchen carrying china plates, their delicate red rose design concealed beneath the black and ivory shells of roasted watermelon and pumpkin seeds. She brought back clean plates, offering leaves of romaine lettuce to be dipped in sweet *sekanjebin* syrup or *torshi* of pickled green apples, unripe plums, almonds, and eggplant. One of the women refreshed the waterpipe, changing the water at its base, adding new home-cured tobacco, swirling the coal in a basket with a long handle overhead like a cowboy's whip to get the coals red-hot before stacking them over the tobacco in the crown of the waterpipe. Although I enjoyed these visits I craved a quiet, private place for my own family — just for me, my parents, and my siblings.

Now married and living in my promised land, in a quiet, private place of my own, I feared the outside even more than I had my childhood garden of orange trees, their limbs stretched toward darkness.

≈

BUSY WITH THE move to New Orleans, adjusting to a new environment, trying to overcome my worries and insecurity, I had been almost oblivious to the worsening political situation in Iran. I had tried numerous times unsuccessfully to get a line. Letters took weeks or sometimes a month to reach my family.

Baba called from Iran about three weeks after we had moved, sometime near the end of July 1978.

"Everything's okay. Nahid's coming for a visit," he said, and gave me the flight information.

I felt a great sense of relief. I wouldn't be alone any more. My father had encouraged Nahid, a medical student, to visit because life was becoming difficult in Shiraz. Jewish students feared attending classes since the anti-Shah propaganda sometimes became anti-Semitic. Then, the schools shut down. Nahid would spend two months with us, returning to Iran in late September.

On August 19, 1978, Cinema Rex in Abadan, filled with civilians trying to escape the unbearable heat of the city, was set on fire. Since all its doors were locked from the outside, no one escaped. The followers of the exiled cleric, Ayatollah Khomeini, the Shah's nemesis, blamed the king, which, in turn, blamed the agitators. The news didn't make a big splash in the media in New Orleans and Baba dismissed my inquiries over the phone, denying that there were any serious problems.

Then, on September 8, 1978, Black Friday, a group of untrained, unprepared soldiers, responded to gunshots from a few demonstrators by opening fire on the largely peaceful demonstration in Jaleh Square in Tehran. According to the government, the soldiers killed tens of protestors, but Khomeini declared the number of dead to be 4,000. He blamed the Zionists for the bloodshed and spread rumors that Israeli troops had committed the alleged massacre. By aligning the Shah with the Jews and Zionists, Khomeini cleverly portrayed the Shah as an outsider, an enemy of Islam. The Shah lost control of the country.

I wasn't following international coverage of Iran so I didn't hear of the massacre for several days. I didn't know then that that event would seal the Shah's fate, and my family's fate along with it.

≈

NAHID AND I took the streetcar downtown to Le Sac at the Hyatt Hotel. My employers didn't mind her presence and they paid her for her time. The flow of shoppers at the hotel corresponded with events held across the street at the Superdome.

Sometimes, there would be long periods of total inactivity when the cash register remained empty. Before Nahid's arrival, I filled these long hours of boredom at work with dusting ostrich-skin purses, cleaning, and rearranging imported leather shoes, but never considered reading a book. America had paralyzed my passion for reading. After her arrival, while the store was quiet, Nahid and I chatted and giggled like two young girls, like the old days when we shared a bedroom in Shiraz.

Other times, there would be a tremendous rush of people stopping by the store before heading to the Superdome. On September 15, 1978, before Mohammed Ali's boxing match against Leon Spinks, hundreds of boxing fans tried to jam into the tiny shop, eager to spend their gambling cash, to buy anything and everything. Laughing and drunk, customers spent thousands of dollars on leather and imported goods in the hours before the match: "Give me this; give me that." They bought without looking at the price tags, throwing hundred-dollar bills on the counter without counting, sometimes not waiting for the change. (Let the good times roll!) I called the owners of the shop: "There's too much cash here. You must come over."

Excited, they gave us a bonus. "Go home. You worked hard."

Nahid and I walked to the streetcar, reminding each other of each crazy customer, laughing.

Norman had gone to see the match and he told us later that the crowd was even more unruly inside.

"A tall blonde walked onto the stage," he recounted, "and dropped her full length black mink coat."

Norman couldn't remember the colour of the high heels she wore, even though they were the only piece of clothing she had left on.

He told us that the governor, Edwin Edwards had stood up alongside the other fans, whistling, jeering, and booing a policeman who tried to cover the blonde woman up with his own coat.

Nahid's eyes grew bigger as she listened. The striking contrast between the woman's shameless nakedness and the strict rules being imposed on women regarding modesty and attire during the revolutionary mayhem in Iran must have been astonishing to my sister. What a difference a day's travel could make!

"You've brought me to such a wild place," I told Norman. "I'd never imagined a place like this."

ON THE NIGHTS or weekends that Norman was at home, we went to the French Quarter to explore New Orleans. When I worked on Saturdays, Norman took Nahid out for a bike ride or to visit friends. But when Norman slept at Charity Hospital, my sister and I barricaded ourselves in the dark living room, away from the bedroom windows, and chatted in hushed voices. Nahid had always known me as the bossy big sister, the one who had defied our parents and family by coming to America and marrying a man of her own choosing. However, Nahid soon learned about her big sister's insecurities, my fear of being home alone at night. We cuddled on the sofa bed in the living room and talked late into the night, ready to bolt out the front door if someone broke into the apartment.

I couldn't see Nahid's big black eyes and long eyelashes on those dark evenings. We spoke with our eyes closed, hovering somewhere between sleep and alertness. Sometimes we laughed as we chatted about family skirmishes. She told me about her friends, her private life, what was keeping her in Iran despite her fears. Sometimes we spoke about serious matters. Nahid told me how our parents were coping in the face of so much uncertainty in Iran. She described how she often heard Maman mumbling her dissatisfaction to herself, cursing those who did injustice to her. Nahid worried that without the support of friends and family our mother's mental and physical health might deteriorate quickly.

Nahid learned about the violent thunderstorms that exploded over New Orleans when afternoon humidity reached one hundred percent. From her, I learned about the political storm hovering over the star-studded Iranian sky. She told me about the political situation, which had dramatically worsened since I had left three years earlier, but which she described as "tolerable." My family members were virtual prisoners in their home, afraid of the streets.

I asked about our little sister Niloufar. She was born after I left Iran and came to my wedding as a two-year-old, crying, clinging to our parents. We sedated her with a low dose of Valium, so that my parents could walk me down the aisle, but soon she was awake and stealing the show. A happy child with a perpetual twinkle in her eyes, Niloufar loved to sing, to ride her tricycle around the walled backyard, and to help our mother with the laundry, but, like the rest of the family, she almost never left the house.

Nahid told me that the streets were hostile, the schools political and anti-Semitic, and that my brothers, eighteen-year-old Freydoun and fifteen-year-old Farzad, also stayed at home most of the time or went to the poultry farm with Baba. As always, my father drowned himself in work.

As my sister told me about the situation in Iran, I realized that my father and I were both dreamers. In Iran, I had escaped reality by living in the world of fiction. Baba escaped the political reality in Iran by creating a fictional world, an imaginary paradise inside the walled borders of his poultry farm and its adjacent apricot orchard.

The information jolted me, exacerbating my worries. What would become of my parents, my siblings? Why would they stay in a such a frightening place? Why did my father tell me that everything would be fine?

I called him. "Don't worry," Baba said. "This shall pass, too. Everything's okay."

TWO YEARS EARLIER, when my father had tried to keep me in Iran and marry me off to someone with deep roots in Shiraz, I had begged Baba to collect the fortune he had invested in his poultry farm and establish a foothold in the west. I told him about the unrest at the university and the hostilities I felt on the streets.

"Since when do Jews attach themselves to the land?" I asked him. "We're wanderers."

"This disturbance will pass." Baba tried to reassure me or maybe himself. "The big question is why you don't have a sense of loyalty to us, to this land? Why do you want to become a wanderer with no homeland or family, a solitary woman among strangers?"

"Leave. Please get your money out," I said. "Instead of trying to keep me here, you should think of loosening your bonds to this land."

"I haven't whitened my beard in a flour mill," Baba said, spicing up his speech with a proverb. "I've seen this before. This time it shall pass as well. Don't worry. America won't let the Shah fall."

≈

NAHID WAS A medical student. And as always, the first sign of a power struggle appeared at the medical school, just a few blocks away from our house in Shiraz.

In the 1960s, my Aunt Sholeh, a medical student, found herself in the midst of a showdown between the clergy and the Shah's soldiers at the university. We were all at home, peeking through the window, waiting, worried about Sholeh, when someone shouted from the street, "Keep inside, away from the

53

windows." Loud pops, like firecrackers during Purim celebrations, shook the glass pane of the windows. The sound vibrated the clotheslines and reverberated off the terrace roofs and returned muffled. We jumped when someone knocked hard on the metal front door.

"Police!"

We were afraid to open the door. *What did they want? Was this really the police?* We heard Aunt Sholeh's voice from behind the metal door, "It's me. Open the door." My mother opened it a crack; my fashionable aunt entered, wrapped in a black *chador* for safety.

Women's presence at the medical school and their *be-hejabi* — their lack of full body covering — became the first agenda for the religious fanatics of 1960, their first target during any uprising. In 1978, the medical school was attacked again. A sympathetic teacher locked the women in the morgue, among the dead, to save them from the attacking mullahs.

Overlooking the continued turmoil in Iran, Norman and I enthusiastically watched the events leading to the peace negotiations between Anwar Sadat, Menachem Begin, and Jimmy Carter at Camp David. Nahid left New Orleans to continue her third year of medical school just before the treaty was signed on September 17, 1978.

I had begged her, "Don't go. Stay. I need you. This isn't a good time to return to Iran."

Norman insisted as well. "Our home is your home. Your sister needs you. Don't go."

My father called. "Convince Nahid to stay in America."

But my sister had to go back. She had left her heart in Shiraz. We kissed; we hugged; we cried. I would next see her in Israel, a refugee.

ON OCTOBER 3, 1978, under pressure from the Iranian government, Iraq banned Ayatollah Khomeini's political activities in

Najaf. On October 10th, his arrival in Paris marked the beginning of a courtship with the western media that publicized his anti-Shah sentiments. His followers in Iran set fire to the British embassy and other buildings in Tehran. Chaos ruled key cities in Iran.

AFTER MY SISTER left, I felt lonesome at the small shop, so I found a position at Adler's, a prestigious jewellery store. Selling gold, silver, and jewels intrigued me, although mostly we needed the money. I bought books describing precious stones, including one on the jewels of the Persian court. I had seen many of these jewels in the vaults of Bank Meli in Tehran during a college tour: fist-size emeralds and rubies and strands of pearls poured over jewel-studded trunks. They were a remembrance of another era, of the conquest and looting of India by Nader Shah.

Adler's was located at a shopping centre in Metairie. On the way to work one day, I had my first automobile accident in the United States. As I tried to cross Claiborne Avenue during rush hour, a shriveled woman with grey hair and trembling hands, barely visible above her steering wheel, hit my brown VW Rabbit on the passenger side. A portly middle-aged policeman arrived. He saw that I was shaking and crying, and, at first, he was very sympathetic.

"Lady, are you okay? Can you talk?" he said, resting his pale hand on the driver's seat.

"She ran the stop sign," I said in my accented English.

The policeman stared at me for a second. His blue eyes became icy. He turned around and walked toward the old woman. Our cars had only minor damage. The woman had rolled onto the main street very slowly; I had slammed on my brakes. The policeman helped her back into the car and stopped the traffic so that she could cross. Then he walked back to me, his skin pasty, his nose bulbous.

"Change your residency to Louisiana. If I see you driving this car again with a Virginia license plate," he shook his chubby index finger at me, "I promise you'll be put in jail." He threw a no-fault ticket in the car and ordered, "Get the hell out of here! You're blocking the road." His right hand rested on his gun. My hands, dark in comparison to his, shook uncontrollably.

I called Norman from work. "The car is registered under your name. You MUST change the licence plate or I'll go to jail."

"No one goes to jail for an out-of-state licence plate. Really, silly. You are afraid of anyone in uniform," he said.

*Not fair*, I thought. Still, it was true, I did fear "anyone in uniform." My father had insisted that especially as Jews we had to avoid confrontations with the authorities.

I knew that Norman, too, had similar fears. On our long journey from Stamford to New Orleans, we had passed through Mississippi. On a stretch of two-lane divided highway, a policeman had stopped traffic, approaching each car with a collection box in hand, asking each driver for a donation to some kind of charity. Norman and I looked for cash in my purse, in his pockets.

"You don't challenge a Southern cop — not in Mississippi — definitely not in Mississippi," Norman said. "Don't say anything; just smile." He chatted amicably with the jolly white cop, adding "Sir" to each sentence when the cop asked about our licence plate, and our destination.

"I thought Virginia was neutral ground between the South and the North," I said.

"Not quite," Norman replied. "The Civil War is still going on here."

After my accident, I refused to drive in New Orleans with a Virginia plate and there was no public transportation to the suburbs. Norman took half a day off to visit the DMV.

ADLER'S JEWELLERS HIRED many salespeople to work on commission only. Men sold the most. Sometimes, customers lined up for a man to serve them while the women stood idle. My accent, however, helped me to sell gold chains, as if the allure of eighteen-karat gold was connected to my foreignness. Knowing the markup, I allowed bargaining. My boss didn't approve of these bazaar-like interactions, but he liked the results.

Salespeople were allowed to model a piece of jewellery for the day. One night I wore a stunning five-carat deep green emerald ring in a nest of pavé diamonds. A woman with no makeup, wearing a calico kerchief around her grey hair, entered with two men on either side of her. She approached me as I stood behind the display cabinet, waiting for customers. My co-workers walked away, assuming there was no need to waste one's time on a poor customer browsing for fun.

"That's a beautiful ring," she said.

Feeling sorry for her, I stretched my hand toward her, "Yes, it is. Not mine, of course. I'm just displaying it."

"Can I try it on?"

I checked the security around the shop. "Sure." I took the ring off. She slid it on. No nail polish, cuticles grown ragged. Definitely not the buying type.

"I was just looking for one of those spinner rings," she said.

*Of course*, I thought, *Just her style to wear a tacky ring*. I looked around the crowded store at the holiday shoppers. Others were busy selling. *Why me?*

I hadn't sold a single piece of jewellery all day. The lone serious customer I had helped before lunch had said politely, "Let me think about it." When I returned from lunch, another salesman was completing the transaction, but I was too shy to ask for my half of the commission.

I took the emerald ring back from my plain customer and handed her the spinner ring. She played with it, smiling, and showed it off to the unsmiling men.

"Okay," she said. "I'll take both."

Surprised, I took her American Express card to the back of the store for the credit check. She was part owner of an electric company. The other salesmen looked at me with envy. What a great night!

Unlike her, most of my customers were fancy ladies from oil-rich Houston. They visited the shop wearing full-length mink coats in the mild winters of New Orleans. Once in a while they patted their powdered foreheads with linen napkins, wiping away the beads of sweat forming on their hairline, but they kept their coats on. Men clad in silk suits came in search of Rolex watches with custom-made gold nugget bands. On good days, during the Christmas season, cash rained down on us like the city's afternoon thunderstorms.

I WAS GETTING comfortable in my new job; the commission from Christmas sales promised a vacation. In the first week of January 1979, when the New Orleans police went on strike, the tourists, fearful of uncontrolled crime, didn't arrive. New Orleans had its wildest Mardi Gras ever. In the absence of huge crowds, Norman and I managed to walk to the French Quarter. Fabulously dressed figures marched up to a raised podium, turned around, bowed and walked down. The crowd cheered.

"Wow! Such gorgeous women; such magnificent costumes!" I said.

"Silly. They're men," Norman said as he clapped and whistled with the crowd.

I was speechless. He pointed to a balcony where two young women screamed to men on the street below, "Throw me something, mister."

Men, sweaty, wobbly on their feet, twirled beads like lassos, "Show me something," they cajoled.

Women, eyes glazed, shrieking in delight, pulled up their shirts, exposing their breasts. They caught the colourful necklaces, yellow, purple, orange, and pulled them over their heads.

Norman pointed to another balcony where a man and a woman, or perhaps a man and a man were having sex. Having grown up in a puritanical society, I walked around in a daze, refusing to let go of Norman's arm for a second, fearing that I might get lost in the crazy crowd. I was embarrassed by the open display of sexuality around me, yet I was having the time of my life. Such a guilty pleasure! No doubt my father would have described the scene as something out of Sodom and Gomorrah. I could picture Baba pointing his index finger at me: "I raised you better."

After our wedding, Norman and I had taken Baba to the Virginia Beach oceanfront. When he saw the women in tiny bikinis, he turned his head. "Promise me that you'll never adopt this American lifestyle."

*What would my father say if he saw me walking through the wild crowd at Mardi Gras?*

A muscular man walked by in a black leather bodysuit that covered all of him except his behind. "My ass is mine, but I'll share today," were the words printed on his skin. He turned around. Observing my stare and open mouth, he winked at Norman with a smile. I giggled.

"Not funny," Norman said.

"Oh, that was so funny." I kept on laughing. Then I saw eight legs in tan leotards, carrying a gigantic dripping plastic penis. Baba's figure hovered over me, his eyebrows pulled together in disapproval. I pushed him away.

"Would you like another drink?" Norman asked as we passed Pat O'Brien's bar. A water fountain inside its courtyard spewed fire and water.

"What is the pinkish red thing in that tall glass?"

"Rum and passion fruit juice."

"That's what I want."

"Be careful." Norman said. "It might taste like lemonade but it's got a lot of alcohol."

It was too late. I had chugged most of my Hurricane. The sweet taste of New Orleans. A few hours later, Norman held my hair back as I knelt by the toilet, heaving.

ON JANUARY 16, 1979, following months of continued and intense protest by his opponents, the Shah and his family fled Iran. On February 1, the king's longtime nemesis, Ayatollah Khomeini, returned to Iran. I couldn't get ahold of my family. Baba called a few days later.

"Allo, Farideh."

"Baba? What's going on? Are you okay? I've been so worried about you. Why don't you …."

"Farideh, stop. It's been a bad month. We're in Israel, staying with your mother's mother." Baba replaced the words "your grandmother" with "your mother's mother" in order to distance himself from my mother's side of the family, whom he disliked, although he rarely saw them.

My mother's family was from Hamedan. They moved to Tehran when they could no longer bear the intense anti-Semitism, but the capital wasn't much better. Living in a poor neighbourhood, they were constantly harassed. Uncle Shemuel had run through narrow alleyways as the neighbourhood boys closed in on him, trying to cut off his ear with a dull knife. He still bears the scar.

Hearing my father's voice, I sat down, relieved but horrified. How could it be that they were experiencing devastation and displacement at the same moment that I was walking in the French Quarter gawking at half-nude people parading down the street.

"I'll be there as soon as possible," I told Baba.

"You don't need to come. Just see if you can get your brothers out of here." He paused for just a second, "and your cousins, too."

"I'll be there," I repeated.

"I don't want you to come," he said more emphatically. "Arrange for your brothers and cousins to come to America."

Ignoring him, I asked "What is Maman-bozorg's address?"

I emptied our savings account, bought a ticket to visit Israel, took a month off, and left Norman for the first time in our married life. Norman wasn't happy, but he understood.

"I feel bad that your first visit to Israel is a sad one." Norman had studied at the Hebrew University after graduating from high school and he remembered the country with fondness. "I'd always imagined showing you around Israel myself," he added.

I didn't know what awaited me in Israel or if I could help my family. *I will find a way*, I thought. *I will find a way to help them.* At the same time Baba's voice echoed in my head, "Don't come." *Why didn't he want me there?*

## FARIDEH
### *February 1979, Israel, Kiriat Sharet*

On the long flight to Israel, I went over my family's predicament in my head. They should have moved to Israel when the political situation didn't demand such drastic action. Now they were forced to leave everything behind, become refugees, and depend on others to take them in.

During his first trip to Israel in 1963, when he was struggling financially, Baba had considered making *aliyah*, a Hebrew word meaning ascent. I was in fourth grade at the time and my family was living off the money we collected from an American couple who had rented the second floor of our house. That year Baba, leaving my pregnant mother behind, took Nahid to Israel for orthopedic surgery. But we knew that he was also checking out the country for possible immigration. He returned six months later when Farzad was two weeks old; Baba was delighted to have another son.

The family had decided to break the eight-day rule of Jewish circumcision so that Baba could attend his son's *brit-milah*. When Baba opened the door, the extended family rushed to greet him. It was the only time I ever saw Baba kiss my mother. My father hugged and kissed all the cousins who had passed me to greet him, as if Baba were *their* father and not mine, not *ours*, his children. I stood in the back until he finally beckoned me over for a hug.

With his last bit of money, Baba had bought two boxes of Israeli chocolates for the extended family, thin creamy rectangles wrapped in shiny colourful paper. What I had mostly known as chocolate had been the sugary, sticky water taffy — not the silky sweetness of Israeli chocolate, which, in that moment, represented the hope of a kinder world elsewhere. *Life is better in Israel,* I thought. *We'll live there as a family — just us — Baba, Maman, me, Nahid, Freydoun, and baby Farzad.*

During the ensuing festivity, aunts, uncles, and cousins gathered around Baba to hear his stories. I retreated to the room my parents shared with my sister, brothers, and me and snuck the tiny chocolate squares, wrapped in green, yellow, red, and black, out of their boxes, one at a time, undressing them to their naked brown flesh. I savoured them slowly and languidly, letting each one melt on my tongue until they were all gone.

Then I returned to join the circle around Baba, who was telling stories about the wonders of Israel, where a factory could produce many chickens and eggs.

"Go get the chocolate," he asked me.

I brought back the empty boxes. "There is no chocolate left."

"The kids must have eaten them." He meant all the cousins.

The taste of chocolate still coating my tongue, I dreamt of leaving Iran. My father, still a young man of just thirty-seven — a reasonable age to start a new adventure — told the family about his plans to open a poultry farm in Shiraz. It was clear we were not making *aliyah* after all. Running my tongue over my teeth to taste the last remaining sweetness, I promised myself: *I'll keep the spark alive. I'll leave one day — by myself.*

SHIRAZ SUFFERED FROM a dire shortage of poultry and eggs. Farming families raised hens in their backyards and took the eggs to food stands early in the morning. The unreliable supply didn't meet the city's growing demand. Baba thought that the mass production he had seen in Israel would solve the problem. Over the next several years he investigated the possibility. While still working as a goldsmith on the outskirts of the *mahaleh*, he experimented with hatching chicks at home. At first, he and Morad transformed our living room into a hatchery. They rolled up the Persian carpet with designs of green and blue paisley and moved it to another room. Out went the green sofa and the coffee table. In came the incubators, eggs, and space-heaters to keep them warm.

One winter night, my father stormed into each room in his striped pajama bottoms and bare chest. "Wake up, wake up. Get out of here. Go outside." The kerosene-operated heaters had malfunctioned and the house had filled up with thick greasy smoke. My mother, grandmother, aunts, siblings, and cousins stood in the walled yard, shivering, as Baba and my uncles opened the windows and aired out the house. Even with the mishap, the chicks hatched, but the eggs were the wrong kind with double yolks. Chicks were not meant to be twins. One by one they poked their little heads out of their joint shells, looking pitiful and slimy. Every single one died. We, the children, were devastated emotionally and my father and uncle financially.

Still ambitious and hopeful, Baba drew sketches of the cages he had seen in Israel, took the design to a local blacksmith, and had him build a few cages for a trial run. He imported chicks. Soon chickens were clucking in their stacked-up cages next to the sour orange trees that lined the walls of the courtyard. The children took turns feeding them, cleaning the droppings to be sold as fertilizer, and collecting eggs – so many eggs. Our chickens were fat with snow white feathers, nothing like the tough colourful chickens that ran around the villagers' yards.

We ate well. Baba's poultry farm was a blessing and a curse. In our family pictures, I changed from a scrawny girl with ribs showing through a thin dress, to a chubby young woman with red cheeks, thick legs, and stooped shoulders. We had been nourished physically but not emotionally.

OUR HOUSE, our meals, and our lives were shared with Uncle Morad and his family. When Baba was eighteen his father passed away, leaving him to work full time and support his mother and his five siblings still living at home. Two of Baba's sisters had been married off before puberty. Morad, who was two years younger than Baba, was a dropout, although this wasn't unusual for a boy his age and social class. My father took it upon himself to stop Morad's youthful ways (hanging out with friends, not earning any money), and forced him to work by his side in the gold and silver business. Baba was a father-figure to his siblings, and he felt that he had to instill in his brother a sense of responsibility toward the family.

Baba might have found it natural to include his brother in this new adventure into poultry farming. Years later he would wonder why. I don't know if he didn't have enough confidence to do it by himself, or if he didn't know how to separate himself professionally from his brother. Perhaps he thought that it was simply the right thing to do.

Baba didn't regret his decision until years later but his children and wife had known about the wrongs in this partnership all along. We all paid a huge price. In his resentment and passive aggression, my uncle periodically unleashed his contempt and hatred toward my mother and her children.

65

Once he sent a teenage apprentice in the jewellery store to collect a wedding gift that my father had given my mother, a gold brooch in the shape of two roses, the petals meticulously crafted of stranded baby freshwater pearls. Morad had a customer waiting for it at the shop; Baba was not there to stop him. Having to obey Morad's order, the brazen apprentice was firm and rude. Maman relinquished the piece, as she would do again and again — nothing nice was hers for long. A few years later, she surrendered her diamond necklace, another wedding gift, to Morad's new bride. My uncle even took a silver vase, a gift from my maternal grandmother, Touran, when Nahid was born. "This is good silver, a waste here," he declared as he headed to the shop to melt it down.

Although we feared him, my siblings and I were deferential to him. Baba insisted on a show of respect to all our elders including his nemesis — even if he himself fought him physically and psychologically.

Maman often complained to Baba but to no avail. Some nights her whispered words of discontent seeped through the walls. "Why can't we have our own place?" was included in every conversation, followed by an inventory of wrongs done to her. My siblings and I had witnessed the violence between my father and uncle on numerous occasions, watching in horror as they clawed at each other. We should have been sympathetic to our mother. Instead, we hated Maman's constant nagging and calls for action. We preferred to endure silently.

Despite these problems, my father didn't hesitate to make plans to share our new house with Morad and his family. We moved to Hedayat Street when I was eight years old. After the cramped two-bedroom house in the *mahaleh*, this house was a palace. Two large tinted glass doors led to a stately curved stairway that faced a tall glass wall. The second floor, with its own private entry door from the street, was designed to look western. The attached living and dining rooms stretched the length of the house and were decorated with hand-painted, handmade plaster mouldings. The built-in china cabinet was made of an expensive rare wood. The master bedroom had a balcony that faced the courtyard; the bathroom had a western toilet (not a hole in the ground) and a bathtub, an item of luxury that was new and exotic to us. But this space was not meant for us.

This fancy house in an exclusive Muslim neighbourhood proved to be a financial burden, alleviated only by the rental income of the lavish, modern upstairs suite. Our renters, an American couple with fair skin, broad smiles, and a strange clean smell, lived in luxury upstairs, while the eleven people of my extended family suffered together in the three-bedroom, one-bath unit downstairs. For many years, my parents, my two brothers, my sister, and I slept in one room; Morad, his wife, daughter, and son took over what had originally been designed as a dining room; my grandmother, Aunt Sholeh, and Uncle Jahangeer slept in two adjoining rooms, the larger of which served as our living space as well. The kitchen had wood-burning stoves and no refrigerator. We had left the ghetto, but the ghetto had not left us yet.

We ate our meals together, prepared jointly by the hostile women, hissing as they passed one another in the dark, dungeon-like kitchen. It was one step lower than the rest of the house, with a strip of small windows high above the ground, giving little light. My mother and aunt drew knives, chopping herbs and cutting meat with a vengeance, slamming meat over and over with a wooden striker and shoving it down the throat of the grinder. They smashed burning logs in the mud stove and threw the cutlery noisily into the washbasin. Meanwhile, my grandmother worried about the *jinn*, the evil demons in the drain in the middle of the kitchen. She screamed *parheez, parheez*, beware, keep away, as the feuding sisters-in-law held the two sides of a large copper pot, draining the rice into a gigantic colander, splashing starchy boiling water like molten metal down the drain.

Ignoring the hostility between the women and their own constant disagreements and competition, the brothers decided once again to embark on the next business venture together.

Why did Uncle Morad go along with Baba's plans? What was he thinking? I could ask him but he has broken his relationship with all of us, punishing us for his hatred toward Baba. Many times I have been tempted to contact his son, whom I could easily find, and ask: *Do you remember me? We lived in the same house. You were my baby cousin. What does your father say about my father? About me? Why is your father so rich, my father so poor?* I have never found the courage to ask these and many more questions. And is it necessary after so very many years?

I often wonder if Uncle Morad felt that his youth was wasted when he could have been on his own, having fun, making his own destiny. Did he feel that my father was patriarchal to the point of being the family dictator? If so, why did Morad accept going into business with his brother for a second time? When they sold the jewellery workshop he could have said no to Baba's new adventure. He was a husband, a father. He could have separated himself from us. After a government office misspelled his last name, he chose not to correct it, instead he embraced the mistake. In essence, he changed his last name to be different from ours, to declare his independence. Why didn't he then change his professional partner as well and go his own way?

I DON'T LIKE flying. I don't sleep on planes. Norman tells me, "You think you can hold up the plane in the air if you stay awake. Give up control. Take a sleeping pill, for God's sake." He is right, but flying time is my thinking time, my praying time.

On that long flight to Israel to check on my displaced family, I went over the events of the past again and again. *I wish Baba had not started that farm.* I thought. *I wish he had never found a suitable piece of land.*

≈

TO MAKE MY father's dream a reality, the brothers bought a cheap piece of land on the road to the airport. My father travelled to Tehran to plead for an agricultural loan from the government. He was savvy. He knew the art of pleading; demanding the Iranian way with respect, firmness, resilience, and even bribery. He finally received the money, but it wasn't enough. Baba and Morad asked their brother-in-law Khaled for a loan. They would pay him monthly interest on the loan until they could pay him back. There were no legal documents drawn; their verbal agreement was based on mutual trust; another mistake that would haunt my father throughout his years in Iran. Demanding that he be made a full partner, Khaled periodically threatened to take the brothers to court.

CHILDHOOD MEMORIES OF ATTACKS on the Jewish quarter prompted Baba to revisit the idea of immigrating to Israel each time an Arab/Israeli war reignited anti-Semitism. The Iranian radio spewed anti-Israel propaganda during the Six-Day War of May 1967. The media reported that Jews were being pushed into the Mediterranean. An awkward skinny fourteen-year-old with two long braids, I was afraid because my father radiated fear.

"*Chekar konim?*" What is to be done? He hit himself on the head with both hands in a sign of mourning.

I hated his despair.

"*Bache-ha beran madreseh?*" As we finished eating dinner that night, Baba asked my uncles if the children should be allowed to go to school the following day.

"I don't know. Are they going to be safe?" Morad answered, leaving the decision up to my father.

The men argued away from the table, the children listening carefully, but not participating in the conversation that would determine our fate.

"If the children don't go, *they*'ll think we sympathize with Israel," Baba said.

*Of course, we do*, I thought. *"They" aren't stupid*.

We were definitely not rooting for Arab countries, and the majority of Iranians wouldn't have either if the war hadn't been against the Jews. Iranians were not fond of Arabs. In our history books we read over and over that we were better than *them*; that Iranians gave the conquering Arabs their culture.

The following day, our men split up in order to escort me, my siblings, and cousins to our respective schools, believing that the school grounds would be safe.

As soon as I crossed the threshold to Namus high school, a close friend ran toward me.

"Israel's destroyed. Jews will be thrown into the sea," she screamed gleefully, jumping up and down.

"No, they won't," I said calmly.

"Yes, they will. My father said they can't fight all those Arab countries."

"Yes, they can. They have America, England, France, and all of Europe behind them." I doubted my own words, but I felt that I had no choice but to defend Israel even though my father had repeatedly told us that morning to avoid such confrontations. My mouth sour, I hated my dark grey uniform that day, its scratchy, starched white collar wrapped around my neck, suffocating me. My friend was no longer my friend. She hated, and I loved, Israel, a country neither one of us had visited nor could locate on the map.

Was there not a place that Jews could live in peace, a place where we could live with a sense of pride in our religion and heritage?

THE SITUATION FOR Shirazi Jews became especially ominous during the Yom Kippur War of 1973. On October 6th, we spent much of the day at the synagogue. Being observant Jews, we didn't listen to the radio. My father and uncles walked the long distance to the synagogue that my grandfather had built in the heart of the *mahaleh*, Kanisa-ye Mola. My grandmother, mother, aunts, Nahid, and I went to Kanisa-ye Rabizadeh, a synagogue that was closer to our new home in the upscale Muslim neighbourhood. My paternal grandmother, Khanom-bozorg, wrapped in her white calico *chador*, suggested that we leave before *Neilah*, the concluding services, to prepare food for breaking the fast before the men returned.

On the way home, my father, hungry and exhausted, stopped by a pastry shop to buy *khameh*, whipped cream sand-wiched between two thin pieces of cake; *shirini-e tar*, yellow cake topped with a layer of Jell-O and fruit cut into squares; and *narangak*, cream-filled puff pastry. Breaking our day-long fast was the only occasion on which we were allowed to have sweets for dinner. In the hallway that had been turned into a common sitting area, we sat on sofas and bent our heads for Baba to bless us before he touched his food: "May you be healthy, marry well — *yehi-ratzon* — may you live to see your children's happiness, your grandchildren." Then he drank a glass of aromatic sweetened *bidmeshk* drink and ate a piece of watermelon soaked in rosewater.

Afterwards, Baba turned on the radio to Kol Israel, the voice of Israel in Persian. Every night we dutifully gathered around the radio to hear two short beeps and one long beep, followed by *inja oorshaleem, sedaye-esraeel* (This is Jerusalem, the Voice of Israel). Menashe Amir was the sweet voice of radio Israel in Persian. Every time I heard him, and each time I heard Hebrew music played on the radio, my heart thumped with love for a land I had never seen, where it was all right, even preferable, to be Jewish. That night, there were no beeps, no music, no Menashe Amir. Instead, a continuous screeching noise irritated our ears. The frequency was jammed — not a good sign. Baba switched stations. The Iranian radio announced the imminent destruction of Israel. I remember bits and pieces of the horrific news that was broadcast with much joy and enthusiasm:

"Arab armies are on their way to victory."

"Thousands of Jews are dead."

"Israel is dead."

The war had raged all day as we had fasted, asking for God's forgiveness and mercy. Thousands had died while fasting men chanted "*Ashamnu*," we have sinned, beating their chests in atonement. Young men burned in their tanks as women in the balcony of the synagogue gossiped and said their "amens." Brothers and fathers to young women my age were blown to pieces as I giggled with my friends in the courtyard of the synagogue. This was the end of us.

Now we understood why the shopkeepers had come outside to jeer and mock us as we passed by them earlier that day. We had assumed that they were hostile because we were walking home as unchaperoned women. Hungry and tired, my feet hurting in my high heels, I felt suffocated underneath the head covering, and I let it slip onto my shoulders. My grandmother said, "Pull up your *rusary* over your head." I obeyed, hoping to stop the harassment, not realizing that the shopkeepers' brazenness stemmed from their belief that Jews were being destroyed.

FRIGHTENED, BABA AND my uncles locked all the doors that night. Our yard was protected by a tall brick wall and locked metal doors but our patio doors made us feel vulnerable. Baba put a piece of furniture behind them.

We still didn't have a telephone connection in our home so we couldn't call others in the community. Baba finally managed to find the voice of BBC. Israel was not dead – not yet.

Again the question was raised, "Should the kids go to school?" I wasn't such a "kid" anymore. I was twenty years old. But I, too, worried about the following day's volatile atmosphere on the college campus. It was decided that everyone was going to attend school because our absence would signify our family's loyalty to Israel and that could potentially be more dangerous for the Jewish community. We would fast again as we had done during the time of Esther and Mordechai, when the evil vizier, Haman, had tried to destroy the Iranian Jewish community.

Baba, again, brought up the idea of immigrating to Israel. During the early stages of his new business, when he was not so successful, when the creditors knocked at his door, when the entire crop of chicks died of a mysterious disease, my father was resilient, hopeful. Now that he was knowledgeable in the field of husbandry, he thought he could start a poultry farm in Israel. This time, I wasn't convinced. If we moved to Israel, my two brothers would have to serve in the army; they would have to fight in another war. That was unthinkable to my father. I realized that Baba was a dreamer. If I wanted to get out of Iran I would have to do it by myself.

Sure enough, shortly after Israel's victory, Baba forgot about the attacks against Jews, the pogroms and *Jude-koshi* of his childhood. He forgot about our vulnerability. Instead, Baba imported incubators from the United States; chicks, fertilized eggs, and feed from Israel. He studied books about poultry diseases and their cures. He dedicated himself fully to his new business and managed to reverse his fortune; he deepened his roots in the land.

Two years after the Yom Kippur War, Baba was our province's authority in the field. He was on the advisory committee of both the local veterinary school and the chamber of commerce. He had purchased a large tract of land in a village outside Shiraz and expanded his business. There, he dug a deep well, against the advice of all locals who thought there were no underground water tables, and brought the dusty land to life. The water irrigated his orchards, creating my father's very own paradise in the desert. Those were some of the proudest and most productive years of my father's life. The idea of seeking a better life in Israel was forgotten as if it had never been conceived.

IN MY EARLY twenties I attended Pahlavi University where I majored in English literature. Disgusted with our constant humiliation, tired of family feuds, and exasperated with the lack of privacy in our collective home, I dreamt of leaving that stifling house and, by extension, Iran. My father, unaware of my thoughts, was engrossed in his business. He left the house as the first ray of light showed through the sour orange trees. Every morning, he donned a freshly cleaned and ironed dress shirt to return long after the last rays of sunlight had disappeared, covered in fertilizer dust, a black ring around his crumpled shirt, exhausted, but happy and fulfilled.

Baba worked hard and took part in every aspect of his business, including inoculating the birds, mixing the feed and storing it in silos, all along breathing in the airborne particles without the protection of a mask. Baba was not at home long enough to know his children's thoughts and desires.

Friday, the Muslim Sabbath in Iran, was a day off from school. On Fridays I made everyone a lunch of macaroni, tomato sauce, and ground beef — my idea of western food. It was also the day I ironed the men's shirts and polished their shoes, the day I swept the backyard with a low broom, and cleaned the bathroom. On Fridays, without wearing plastic gloves for protection, I rubbed benzene on the ring around the collars of Baba's and my uncles' shirts to get the dirt and grease out,

I dutifully left for classes on Baba's day of rest, Shabbat. Once extremely close to my father, I felt as if I no longer knew him, was no longer involved in his adventures. Now, he took my brothers with him. He expected me to follow the established path for a woman: go to school, return immediately, help my mother with housework, stay away from friends, keep a low profile in the community, and act modestly and obediently until he approved of a husband for me. We stopped chatting and communicating. He didn't tell me about his days on the farm. I didn't tell him about my friends, my education, my dreams.

To fill the void, I lived in the dreamy world of western novels. The first time I visited the university library, I promised myself that I would read every single piece of literature they had in translation. I read them systematically, alphabetically: Dante, Dostoyevsky, Gogol, Hemingway, Homer, Hugo, Kafka, O. Henry.... The sections filled with Iranian literature went unnoticed. I wasn't interested. I was *gharb-zadaeh*, a term coined later by the revolutionaries; I was intoxicated by western ideas. I needed to stretch my wings, to get to know those mysterious worlds so I started making serious plans to leave Iran. Joseph Adams, a professor from Kansas, taught American literature at Pahlavi University — we studied *Walden*, the dream of self-reliance by a pond, and *Huckleberry Finn*, escaping oppression along the Mississippi river. Dr. Adams, with his grey hair, penetrating eyes, and big smile, soon became a father-figure who listened to me, encouraged me, and helped me with my plans to transfer to an American university.

Baba remained distant, occupying his time with work alone.

Neither one of us realized that he, too, was escaping the house. Whenever we saw each other, mostly during meals, his critical eyes, narrowed in concentration, scanned my behaviour, and tried to find the slightest misconduct.

Returning home one afternoon, happy after spending time with my friends, I was startled when Baba grabbed my tote bag and pulled out a wet bathing suit. "What's this? You're baring yourself in front of strangers?"

"Baba, it's a women's swimming pool."

"You're desirable because you're fair." He pulled on the collar of my shirt, and pointed out a patch of peeling skin on my shoulders. "Look what you've done to your skin." He threw my bathing suit in the garbage. I bought another one, asked a girlfriend to take it home after each swim lesson, and tried to stay in the shade.

Another time my father saw me on a side street, a tennis racket under my arm. I was walking to the university tennis courts, wearing a light-blue and white checkered tennis skirt. He followed me in his car and honked the horn to stop me. "Do you see how people look at you? No more!"

I would dwell on this particular incident more than any other. Norman, finally, tired of hearing it, once asked me, "What's keeping you from playing tennis now? Do I tell you not to? Go take some lessons for God's sake."

THE PLANE HITS an air pocket. My heart drops. My mind returns to reality. I pray, "*Ya-khoda, ya-arvaye-baba-ye baba. Shema Israel, Adonai eloheynu, Adonai echad.*" I often think that I am not that religious until I fly on a windy day. Then I imitate my father. I ask God for help; I conjure the spirit of my great-grandfather; I say my Hebrew prayers: "Hear, O Israel. Adonai is our God; Adonai is one."

The turbulence disappears, but most of the passengers are awake now. A young man in front of me turns up the volume on his headset; I can hear the music.

≈

IN OUR HOUSE in Shiraz, we rarely listened to music. Only news was worth listening to. When in college, I tried to learn to play the guitar. Baba saw me studying the notes. "What's this? My daughter isn't a *motreb*." A generic word for an entertainer, *motreb* has a very negative connotation. I gave up guitar. Years later, when I had already left for the United States, I learned that Baba had bought a violin for Freydoun, a guitar for Nahid, and had paid for private lessons. Maybe he thought the musical instruments would keep the rest of his children in Iran.

Reacting to my father's strict rules, I became secretive, a total recluse among the family. With my friends, I went to the movies, which Baba had prohibited, and told him that I was at school. I ate non-kosher food at restaurants or at the homes of my Muslim friends. I stopped fasting, first for the fast of Esther, then the fast of Yom Kippur. I was rebelling against everything Baba believed. My mother enjoyed watching our crumbling relationship. She brought me food to the back room when I told her I didn't want to fast.

I read ferociously. To avenge a time in high school, when my father had burned my western novels in translation, I left an English copy of *Lady Chatterley's Lover*, a book once banned in England for its sexual content, on top of my textbooks on the coffee table. I knew that Baba couldn't read English, and that he probably assumed the novel to be just another textbook.

The more time my father dedicated to his farm and his paradise gardens, the more time I spent at the university, often staying at the library until it closed. My father planted. I cut away my roots, giving away as many of my belongings as possible. We both dreamt of magical worlds. Baba, hands folded behind his back, strolled between the rows of apricot trees in his garden; I, a book in hand, crouched between the library stacks. We both thought we were in charge of our own destiny.

The majority of my friends were upper-middle-class Muslims. I couldn't help but notice the differences in our lives, especially the strains of an overcrowded house, where everything was shared and nothing was private. My father reinvested his huge profits in his business, in a bigger facility, a larger farm, acres of land outside Shiraz, orchards, deep wells. Despite their financial prosperity, neither Baba nor Morad could accept the idea of leaving the house they had built together. They were both attached to the key-shaped decorative pool and its water fountains in the middle of the walled yard. They both loved the tall, majestic sour orange trees that lined the two sides of the house. They both enjoyed watching the red and yellow clusters of grapes, hanging from a trellis over the carport in the back yard. They both were proud of the variety of roses, red, yellow, and white, that they had planted with their own hands, and had grafted one stem at a time. Neither would agree to move his family to a single-family home. Both families could have bought nice homes, but Baba and Morad were attached to their joint achievement of building *this* house. Our families lived together in a misery created by two stubborn men and my unyielding grandmother, who insisted on having the entire family under one roof.

During communal lunch, women bickered over a non-event in the kitchen. I had stopped listening long ago.

My grandmother asked me in front of the entire family, "Did anyone rinse the dishes you washed?"

Menstruating, I was *tamei*, impure. She had a sharp nose for such things. As much as I tried to hide it, somehow she knew.

I blurted out, "I am leaving for the United States after classes are done."

A hush blanketed the common area we had set up for lunch.

My father's eyes narrowed. "Nonsense!"

Everyone at the table went back to spooning rice, and pouring the eggplant and tomato stew over it.

My grandmother said, "Don't sit next to me."

*She's become a man,* I thought. The religious rules barred me from touching the men, passing them a dish, or sitting next to them when I had my period. She had included herself in the male category, since she was our elder and had long reached menopause. I stood there staring at everyone.

"I'm leaving. I've got my passport, my exit visa, a ticket. I'm leaving."

Without touching the food, I gathered my books and rushed out to catch the bus to school. I had paid for the plane ticket with money my father had paid me to translate his poultry farm manuals, my stipend saved from university for being a good student, and a loan from a dear Muslim friend, Fatemeh.

When I returned at the end of the day, my father had searched my belongings, but I had all the documents locked in a friend's cubby at school. The word was out. My aunts and uncles chastised my father for his crazy, undisciplined, and out-of-control daughter. I would never have dreamt that most of them would follow my path in a few years.

I left for the United States on July 4, 1975, exhausted from the long arguments and yelling matches with my father, and relieved to be flying to my utopian America.

The foundations for the Iranian Revolution were being poured even then. The government of Mohammad Reza Shah, the king who had enabled the Jews to live comfortably in Iran, would topple less than three years later, when the royal family left Iran on January 16, 1979. The Shah's nemesis, Ayatollah Khomeini, and his entourage returned from exile on February 1, 1979. Baba, Morad, and their families left Iran for Israel on the last El-Al flights amidst the chaos of these historical departures and arrivals.

≈

SOMETIMES I TRY to imagine my family's first night in Israel. They took two taxis to my maternal grandmother's four-room apartment. Touran's place had a joint living, dining, and kitchen area that counted for two rooms in Israel, two small bedrooms, and one dingy bathroom. My mother, Nahid, Farzad, and four-year-old Niloufar descended on my grand-mother, bringing along Uncle Morad, his wife, and their five children. My father and Freydoun, a freshman in the engineer-ing department of Pahlavi University, would join them later after obtaining an American visa for my brother, ensuring that he would be able to continue his education in the United States. The rest would return to Iran, Baba thought, when the situation calmed down.

ON THAT DARK night in the winter of 1979, my groggy, fright-ened grandmother hesitantly opened the door to her tiny apartment in Kiriat Sharet, and was shocked by the sight of her daughter and Niloufar, whom she had not seen since my wedding in 1977, the rest of the grandchildren, whom she didn't know, and, of course, the entourage. When Maman saw her brother Shimon, a hunchback with short arms who stood barely three feet tall, standing next to my grandmother she ran downstairs, telling everyone, "I feel sick." Had she forgot-ten about him? My uncle Shimon was a possible victim of thalidomide, an experimental drug given to pregnant women to prevent nausea. A major side effect of the potent drug was birth defects. The family had tried to convince my grand-mother Touran to give Shimon up to a travelling circus, but she had refused.

I am not sure what happened in Kiriat Sharet afterwards. When my father joined them a few days later, he begged

Shimon, who had given up his room for them, to remain hidden inside so as not to embarrass him in front of his brother's family and other visitors. And so Shimon stayed with my grandmother in her room as the others took possession of the rest of the apartment. I don't know how my father, a compassionate man to the poor and needy in Shiraz, could have asked my uncle to make his twisted body disappear. Maybe he asked my grandmother to have mercy on their sensibilities. Deformities were looked down upon in *our* Iran. Israelis, however, with their share of people injured in the wars, respected them. The Israeli government had given Shimon a car with custom-built modifications that enabled him to drive to the job the government had provided for him.

ON MY FIRST flight to Israel to visit my refugee family, I could not stop thinking of "fate," the predestined path in life in which my family, like many other Iranians, so firmly believed. I thought of the recent unbelievable turn of events, of their uncertain future, and I thought of its impact on my own life. New Orleans felt like a faraway place in a novel I had read and then shelved.

IN PREPARATION FOR landing at Ben Gurion airport, Israeli music filled the cabin. A group of teenagers on an organized trip started singing *Yerushalayim Shel Zahav, Jerusalem of Gold*. My eyes were moist. *I am here, finally*, I thought, *my first trip to the Holy Land*. My father picked me up from the airport in a taxi. In my hazy, jet-lagged memory I recall the airport being filled with dazed Iranians. Baba had deep wrinkles around his eyes. He had lost weight. He looked unkempt, untidy. A forced half smile crossed his face. His embrace was tentative, as if he had lost strength in his arms.

We remained mostly silent in the taxi. My grandmother's apartment on the top floor of an old rectangular drab grey concrete building, a legacy of Israel's early socialist experiment, felt like a house of mourning. My wide smile and eager embraces felt out of place even to me.

To my grandmother I was just another person in need of a bedroll, another guest to be fed and entertained. Grandmother Touran was, as I always remembered her, *akhmoo*, serious and abrupt. She did not speak a kind word even though she had not seen me since my wedding in May of 1977. Hair severely pulled back, she ran back and forth from the fruit and vegetable stalls to the kitchen, cooking, cooking, cleaning. I tried to help. "Get out of the kitchen," she screamed. I thought she resented my presence, but she was probably just refusing help from a guest. I can't imagine the emotional and financial burden to which we subjected her. Those days, however, she was simply an unfriendly face to me. *Maybe Baba was right*, I thought. *Maybe I shouldn't have come.*

The following day I awoke to find my father and Morad standing by my grandmother's window staring out silently, aimlessly. Shimon had liberated himself from his temporary imprisonment to go to work. Freydoun sat in a corner, his legs folded into his chest, hands wrapped around them, his head resting on his knees. Having hardly any room to move or play, Niloufar leaned against a pillow on the sofa, looked at the wall with blank eyes, and sucked her two middle fingers.

I asked Maman, "What about enrolling Niloufar in kindergarten? She needs to learn Hebrew and to play with other children."

"I don't know," she said. "Your father hasn't made any decisions about our lives. We don't know what to do."

I knew I had to get Neli away from the unhappiness that saturated the air of the tiny apartment. That was something I could do. None of us had ever attended preschool, but we hadn't been displaced as children either. She needed to acclimate to her new society.

Maman and I walked her over to the nearest childcare centre. Neli was excited to see potential playmates and lots of toys. She ran to play, jabbering to the other children. As we turned to leave, she must have figured out that those children were different; they spoke a different language; they had already recognized her foreignness. She ran after us, "Maman, Maman," she screamed, begging to go home. The teacher held her in her arms and tried to comfort her as we left. We could hear her shrieking, "Maman *raft*. Maman *koo*? Mommy left. Where is Mommy?" She had already gone through the trauma of leaving her home, her bike, her familiar surroundings. She had to get used to these departures. Although we didn't know it that day, she was destined for many more separations.

I took long walks with my other siblings, speaking to them in English. I don't know why. Maybe because it was different from the language of our homeland that had betrayed us, and of the house we had unhappily piled into even though everyone now missed its familiarity, or maybe because we needed change. To converse in a foreign tongue was soothing because it promised a new beginning. We have retained that habit until today.

Farzad was almost the same age as Morad's son and daughter. I asked my father and uncle, "What about the kids? Have you found them a school? They can't just sit here all day long, doing nothing." They had already missed months of schooling in Iran.

"People who run these schools are hateful," my father said.

My uncle chimed in, "They told us to send the kids to a technical school."

Baba added, "They think Iranians are stupid. Our children are bright. If they stay here they'll have no future."

I couldn't believe my ears. How could that be? We had loved Israel. Did Israel not love us back?

"Take them to America with you," Baba said. "I told you not to come. You should have found them a high school there."

"People say that all schools are free in America," my uncle added, assuming that my hesitancy had something to with the expense of bringing my brothers and cousins to America.

Morad, who had not given me a wedding gift out of his hatred for Baba, went out the following day and bought me a pendant as a bribe. Maman noticed his effort. "Your uncle thinks you don't want to take his kids because he didn't give you a wedding gift." I was astonished. I feared taking those naïve young people to a violent city, where I had heard that public schools were places of mayhem, drugs, and abuse. Private schools were exclusive and expensive. The middle class, who could not afford them, enroled their children in religious schools, still at a great financial sacrifice. And where would these teenagers live? In our small one-bedroom apartment? Would I dare let them live in an apartment by themselves in New Orleans?

I had contacted the New Orleans Jewish Federation before my family left for Israel, asking for their financial help and support with the logistics of getting my young cousins and siblings American visas. Although they had solicited our financial help with the immigration of Russian Jews to the U.S., they flatly refused, "Let them go to Israel." I knew I could not count on their assistance.

I suggested that we look at the American school in Kefar Shmaryahu , which catered mostly to the children of American government staff and some wealthy Iranians. Although the expenses would be a huge sacrifice, I assumed that it would not be higher than private schools and housing in New Orleans. Farzad, my cousins and I took the long bus ride to the school, filled out the forms, and registered for placement exams. The school did not offer housing options.

Trying to keep Farzad and my cousins happy and carefree a bit longer, I suggested walking around the neighbourhood, delaying our return to my grandmother's tiny apartment. We wandered around the city, looking at beautiful homes with tennis courts, stopped by a little café for refreshments, chatted and laughed, tried to forget the dire situation. I felt very close to my cousins that day. I never imagined that our fathers' animosity would soon spill over our lives, that we would become total strangers; that our children could potentially pass by one another on the street, not knowing that they were family.

When we returned home and giddily retold our adventure to our preoccupied families, Baba turned his back and stared at the horizon outside the window. Morad said, "Well, maybe their education could be our sacrifice. We'll spend everything we have and don't have on it." Baba didn't react. Maman cleaned the rice on a round tray, not listening or participating in the conversation. My grandmother shook her head. "Kefar Shmaryahu? So far away?" The atmosphere returned to its gloom.

My displaced family never responded to the suggestion that they move to an area where they didn't know anyone, where the lifestyle was expensive and unfamiliar. The tuition plus the daily four-hour bus ride to attend classes made the arrangement impossible. They didn't tell me this, but they didn't have to. Their thoughts were conveyed through their silence.

My father and uncle had been in Israel long enough to encounter intolerance and scorn toward Iranian Jews. They were adamant that the children had to leave for America. I was shocked to discover that the discrimination my family faced in Israel was similar to what I had experienced in Iran, the double discrimination for being a Jew *and* a woman. My calligraphy teacher in high school recited anti-Semitic poetry in class and rarely gave the Jews a grade higher than 10 out of 20.

At Pahlavi University High School, I had an American-educated math teacher who repeatedly asserted that women must get married and have babies rather than study math. Women were separated from the class to study home economics, to sew, knit, and gossip while male students attended physics and mechanics labs. The lower grades given to women were then used to argue that we were not suitable for studying math and physics.

I had naïvely thought that all Jews would be equals in Israel. This discrimination was unacceptable.

I had been silent about my discontent in Iran, but I had to protest the treatment of my family in Israel. The day after we visited the American school, I told my father and Morad that I was going to take my brother and cousins to Tichon Hadash, which was considered to be one of the finest schools in Israel. I marched into the school office and shouted at the principal in English. I had been in Israel for just a few days but had quickly learned that Israelis liked a good argument and that they venerated Americans. In that office, I was an American, not a *Mizrakhi*, an Eastern Jew.

"These are smart kids. Why do you refuse them?" I asked the woman behind the desk.

"The other school is good, too," she smiled.

"Not good enough. My brother and cousins are college smart. You're condemning them to inadequate education; you're taking away their future."

She shook her head. "It isn't just that, you know."

"What is it then?"

"They are going to get free education and leave the country. They are not worthy of our investment."

"If you don't take them, they'll leave for America now."

"Okay. We'll take a chance. Maybe they'll be of the few who remain in Israel after we've spent our resources on them. Maybe they'll surprise us by resisting the lure of America. They may register for classes."

FARZAD AND MY cousins were accepted but first they had to begin their *ulpan,* their study of Hebrew. But Morad was suspicious and believed that I had hidden plans to take my brothers, and not his children, to America. Soon after he made separate arrangements for his own children at an orthodox Jewish institution in New York that accepted young Iranian refugees, partly to indoctrinate them into a more religious branch of Judaism. My cousins left for America as the principal of Tichon Hadash school had predicted.

Nahid had finished her third year of a six-year medical school program in Shiraz before the revolution interrupted her education. I accompanied her to Tel Aviv University, trying to convince them to permit a transfer. "No room ... too many applicants ... inadequate educational standards ... why don't you study biology ... leave your papers here ... let's wait and see." We didn't hear back from them by the time I left Israel.

Freydoun had been an engineering student, a highly competitive field in Iran. He had barely finished the first semester when his education was disrupted by the unrest. Leaving a class one day, he was surrounded by revolutionary students, booing and jeering those who had attended classes. He did not return to school.

According to Iranian law, men his age who were not enrolled in school were eligible for military service. To avoid that, months earlier, I had secured an acceptance letter for Freydoun from Queens College in New York. Baba and my brother delayed their travel to Israel by two days in order to obtain a student visa for Freydoun from the American Embassy in Tehran. Although they had camped outside the Embassy, soon it became clear that there were too many applicants for the limited number of visas available. My father again used his street smarts. Pulling aside a guard, he discreetly handed him a few one-hundred dollar bills. Visa in hand, they were lucky to have caught the last flight to Israel before the airport shut down.

I RESISTED MY father's desire for Freydoun to study in the United States. I suggested that instead my brother should try to enrol at Technion, an engineering school in Haifa, the equivalent of MIT in the U.S. The thought of my brother, who had never been away from home, living alone in New York was frightening to me. The two of us took the bus to Haifa and met with the head of admissions, who told us that Freydoun could not apply before finishing his Hebrew *ulpan* and serving for three years in the army. Even then there were no guarantees that he would be accepted. Under normal circumstances these demands might have been justifiable, but at that particular time in our lives, when my brother's life was in turmoil, those were not acceptable conditions. Freydoun's best option, I agreed with Baba, was to continue his education in the United States. We bought a ticket for him on my return flight. Nobody asked him what he wanted to do.

There was nothing more to be done. I had planned to stay in Israel for a month, but living at my grandmother's apartment was becoming unbearable. Because of the time difference, I had rarely spoken to Norman. Whenever he managed to get ahold of me on my grandmother's landline, the sad dark eyes of my family members looked at me with longing curiosity. As they listened, in that cramped living room, I didn't feel comfortable talking to Norman about the anxiety and gloom that filled the apartment, feelings that threatened to suffocate us like the smoke from the incubators in Shiraz. Each time Norman said, "You must try to experience Israel, to see its beauty. I was hoping that your first trip would be with me," his optimism grated on my nerves. I wasn't sure why he couldn't grasp the severity of the problems my family faced. Was it because of his comfortable upper-middle-class upbringing in America? A Zionist, did he think that all problems could be solved by simply being in Israel? Maybe at twenty-seven he was just too young to imagine such a great loss.

We were both young. Norman's youth had been filled with United Synagogue Youth conventions, Camp Judea adventures, soccer with neighbouring boys on the streets of his suburban Portsmouth home, and trips with his twin brother. I hadn't shared the details of my youth with Norman. I didn't tell him about the restrictions that were set upon me in Iran. Without the knowledge of my childhood experiences, he couldn't understand that I had no choice but to commiserate with my parents, my siblings, and other Iranian Jews on the streets of Tel Aviv.

Norman's parents, who were visiting Israel through a Jewish Federation trip, called me. "Your husband told us that you must get away." The words "your husband" sounded like a command. They were in Israel with their friends to have fun; this was their big vacation. They paid extra to include me in their plans. As their guest, I visited the Knesset, the Israeli Parliament, and we met with the President as a group. I listened to high-powered Israeli politicians discuss the "Iranian Jewish problems." My in-laws, along with other prominent American visitors on this mission, were courted and solicited for donations to the State of Israel. Israeli officials used the Iranian refugee problem as a fundraising hook. I sat there silent, and I listened, and I didn't know who I was and what I should do. I was dining with those who watched Iranian refugees on the big screen of the large convention hall. They watched my people with the distant curiosity of the benevolent. To everyone else in that large convention hall — those people sipping wine, cutting through stuffed chicken breast, and spooning wild rice — Iranian Jews were a news item, a novelty. What a stark contrast to the parallel world I was living in!

Shortly after attending lavish dinners at five-star hotels and passionate speeches by Israeli and American politicians, Norman's parents took time off from their very busy travel schedule to visit my parents in my grandmother's tiny crowded apartment with my hunchbacked uncle locked in his room.

They sat there silently, not having much to say to one another. My in-laws didn't speak Hebrew or Persian; most of my family didn't speak English. My father had a false, self-conscious smile on his face; his shoulders remained in a long-held shrug. As we piled onto the one sofa in the room for pictures, I was embarrassed for my parents, my grandmother, and myself. I felt sad for my grandmother who had to entertain these fancy Americans, passing tea and biscuits on a cheap metal tray. My in-laws were in a hurry to get back to Tel Aviv and catch the bus to their next destination. They refused the food politely. My father and I escorted them back to the main road to catch a taxi, then we walked back and silently climbed the stairs.

"I hope your in-laws know that we are better than this," Baba finally said.

"Don't worry, Baba. It's okay," I said, although I didn't mean it. Once again, I was straddling two diametrically opposite worlds, and I belonged to neither one.

It would take decades and another trip to Israel for me to find and to accept an identity of my own, a place of my own in the world around me, to accept that I belonged to many cultures, to embrace my American, my Iranian, and my Jewish identities, to see them like tiles in a mosaic that only together can complete a scene.

I THOUGHT BACK to my engagement party held just two years earlier in Norman's apartment in Charlottesville, where he attended medical school. Amos, a good Israeli friend and a student of International Law, a *yekke* (a descendent of German Jews in Israel) could not hold back his intense emotions. As people raised their glasses to toast us, he objected. "You don't know what you're getting yourself into," he told Norman. "You're marrying a woman from a primitive culture. This marriage won't last."

I remained silent. Norman ignored the comments. The party went on.

I WONDERED HOW my in-laws had viewed the scene in my grandmother's tiny apartment, in the dilapidated neighbourhood of Kiriat Sharet. I knew that they were open-minded, and because they embraced diversity, they had encouraged a union between their son and me; but I wondered.

A few days after my in-laws' visit, another incident intensified my insecurity. Our good friends in New Orleans had given me a gift to deliver to their parents in a beautiful, quiet neighbourhood in Tel Aviv. Their apartment was orderly and tastefully opulent. They were also *yekkim*. The mother was educated, beautiful, and sophisticated. Her nails were polished in the colour of onion skin, her hair nicely cut. She wore elegant brown pants and a beige silk shirt; her smile showed white teeth and just a touch of pink lipstick. Although anxious about all that needed to be done for my parents and siblings, I put on my friendly mask. We chatted amicably in English.

"How did you and Norman meet?" she asked.

"Oh, on a blind date." They had their own accent, and, I guess, didn't realize that mine was not American.

"Are you visiting family in Israel?" She offered me tea in British bone china; I prefer my tea in clear glass so that I can enjoy its colour as well as its taste.

"My family just escaped Iran. I'm trying to help." I extended my arm to receive the cup, but she put it down on the coffee table. Her soft beautiful voice rose just a bit as she complained about the poverty-stricken and ignorant immigrants who were ruining Israeli society.

"They're such a huge burden. We've tried so hard to make Israel a country of intellectuals and here come the uneducated, uncultured people, drawing on our resources, lowering the country's intellectual standing in the world."

They were both aghast that an American physician would have married an Iranian, and although they didn't say the words, I heard "primitive" in my head, and its essence filled the room. I thanked them for their hospitality and left without drinking the tea.

I don't think they knew how hurtful they were. Many Israeli people of European heritage viewed themselves as intellectuals, resentful and embarrassed by the "primitive" immigrants of the Middle East and North Africa although they did not know our histories. That day I didn't wonder how such nice people could behave so badly. *Was it me?* I thought. *Was it something I had done?*

I HAD BEEN in Israel for a few weeks when Norman started to call more regularly.

"Come home, please."

"I will, next week."

"No, *now*. Please come home."

"What's going on? Are you okay? I'll be home next week." I reiterated, not understanding his persistent request. Wrapped up in my family's problems, I paid little attention to Norman, who was so far away, who was often too independent to need anyone. I didn't hear the despair in his voice.

"I need you now. Please come home," he insisted.

Everyone needed something. I needed to finish what I had started.

"I can't. I'll be back soon enough."

TWO EVENTS MARKED the day Freydoun and I were scheduled to leave.

My father asked, "Do you remember your great-aunt Khatoon-jan? She died. Do you want to go to the funeral?"

I said, "No."

Baba put his shoes on by the front door. "I'll try to be back in time to go to the airport with you." He paused, opened the door, and before leaving said, "You know she loved you very much." Then he closed the door and left.

My paternal grandmother, Khanom-bozorg, had told me many times how her sister had sold her jewellery to lend them money. She had been instrumental in my family's survival when my grandfather passed away. I remember my great-aunt's departure for Israel when we were still living in the *mahaleh*. I remember her sorrow when she left us all behind. I remember her hugging and kissing me over and over, begging me not to forget her.

In those days, the Jews were housed in Beheshtieh (Paradise), the Jewish cemetery in Tehran, while waiting for their papers to be processed. Away from the centre of the city, the makeshift lodging gave them sanctuary before they left quietly for the Holy Land. My aunt had wandered through the graves, lighting candles and praying, a part of her dying as she left her old life behind. She was reborn in Israel.

I remember a letter Khatoon-jan had asked a scribe to write when she reached Israel. "I got a glimpse of the *Kotel* today," she wrote. At the time, the Western Wall of the Jewish Temple that had survived the ravages of time and war was under Jordanian rule. Worshippers could see it from a distance. "I prayed for you," my great-aunt had written. "I prayed for your health and well-being. I miss you. I miss Iran. May it be G-d's will that we be reunited."

I don't know why I didn't want to be at her graveside, saying goodbye. I wish I could go back in time and reverse my decision. Then, I was still trying to distance myself from the old ways. Even though my parents' exile after the Iranian Revolution had forced me back into the family and Iranian problems, I tried very hard to be American and nothing else, to shake off the Iranian dust that settled on my consciousness.

The second event was the strike by Israeli airport workers for better pay. When I called the airport to check on my flight, a disgruntled employee refused to answer my questions. "Call tomorrow," she said. "The airport is closed." My brother and

I didn't go to the airport that night for our midnight flight. However, the airport did reopen temporarily that night so that Prime Minister Menachem Begin could leave for Washington to attend the preliminary peace treaty negotiations with Egypt's Anwar Sadat.

Escorted by my entire family, who wanted to say goodbye in the Iranian tradition, we showed up at the airport the following night only to be told that we had to purchase new tickets since we had missed our flight the previous night. My maternal uncle, Daee Eliahoo, tried to reason with them in Hebrew. Even though I didn't speak the language, I knew that his lack of language skills presented him as an uneducated Iranian immigrant. The officer made faces and said, "NO!" adamantly, at which point I rudely pushed my uncle aside and screamed at the officer in English. "This is *your* fault. Is this the way you treat your tourists? I called last night. Someone said the airport was closed. What was I to do? You MUST put us on this flight." My American chutzpah worked again. Freydoun and I were on that night's flight to the U.S. without paying an extra dime.

I WOULD SOON realize why Norman's voice had been so sad. Just as I had not shared the story of my family's woes in Israel, Norman had saved his own sad story for my return. He met me at the New Orleans airport. He looked pale; he had bags under his eyes.

"Our apartment was broken into," he said.

"Oh, my God!" I screamed. "Are you okay? What did they steal?"

"You'll see. I haven't be able to sleep well for weeks. I even bought a gun."

"You bought a gun?"

"I returned it. It's dangerous to have a gun you are not willing to use on a human being."

The apartment looked ransacked. The robbers had been watching our house, waiting for Norman to leave. Noticing that he was on call at night, they broke through the glass on top of our bedroom window — just the way I had imagined it, as if I had conjured them — found the key by the bed and opened the back door. Norman's schedule had just changed. He returned home at midnight to see the Persian carpets rolled up and the electronic equipment unplugged. He slammed the door, ran out, and woke up an unhappy neighbour to call the police. In their haste and surprise, the burglars only took one Persian carpet, some jewellery, and, thinking it was marijuana, a few bags of Iranian herbs that I had stored on the top shelf of our bedroom closet. The police said that it was an inside job.

I tried to go through my memory to see who knew about my departure for Israel — my co-workers? The insurance man who sold me extra protection? The neighbours? The gardener? *What if I had been at home*, I wondered in fright. We felt violated; we had to move. A new apartment on the second floor of a house promised better security after the installation of metal bars on every window and entry door. I found a job at a gift shop, called "20th Century," on St. Charles Boulevard by Lee Circle in the uptown area of New Orleans that I could take the trolley to. Now I didn't have to work at night. When Norman spent the night at the hospital, I locked myself in behind the bars.

THE ATTACK ON the American embassy in Iran on November 4, 1979, caused me undue stress. Nice southern ladies visited the gift shop after lunch in twos and threes to buy Limoges and Villeroy & Boch china. They inevitably asked me, "Nice accent. Where are you from?"

"Iran."

"What did she say? I-ran?" A customer asked her friend as if I didn't exist.

"Yes." The friend responded.

"Those horrible people. I've got to talk to Carrie, the owner. I've known her all these years. I can't believe she hired an I-rain-ian woman after what they've done to us."

My boss, a very proper southern woman always in high heels and bright lipstick, tried to defend me, informing them that my family was suffering as well. Sometimes customers shouted at me; sometimes they threw the merchandise on the table and left the store without a purchase. Many Iranians had started to introduce themselves as Persians to avoid similar confrontations. I didn't like that idea. I feared sooner or later someone would ask about the location of Persia on the world map. *Oh, it was a great empire that dissolved hundreds of years ago,* I would have to say. *Oh, that's a name the westerners used to call my country of birth before Reza Shah changed it to Iran.* I had to find a better way to deflect the abuse. I decided to become French. Parisian, Persian — close enough — although not such a wise decision in the Cajun country, where people knew some French. And when the customers decided to practise their French on me, I said "No, no. Peeleese Eengeleesh. I te-ray to learn. Please."

≈

BABA CALLED FROM Israel. "Did you take Freydoun to see a doctor as I'd asked you?"

"No, Baba. It's been busy, and now he's in New York."

He sounded agitated. "What about his cholesterol? I asked you one favour, one. You know I worry about his health." With so many unsolvable problems, Baba concentrated on my brother's cholesterol level for months.

"I'll do it later, Baba. When I see him again."

His voice trailed off. Disappointed, he had nothing else to say. A voice inside my head cried out: *What about me? Aren't you worried about me? Baba, you're putting me in charge of my siblings the same way your family put you in charge?*

≈

NORMAN FINISHED HIS residency at Charity Hospital in the winter of 1980. We took February off to visit my family in Israel before Norman had to start a GI fellowship at Ochsner Clinic. I didn't know that I was pregnant with our first child until the smell of falafel hit me. Nauseated, I had to cross the street every time I saw a kiosk displaying containers of cut-up pickles, tomatoes, hot peppers, and everything else that Israelis stuff in their pita.

It was an unusually cold winter. Blanketed in snow, Jerusalem looked solemn without its usual heavy traffic and international tourists. Part of the time we stayed with friends in Rekhavia, a ritzy neighbourhood of Jerusalem. With no central heat, I often stood on the balcony to warm up since the stone facades of homes in Jerusalem chilled the inside like a refrigerator. We went to bed in our hats and sweaters, shivering.

I tried to spend time with Nahid, who was recuperating from surgery at Alyn Orthopedic Hospital in Jerusalem. We visited my parents, Niloufar, and Farzad, who had finally left my grandmother's apartment and lived in a dingy ground-floor, inexpensive apartment building in Kiriat Sharet.

Niloufar, five years old, greeted us, wearing the mask of a laughing clown. When she removed her mask, Norman commented, "Your sister's eyes are so sad." My sister was caught in the family's collective turmoil in a house without laughter.

Baba asked Farzad to sleep in the living room so that Norman and I could take over the tiny bedroom. We huddled around a small table in the kitchen to eat the delicious meal my mother had made for dinner. Baba searched for a piece of meat in the green stew to put on top of the rice on Norman's plate.

"Tell your husband that it is difficult to find good meat in Israel. I don't want him to think that we couldn't afford any," Baba told me.

"Don't worry, Baba. He knows. He's lived in Israel before. He knows that Israelis don't eat much red meat."

Flies attacked the food like kamikaze pilots, drowning themselves in the stew, looking like raisins on the rice. My father desperately tried to shoo them away. He shook his head.

"Dirty Israelis," he grumbled. "They drop their garbage everywhere, and this is the result. We're all going to get sick from these filthy flies."

I was shocked that my father was blaming Israel for his poor surroundings. This would eventually become a habit. Feeling rejected as a Jew in Iran, my father projected his internalized feelings of inferiority and shame onto Israel.

Baba was obviously embarrassed to have to entertain his son-in-law for the first time in such a poor neighbourhood. I wonder how much his return to Iran just a few months later was motivated by this degrading experience. The depression hovering over the house was unbearable. My parents had anxiously awaited our arrival, hoping that by virtue of being American, we could offer solutions to their misery, but we had nothing to offer. I begged my father not to return to Iran.

Norman knew just a handful of Farsi words and my parents had not yet learned Hebrew. Feeling left out of the conversation, Norman made himself busy looking at an Iranian Jewish calendar on the table that included the *brakhot*, the prayers for the Rosh Hashanah Seder. On its first page, a letter from the Iranian Jewish leaders denounced Israel and welcomed the new Islamic government. I translated for Norman. Appalled, he asked, "How can they denounce Israel in the foreword to a collection of prayers that besiege G-d not to allow us to be humiliated in the face of those who hate Jews?"

"They've got to do whatever is necessary to stay safe," I said.

"I don't understand how Jews can live in Iran without dignity."

"Norman," I responded, "You're lucky you never experienced what your Russian grandparents went through. I'm sure they blessed the czar as well."

WE LEFT MY parents and visited Norman's sister, who had been my pen-pal when I lived in Iran and who had made our meeting and eventual marriage possible. She had married an Israeli. We visited friends, including Amos, the lawyer who had warned Norman not to marry me. Ignoring me once again, he asked Norman about the impact of the Iranian Revolution on our lives. His eyes communicated his previous sentiment that Norman had married into trouble. "I told you so," hung in the air but was not uttered. Like many other Israelis, he made fun of "idiot" Iranian Jews who had sent carpets to Israel instead of saving themselves. Apparently there were images of rolled Persian carpets arriving at Ben Gurion customs without their owners that had been broadcast repeatedly on Israeli TV and had become merriment-making fodder for comedians both in Israel and abroad.

I thought of defending my people by explaining that banks were closed. Smart Iranian Jews did not trust the fruits of a lifetime of hard work to Iranian banks, the way my father had so unwisely done. A Jew could not be attached to land; a Jew had to remain mobile — a lesson my father chose to forget with devastating consequences. Persian carpets could be sold to pay expenses. This was similar to German Jews shipping artwork abroad for financial security during World War II. My father had managed to send me two red Kashans. In a desperate moment of financial panic, he would later ask if I was interested in buying them, which I did, paying him retail, knowing that he needed the money to visit the United States and Iran.

I wanted to let all Israelis know that the majority of our people had lost everything. I wanted to tell Norman's *yekke* friend that I had seen proud Iranian men on the bus, on the streets, looking dazed, crying openly for their losses, their unexpected displacement. Were his parents not Holocaust survivors? Shouldn't that have elicited a bit of sympathy?

But I remained silent.

Before returning to the United States, I tried to convince my father to leave it all behind. "Baba, don't go back. It isn't worth it." My father's eyes filled with fury. Couldn't I see what had happened to him, that he had lost so much, that his brother and the government had taken away his life's work? Frustration danced in his eyes, but he smiled and told me, "Don't worry." I could see that he felt the weight of being the patriarch; he felt solely responsible for everyone's well-being, for their expenses, for their health, for their happiness. He had a daughter suffering at a hospital in Jerusalem, two unhappy children at home, a nagging wife who demanded they leave her mother's home for an independent apartment even though they were running out of money, and an elderly mother living in Iran for the first time without his care and protection. He felt that he was failing miserably at the responsibilities he, his family, and his culture had assigned him.

Baba left for Iran a few months after our departure in October of 1980. He told my seventeen-year-old brother, Farzad, "You are now the man of the house. Take care of your mother and your sister."

## '03

## BABA
### *September 1980, Tel Aviv*

My lungs burned as I struggled to inhale the humid, exhaust-filled air of Tel Aviv. It had been five months since my family's rushed exodus from Iran amidst a revolution that turned our lives upside down, and I was still lost, sleepless, dazed. I missed Shiraz, the crisp, dry breeze sweeping down from the mountains to the valley that had been home to my ancestors for thousands of years. Exiled to Babylon after the destruction of the First Temple in Jerusalem, my people were set free in 539 BCE by the Persian King, Cyrus the Great, and they followed him to Persia. Like my forefathers, I had prayed for a return to Zion every holiday, every Shabbat, every day. At the end of each Passover Seder, I would say wholeheartedly, "Next year in Jerusalem!" But now that I was finally in the Holy Land, I yearned to return to Iran.

I walked along the narrow alleyways of *Takhanat Merkazeet*, the central bus terminal in Tel Aviv, where time had stopped and modernity didn't dare encroach. Travellers tried to find their connections in the winding, confusing maze of alleyways that were lined with small shops. Shoes, bolts of fabric, and household knick-knacks filled the small shops and poured onto the sidewalk. The shopkeepers sat uncomfortably on metal chairs or low stools, chatting with each other or with the familiar faces in the crowd. The smell of falafel, kebab, herb polo, and freshly squeezed juices — orange, pomegranate, carrot — blended with the pungent odour of Noblesse and Marlboro. I reached into my shirt pocket for a cigarette, the last of a pack I had brought from Iran, and held it between my fingers, but resisted lighting it.

*Avateeachhhhh, tut sadeh,* vendors yelled, watermelon, strawberries. My little daughter Niloufar loved strawberries — a new, exotic fruit for her.

Waiting for buses to take them to the beaches or to Jerusalem for sightseeing, tourists chatted in languages unfamiliar to my ears. Their exuberance stood in stark contrast to the gloom hanging over the refugees whose language I understood, whose pain I shared. We didn't laugh or bargain at the gift stores or linger at the cafes. We looked haggard; we had withdrawn to a deep pain within.

*My name is Esghel Dayanim, the son of Mola Meir Moshe Dayanim, the chief rabbi and judge of the Jewish community of Shiraz, a holy man, like his fathers for many generations, revered by Jews as well as many Muslims. Now I am an* avareh, *a wanderer.*

TO US, the wandering Iranian Jews, westernized Israel was surreal and not what we had imagined of our promised land. In our country, *hejab* was mandatory for women, but here young women scurried around in shorts and tank tops beside *Chasidic* men, dressed in the heavy black gaberdines of bygone eras and Eastern European winters. With beads of sweat dripping from their sidelocks, these men averted their eyes from the semi-nudity displayed so brazenly. Pasted on walls and buses, posters of apparently famous actresses or models sold one thing or another with their nakedness. We were shocked to see this culture in the country we regarded as the Holy Land.

We came to *Takhanat Merkazeet* every day to find someone to talk to and to be comforted by other refugees who were as confused as we were. Fearing the future, no longer knowing what "home" meant, we sought advice from other *hamvatan*s, our fellow countrymen. We had lost our sense of purpose. We felt defeated because we lacked both the emotional strength and the financial means to support our families.

We anxiously repeated the same questions. Was it time yet? Was it safe enough to return to our homes and businesses? Was it dangerous to return to Iran? We were running out of financial resources but too proud to admit the shame. We missed home, the routine of our everyday lives, the family members left behind, and a world that had been ours.

IN THE BEGINNING, the Revolution didn't seem to be anti-Semitic. After his return from exile in Paris to Tehran on February 1, 1979, Ayatollah Khomeini decreed that he would protect the acceptable religious minorities such as Jews, Christians, and Zoroastrians — but not the Baha'is. Many minorities, apprehensive about the possible danger hidden underneath these conciliatory words, took cautionary measures by leaving Iran, hoping to return soon. Hearing about the execution by firing squad on May 9, 1979, of Habib Elghanian, a well-known businessman and president of the Tehran Jewish Society, made the Jewish minority feel even more insecure. We tried to rationalize his demise. He'd known people in the palace; he'd given financial support to Israel; he was a millionaire, and while many suffered in poverty in Iran he had kept a high profile, forgetting that Jews had to show humility. In contrast, we had no special importance, no ties to the Palace, and no substantial fortune. If we followed the laws of the land, such as adhering to the *hejab* for women and if we knew our place as Jews and acted in meekness, maybe we would be safe.

Mehdi Bazargan's appointment as prime minister in the first year after the Revolution established certain liberties and stabilized the conditions for Iran's Jewish population, who slowly became accustomed to the new Islamic rules and lived without much fear. Many Jews were granted passports seemingly without any bias toward our religion. Most of us believed that this was indeed a holy revolution that ended the Shah's suffocating dictatorship, and maybe we would enjoy more freedoms under the new government.

Several Jewish families legally left Iran with passports and exit visas during this period of Bazargan's reign. Some left when the Shah was still in power and there were bi-weekly nonstop flights from Tehran to Tel Aviv. Iranians often travelled to Israel to conduct business, to visit family, to make pilgrimages to holy sites, and to use the Israeli health care system as it was superior to Iranian medical practices. When the new government stopped these flights to Israel, the Jews flew with Iran-Air to Istanbul or Athens and bought round trip tickets through small companies to Tel Aviv. The Israeli authorities were conscious of this disobedience of Iranian laws and did not stamp their passports, allowing Iranian Jews, and a few Muslims too, to conceal their travel to Israel.

I took my family to Israel on February 4, 1979, just as Khomeini arrived. All the schools had been closed down. My children were cooped up at home listening to the sporadic gunfire and the chanting of revolutionaries marching by our home on Hedayat street. Coming home one day, I noticed their chewed nails, wringing hands, lackluster eyes, and their constant silence. It wouldn't be a bad thing to leave for a while, I thought. I discussed my concerns with my brother Morad, with whom I shared the poultry business and the house. He and his family joined us on what we thought would be a temporary relocation to Israel. A few months later, two of my brother's children and my oldest son left for America to continue their education. I would have returned to Iran soon after, but Nahid underwent major surgery with complications that kept her in the hospital for about a year. Even though Nahid insisted that I leave, I couldn't. My brother, his wife, and younger children returned to Iran. I waited for Nahid's recovery, comforted that Morad would oversee the everyday work at the farm.

Then the situation in Iran changed rapidly. On November 4, 1979, news reached us that the U.S. Embassy in Tehran had been attacked and the Iranian students had taken the Americans hostage. Consequently, Bazargan resigned from the government in protest. He was later quoted in the *New York Times* as saying "don't expect me to act in the manner of Khomeini, who, head down, moves ahead like a bulldozer crushing rocks, roots and stones in his path." His successors, including Mohammad-Ali Rajai, had deep-seated prejudice against the Jews. Rumours circulated that about seventy Jews, after receiving their passports and exit visas, had boarded an Iran-Air plane to leave the country. After ten minutes in the air, the pilot was ordered to return to Mehrabad airport. The Iranian Revolutionary Guard Corps had opened an office at Mehrabad airport. We heard that a few guards had boarded the plane and asked the Jews to disembark before allowing the plane to take off. They confiscated the Jewish passengers' passports and labelled them *mam-nu-ol-khoruj* — citizens forbidden to leave the country.

The Revolutionary Guard interrogated Jews returning to Iran, claiming that they had all visited Israel and that they were all spies for the "Zionist entity." Even those who had never visited Israel were not spared. Then the Jews were denied new passports. The doors closed on Iranian Jewry, confining them to Iran. Many felt that they were not wanted and yet they were not allowed to leave. These unprecedented events marked the beginning of the change in a government whose policies of hatred would destroy many innocents of all religions. Fear spread its shadow over Iranian Jews like the sudden darkness created by the flight of locusts on a sunny day.

AROUND YOM KIPPUR, on September 22, 1980, the war between Iran and Iraq set the area on fire. Mehrabad, Tehran's international airport, shut down. The war added another layer of worry to our lives, intensifying our concern for the welfare of dear ones we had left behind.

That autumn, a gentle wind slowly took over the intense summer heat as the Jewish holidays approached. This year, the holidays had a deeper meaning for me. The Rosh Hashanah prayers repeated in my head: "Who shall perish by fire and who by water; who by sword, and who by beast; who shall be brought low and who shall be exalted." The ground underneath me had shifted, and I was uncertain about my future – my chest was heavy, my stomach ached. I felt nauseous. The anxiety that I had experienced the year my father passed away came back. Barely out of my teenage years, I had suddenly found myself to be the sole provider for my mother and seven siblings. I prayed that I would not be left alone in my old days and I cried, knowing that I had abandoned my elderly mother in Shiraz.

After fasting, praying, and asking God for forgiveness for my sins that Yom Kippur, I met again with other refugees at the central bus terminal. Although the Iranian shopkeepers provided us with a sense of community and a place to gather, they were not unhappy about our miseries. They had immigrated to Israel years earlier out of hopelessness. They did not hide the long-held opinion that those of us who had remained in Iran believed that Israel belonged to the desperate, to the needy, to the disposable. They resented that we had not helped to improve their lives in Iran. Instead we had encouraged them to leave. And now we too were displaced.

From time to time, someone yelled from across the street, from the open window of a crowded bus, "Here you are! Behold how the mighty have fallen!" And of course, they were better off than us; they had survived the shock of displacement and they had already made Israel home. We had much to atone for. Although I had always helped the community and those in need, the sins we ask God to forgive include our collective, communal transgressions. Maybe I could have tried harder to help the poor in Shiraz, but not knowing the pain of *ghorbat* those days, of exile, I believed that Israel could support them better; that Israel was the solution to all Jewish problems, including poverty.

In the post–Yom Kippur excursion to *Takhanat Merkazeet*, Mr. Pouldar, another *avareh*, had a plan. "*Negah konid,*" he said, excited, "Look, there is a war going on and the Revolutionary Guard must be busy." He sucked on the sugar cube between his molars as he sipped his tea. "Let's go to Iran by bus through the Turkish border. Who is going to know where we are coming from? People go back and forth, taking vacations in Istanbul all the time."

"He is right," someone said.

"He has a valid point," we all said. "It's a good idea."

Suddenly the air was clear. What a relief to be able to act! We would fly to Istanbul in groups, spend the night, and hire buses to cross the border. The first group was to contact us as soon as they entered Iran to signal the next group's departure. I was in the last group, the largest, twenty-four people, and composed mainly of families.

I hoped to find my homeland hospitable enough to have my family return and to resume our old lives. Otherwise, I would have to sell my poultry farm and the vast land I had turned into fruit orchards — the culmination of forty years of love and labour — and, of course, the house, the car, and if I was lucky, the furniture and Persian carpets. I wasn't sure if anyone would buy the land at a time of such uncertainty, and it pained me to think of letting go of my business, my home, and, most important, my country.

In my absence, my brother Morad, who had accompanied us in our rushed exodus, managed the business. We had asked one of the workers to oversee the farm before our departure. Not having heard a word from either one, I was now returning to a very uncertain life, having entrusted all my personal property to others.

The first group left Tel Aviv for Istanbul. Through an acquaintance residing in the United States, we heard about their success crossing the Iranian border without trouble. The second group left; we didn't hear anything and assumed that no news was good news. Putting my faith and my family's well-being in God's hands, during the week of the holiday of Sukkot, I left Tel Aviv. This was the first year I had not built a *sukkah* in remembrance of our wanderings, our destined homelessness as Jews. The world was my *sukkah* that year. I left my wife who had never lived alone, a daughter who was recuperating from major orthopedic surgery at Alyn Hospital in Jerusalem, and my youngest daughter, who was just a child. I did not know that I would not see them for six years and that when I saw my little one again, she would have little memory of me and could not speak to me in our own language — I would be a stranger to her for years to come.

OUR GROUP BOARDED a Turkish Airlines flight to Istanbul. There were eight of us from Shiraz who had known each other for many years: Basiratmand, his wife, and his twelve-year-old son; Bashi and his wife; and the Rason family. The rest were from Tehran, Kermanshah, and Isfahan, and I knew them only through other acquaintances from our meetings at the central bus station.

After landing, we took taxis to Hotel Washington, a modest hotel that one of the travellers knew about from his previous trip to Istanbul. Suspicious of a group of Iranian refugees, the owner demanded to keep our passports and payment in cash for two nights in advance. The eight Shirazis created our own small cluster. Basiratmand and I volunteered to buy dinner. In a coffeehouse we ordered tea and watched the crowd of hookah-smoking, backgammon-playing customers in fascination and delight. The scene reminded me of all those lazy Saturday afternoons during the hot summers in Shiraz. After Shabbat morning services, the extended family would pack up the steamy *khaleh-bibi* that had cooked all night and head to one of many gardens in the outskirts of the city to play rummy and *takhteh nard* and drink *araq* with *ma'ze*, salted cucumbers sprinkled with lime juice. Silently, both thinking of Shiraz, Basiratmand and I left the coffeehouse. We bought Iranian flatbread, yogourt, and cheese for our group from a small kiosk, the best we could do to keep kosher.

The following day we gathered at the hotel's cafe for breakfast and chose four among us to find transportation to Iran. The name of an Iranian tour company, Mihan Tour (Homeland Tours) was reassuring. We paid cash for twenty-four passengers and two drivers to leave on Friday morning. It wasn't a good omen to travel on Shabbat but we had no other choice.

None of us could eat much that morning. We rushed outside the hotel, jubilant and anxious, happy to return home and worried about the border crossing. The women especially looked frightened. What kind of men were we who could not comfort them? We were all impotent in the face of danger; God alone was our protector. And so we waited to face our fate.

We recognized the driver immediately and asked him where the second was. He promised that his assistant would join us in Ankara. We had chartered a private bus so that we would not be exposed. The driver stopped on a side street and allowed a middle-aged man with a long beard and worry beads in hand to join us. The driver called him *Haji*-Agha — a title given to someone who has made the pilgrimage to Mecca, a religious man. Haji-Agha boarded the bus. Pulling on his scraggly beard, he stared at us for a few seconds before sitting next to the driver. With their heads together, they chatted in hushed voices.

We passed by the Black Sea before entering Ankara at sunset. The water looked dark and ominous, but also beautiful. The driver didn't stop to pick up his assistant as he had promised. Instead, he headed straight for the Iranian border at Gozargah-e Bazargan. The closer the bus got to the Iranian border, the more desolate the landscape became. The bus struggled through narrow and twisting roads in the mountains of Ararat. I wrapped my jacket tighter around me to keep away the chill and to stop my persistent coughing. We feared bandits every time the bus stopped. But it was always one or two policemen who entered the bus, checked us out, spoke to the driver, and received a carton of cigarettes as a bribe before allowing us to continue.

We had not taken provisions with us and we were starved, but the bus driver wouldn't stop for us. He had been driving now for over fourteen hours without a break. We feared that, exhausted, he would plunge us into a ravine. Finally, at half past midnight, he pulled the bus over at a coffee shop but he wouldn't disembark. "Whoever wants to go, go now," he said as he waved us off. A few of us went to check out the place. The coffee shop reminded us of a scene from *Haji Baba* stories. Big men with bloodshot eyes and long mustaches stared at us from their seats. Frightened, we quickly used the bathrooms and left without eating.

Shivering, we returned to the bus and realized that it didn't have a heater. The driver and Haji-Agha had wrapped themselves with blankets. When we protested the conditions, the driver ignored our complaints and chastised us for having forced him to stop in a place that was a den of thieves and murderers. The previous week, he told us, two Iranian buses were robbed on their way to the border and a few passengers had been killed. We must leave, he said emphatically, without stopping until we reached the city of Van. There, we could find a hotel, he added. We told him that we were worried about him as he had been driving without any rest, but he said that he was used to it. Cold, frightened, and exhausted, we had a sleepless night. At dawn, we still couldn't see anything but the vast expanse of uninhabited land. Again and again, we were stopped by policemen who entered the bus for their cigarettes. Around four o'clock, we saw greenery from a distance. We entered Van before sunset.

By the time the bus stopped at the hotel, we looked half-dead. The driver informed us that the following day he would pick us up at 9:00 a.m. to head for the border at Bazargan. If everything went well, we would leave for the Iranian city of Tabriz, spend the night there, and then leave for Tehran, where we could find connecting buses to our own cities. He said good-bye and left with Haji-Agha. A few in the group showered, some went in search of food to share with those who were too weary to seek sustenance. We retreated into our own minds. I don't know if the night was too long or too short. It was a restless night that mercifully ended. The following day we looked as if we had just left *Neila* services after a long day and night of fasting, barely able to wish each other a good morning. After grabbing a quick breakfast of tea, bread, and cheese in the hotel lobby, we were surprised to see the driver and Haji-Agha emerge from the same hotel room.

The bus arrived at the border at 11:30 a.m. The driver let us out by a large salon that served as customs and immigration and told us that he would wait in the parking lot on Iranian soil. He and his guest disappeared behind the gates and that was the last time we saw Haji-Agha.

Our passports were stamped by the Turkish authorities and we entered Iran, where our luggage had been unloaded for thorough inspection. I had nothing but my clothes and didn't worry. As we passed the passengers who were leaving Iran, a few dared to whisper that we were crazy. They were escaping the war and the harsh life in Iran and were surprised to see returning citizens.

We scattered among other travellers and sometimes spotted each other from a distance. I was even more suspicious of Haji-Agha now, since he had not gone through customs. Was he a representative of the Islamic government, travelling back and forth, reporting to the central government? I saw my friend and his family a few rows in front of me, speaking to immigration officials. They left without a problem. I was relieved.

When I reached the front, I greeted the man in uniform with a slight bow, my right hand on my heart. I handed over my passport with both hands in a show of humility and respect. He passed it to another policeman in a narrow dark room behind him, who opened a large ledger, looking for my name. He passed it to a third person to double-check the information, and then back to the first man, who stamped it. As I was about to receive my passport, a man in civilian clothes approached the customs inspector and whispered something in his ear. Although my passport had already been stamped, the policeman leafed through its pages again. Once in a while, he stopped and stared at me. He finally set it aside without speaking to me and continued to process other passengers.

My heart was in my mouth and I could feel the blood drain from my face. After a while he stopped again, and without looking at me, he handed the passport back to me. My colour returned. I smiled and bowed as I reached for it. I was about to put it back in the inner pocket of my jacket when someone grabbed my hand from behind. I turned around. A grim, bearded young man around the same age as my oldest son scrutinized me with hate-filled eyes. He demanded to have the passport, and without waiting, snatched it from my hand. Grabbing the back collar of my jacket, he shoved me behind the metal bars, locked the gate, and told two guards to watch me. He took a step, paused, and turned around. "Are you Jewish?" he spat the words at me.

"Yes." What else could I have said but the truth?

"Are you coming from occupied Palestine?"

Frightened now, I said "No."

"Liar!" he hissed, walking away.

A few minutes later, I heard him say in a loud voice to the other travellers, "Jews, raise your hands."

No one did.

He repeated his demands, louder this time.

No response. No one moved.

He asked the Muslims to separate themselves.

They didn't.

Again.

No one moved.

Then he said that he would take care of this situation himself.

I saw my friends, the Rasons, get stopped by policemen. One by one, my travel companions were singled out and their passports were confiscated.

I don't know how we were recognized so quickly. Weren't we all Iranians, all sons of Abraham? We all looked Semitic with our dark hair, brown eyes, and olive skin. Looking back,

I think that maybe it was our body language, the humble curve of spines, lowered heads, downcast eyes, and trembling hands that gave us away. I felt as if I were in one of the news clippings I had seen about the Nazis. We had committed the crime of being born Jewish. All but one family from our bus were eventually picked up and thrown in a closed room, where we remained for hours. In the process of interrogating us, the policemen discovered two Christian Armenians and released them.

They asked me why I had visited Israel. I told them that I had not done so illegally. I had a valid passport and an exit visa in order to take my daughter for surgery. I had bought my plane ticket in Tehran. The interrogator, his eyes blood-shot with anger, used expletives I had only overheard from drug dealers, drunks, and hoodlums on the streets. I had a feeling that if the customs were not so busy, and if he didn't have so many witnesses, he would have kicked me until I resembled chopped meat. Hatred burned in his eyes, his hands were clenched into tight fists, and I sensed that he was struggling to control his impulse to strangle me. We *were* brothers, Cain and Abel.

He made me take off my clothes and I stood there naked and humiliated. He found a one-hundred-dollar bill in the pocket of my jacket and slipped it in my passport and ordered another man to tear my shoes apart for evidence, all along calling me an Israeli spy, deserving to be hanged. They tore my belt and my clothes apart, but didn't find anything — intensifying the young guard's anger. They asked me to identify my luggage. It took hours for every item to be scrutinized, every lining torn, the hems of clothes inspected. We were there until nightfall. Finally, a man escorted us to the waiting bus. Our passports, mine with the hundred-dollar bill inside, were confiscated, and we were told to report to the Islamic Revolutionary Court in Tehran. Having seen each other's nakedness, we were ashamed to make eye contact with one another.

WAITING IN THE bus behind the immigration and customs building, the driver had heard a little about our situation and expressed sympathy. The Basiratmand family had escaped the fiasco by finding a secure spot to hide, and now they came from their hiding place to join the group.

We should have been in Tabriz that night, but of course we had spent most of the day being interrogated. With nightfall, the temperature plummeted. Leaving the balmy climate of Tel Aviv, I had not thought of packing warm clothes. My teeth chattered from the chill outside and the cold fear within my body. In the dim light emanating from the customs house windows, we hoisted our luggage to the top of the bus, but a few gendarmes led our driver away to their office. He returned after an hour announcing that we did not have permission to leave because Iraqi commandos were hiding in the area, terrorizing passengers at night. We told the gendarmes that we lacked adequate clothing and a place to sleep, that we had not eaten all day. One of the gendarmes took pity on the group and agreed to escort us to a small cafe. He convinced the owner to give us shelter for the night. A few bus drivers sipped tea in the austere dining room . The owner of the cafe gave us one of the two rooms on the second floor where he lived with his family. He brought us extra blankets and a few pieces of flatbread and tea but no dinner. The aroma of baked chicken and rice filled the hallway. Our mouths watered; our stomachs gurgled. We protested. Couldn't we have just a bit of rice? He said the food was preordered. Shortly after, the man responsible for our miseries at the border stopped by with his two gendarmes to pick up ten braised chickens and a pot of *sabzi polo*.

The bedroom was not big enough for all of us even if we slept side by side, and the owner wouldn't allow us to occupy the dining area. The youngest four offered to spend the night on the bus. Around midnight, repeated thumping on the window woke us up. The four stood at the bottom of the window screaming that they were getting frostbite.

"The owner won't open the door to the cafe. *Bee-mazhab, bee-deen*," they cursed him, calling him a man of no faith.

We threw our blankets to them. At least we had a roof over our heads even if the room was cold. Thankfully, the night ended.

Around 10:00 a.m., the bus started its journey on the frozen and slippery road; icicles hung from the bus windows. The driver dropped us off by an inn on the outskirts of Tabriz around 7:00 p.m. I was surprised to see that in our oil-rich country the line for purchasing gasoline stretched for a kilometre around a gas station across the street. The exhausted driver had family in town and decided to spend two days in this location.

Late that night, the sound of repeated explosions reverberated through the building, waking us in fear. The inn, the city, fell into deeper blackness; the only light was from the fireworks in the sky, sickeningly beautiful. Wrapped in our blankets, we rushed into the corridor and waited there, not realizing that if we suffered a direct hit, the narrow hallway would not give us much protection.

Finally, another night ended. The planes returned to their base. We swarmed the cafeteria for breakfast. Since all was calm, we ventured to the city on local buses to buy fruit, vegetables, nuts, bread, and canned tuna, so that we would not suffer hunger again on our trip to Tehran. After an early dinner in town, we returned to the inn around 3:00 p.m., hoping to have a much-needed rest — but once again we faced the previous night's nightmare of bombing raids. The bus left for Tehran the following morning at 9:00 a.m.

We mostly slept on the bus — tired, suffering from deep depression, facing a very uncertain future. The sun was disappearing behind the Damavand Mountains when we reached

Tehran. Rason and his family left for a relative's home. The rest of us Shirazis rented two rooms, one for men, another for women and children, in a hotel I had known from my previous trips. We bought boiled eggs, pickles, and bread for dinner before a city-wide blackout in preparation for Iraqi attacks.

The night was cold. The government had rationed heating fuel since Iraq had repeatedly attacked the region of Khorasan, which housed the refineries. The hotel manager agreed to turn on the heat at nine, but it had to be turned off at eleven. I woke up with a chill in my bones that night. My lungs ached.

The following day we gathered around a table at the hotel's cafeteria to assess our situation. The Basiratmands were fine since they had managed to escape the wrath of the Revolutionary Guard. Bashi, a simple shopkeeper, feared the courts and decided that he would return to Shiraz and remain in Iran permanently, never travelling abroad, rather than facing another government official. My situation was the worst since my family remained in Israel and it was now too dangerous for them ever to return. I had to find a way to reunite with them outside Iran.

The thought of appearing before the Revolutionary Guard terrified me. I feared torture or imprisonment at the infamous Evin prison like so many others — Jews and Muslims alike. I had not informed any family members of my return and so if I were imprisoned, no one would know of my fate and, if executed, I wouldn't have a Jewish burial. At the same time I couldn't contact anyone in Shiraz, fearing that the knowledge of my return would warn those who hoped to confiscate my property, and tempt them to report me to the authorities (as had happened to others) with false accusations, and expedite the process of my possible imprisonment.

I wandered around Tehran contemplating my options. I knew the city well since I had visited often for business, for research on establishing the farm, and for obtaining government permits and loans. And yet I felt as if I had travelled to a strange city, as if I were in an Arab country. Once, well-dressed, western-looking young men and women, full of life and optimism, had roamed fancy boutiques and fine restaurants on Lalezar and Istanbul streets, which were often compared to Parisian avenues. Now the passersby were mostly unshaven men, wearing shabby clothing, looking serious, if not depressed. Even the storefront decors had changed, no longer exhibiting the latest styles. It was as if the city had taken a step back in time. Just like the well-groomed Tehrani women, the fancy female mannequins had disappeared from public view. Tehran and its inhabitants had lost their zest for life; they had lost the vibrancy that had been the most intriguing aspect of the city for me. The capital's sad condition intensified my anxiety and despair.

When I returned to the hotel, Basiratmand was awaiting me, quite excited. His brother, Iraj, he told me, knew an expert in dealing with the government bureaucracy and confiscated passports.

I knew Basiratmand's brother, whose wife was also from Hamedan and was a distant relative of my wife's family. A gracious man, he invited me to meet his family over Shabbat dinner, where I met another man, Mr. Liaqati, who claimed that he had been at my wedding and was also a distant relative of my wife's family.

They both reiterated that going to the courts was extremely dangerous, and that I had to avoid them at any cost. They recommended a Jewish man named Rabizadeh who would be able to solve my problem. The man was out of town. They reasoned that I should proceed to Shiraz. They would call as soon as Rabizadeh returned so that I could return to Tehran to meet with him. Rabizadeh would be able to return my passport in a short time. "Don't worry," they repeated, and I believed them because I needed to.

Comforted and reassured, I bought the first available ticket to Shiraz for that Sunday. Iraj invited me again to his house for another wonderful dinner, where I met other family members. After such a long period of anxiety and discomfort, my inner calm returned. I called my elderly mother to let her know of my return, so that she wouldn't be shocked by seeing me so suddenly. I left the following day for Shiraz with a deep sense of optimism.

≈

I ENTERED SHIRAZ through the Qu'ran Gate. Passing by the Saadi intersection, I saw the famous poet's monument in the middle of a well-groomed traffic circle, attesting to the true nature of my city, the city of poets and writers, of roses and nightingales. At such a late hour, my mother was still awake, awaiting my arrival. But even her embrace did not ease my anxiety. Fearful and worried about my uncertain future, I lay awake that night and the following nights. When I did fall sleep, the sound of my own screams woke me up. The nightmares felt real and remained with me throughout the day. My mother tried to shake me out of these vivid visions of death and destruction; but awake, I had to confront the darker reality of having to face the judgment of the Revolutionary courts sooner or later. I felt watched. Expecting to be summoned any day, any minute on charges of treason and spying for Israel, my heart skipped a beat whenever someone knocked at the door. I feared leaving the security of the house.

After a week of indecision and living in my house pajamas, I finally forced myself to get dressed and visit the poultry farm. We had had 40,000 chicks and a large accounts receivable before I left Iran. All of the silos had been full of feed. When I arrived, I found that my brother had sold most of the poultry and eggs and had allowed the silos to get low, but I had not seen a penny of the profit. "There is no ledger," Morad told me, "No money." I had been gone for a year and had no choice but to accept that I had lost that year's profit. Now it was almost impossible to buy chicks or eggs for hatching from abroad, especially since we had imported them from Israel. The farm was working below capacity, providing few chickens and eggs, which we gave away for free to the family. The orchard produced plenty of Persian apricots, which we also distributed among friends and family. I was sad to see my dreams in ruins, but as I roamed through the orchards, the feel of the land and the smell of freshly cut grass calmed me. "This is still my homeland," I repeated to myself. "This is my land. This is not a dream. I am not lost. I belong. To this land, I belong."

After a month of not hearing a word from my acquaintances in Tehran, I contacted Iraj Basiratmand and made arrangements to return to Tehran to meet Mr. Rabizadeh. Iraj accompanied me to the lawyer's office on the second floor of a building at the corner of Takht-e Jamsheed and Shemeeran Boulevard. A sign outside the door read, "Electrical Keys and Locks." Apparently Rabizadeh also imported and distributed security locks. I thought this was a good omen. Maybe he could unlock my problems as well. Persian carpets furnished the lawyer's office. His secretary, a beautiful woman dressed fashionably with tasteful makeup and coiffured hair, looked like another decorative item. Her presence made me nervous — I knew that the *Basij*, a volunteer militia group loyal to Khomeini, controlled the area. What if they raided the office and caught me with this immodestly dressed *be-hejab* woman? All women were required to cover themselves, and if even one strand of hair showed from underneath their *chador*, *maqna'eh* or kerchief, they risked arrest, the Islamic courts, and possible flogging. No woman dared to act western the way this secretary so brazenly displayed herself in front of male customers. Amazed by her and by her employer's audacity — that he had hired such a daring young woman — I surmised that she represented her boss's power, a display of his cleverness in circumventing the established rules, reassurance to the customers that the man knew how to manipulate the system, that he had the elusive key to these new and mysterious locked doors. The fashionable secretary informed the few of us there that her employer would be late. We waited.

Mr. Rabizadeh arrived around eight o'clock that evening. A dapper man of forty-five, he was wearing a dark suit and the forbidden western tie, once again a sign of his defiance and his connections. Those days, even the most fashionable government workers wore shabby clothes and rubber flip-flops to show their humility, religiosity, and unity with the Islamic government. We waited for another two hours to be admitted to a large salon, furnished lavishly with expensive furniture and fine Persian carpets. Rabizadeh sat behind a heavy hand-carved wooden desk that stood majestically opposite the entrance, the black receiver of the phone tucked between his right ear and shoulder as he shuffled papers. He nodded to us and rose from his chair and bowed in a show of respect and pointed to two chairs for us to sit: "*Salam. Khosh amadeed,*" he welcomed us mechanically and resumed his conversation with the person on the other end of the line. After a few minutes, another phone rang. Rabizadeh asked the first person to hold, spoke to the second person and told him to wait. Then he finished his first conversation and started a new one with the caller on the second phone.

"Yes, yes. I went to Evin prison today on your behalf and spoke to the revolutionary prosecutor and he agreed to free … Not home yet? Nooo! I was promised that he would be free by tonight … I am sure he'll be home a bit later … and if he doesn't return by tomorrow morning, please do give me another call, and I will pursue it further. Please don't worry."

He then hung up and dialed another number, speaking in less formal language. I presumed that he was speaking to a lower-ranking secretary at the prosecutor's office. He sounded friendly and amicable as if the two were close acquaintances, even friends. He finally said goodbye, placed the phone on its cradle, apologized and welcomed us again to his office.

My friend explained how my family was in Israel and that I must return to them. Mr. Rabizadeh turned to me and asked, "Dayanim, are you adamant about this?" I affirmed my desire to obtain my passport in order to reunite with my family. He reassured me that my problem could be resolved quickly. He could request that my passport be sent to his office through just a simple phone call. "However," he added, "I don't want to bother the prosecutor's office and use my leverage with him for such a small issue."

Teary-eyed and despondent, I held his hands in mine, "I swear by the soul of my father, may he rest in peace, my life, my children's well-being, are in your hands."

He looked moved. "You embarrass me with such show of deference — please stop — no need." He called the secretary to bring us chai and told us of his own life and his accomplishments, about his own visit to Israel and his hope to return for a pilgrimage. He asked about Shiraz and its Jewish community.

He said that he had to make a few phone calls to find out who was in possession of my passport. "I'll have it here by tomorrow night," he said. Then he called someone who didn't answer. "It's late at night," he said. He retrieved a notebook from his pocket, made a few notes, and promised that he would call again in the morning. "Tomorrow, *insha-allah*, God willing."

"*B-ezrat Hashem*, with God's help" I said.

He continued, "If that doesn't work, I'll personally go to the prosecutor's office and bring the passport back. Now go home and come back tomorrow night."

Desperate, I told him that I would pay whatever expenses necessary. He said, "No, no. This is really a very unimportant case, *aghay-e* Dayanim; it doesn't require any exchange of money. *Khejalatam nadeed*; don't embarrass me with your kindness. I just wanted to know if this is important enough for you that I should ask my friends for favours. Since you are affirming its importance, I'll do this for you as a favour."

Then he stood, shook hands with us, and we parted. Convinced of this man's importance and capabilities, believing that he had the key to the prosecutor's office, I slept well that night. Such a generous man; such a gentleman!

The following day I returned to the lawyer's office alone and waited for an hour. The secretary said that she didn't think Mr. Rabizadeh was coming that night since he had a busy day. "That happens all the time," she emphasized, "Nothing to worry about." Mr. Rabizadeh visited various government offices all day, negotiating with the bureaucracy, and he often ran out of time to visit his office at the end of the day. "Go home," she recommended, "Come back another day."

Days went by but Mr. Rabizadeh didn't show up at his office. Finally, on Thursday, the secretary announced that he would be at his office that day with certainty. After I waited for hours, he did enter. Overjoyed, thinking that he must have secured my passport, hence the reason for long days away from his office, I jumped from my seat to welcome him. Mr. Rabizadeh said that, unfortunately, Tehran was suffering from a "critical condition" this week and many people had been arrested and thrown in prison. The Ministry of Justice was very busy and there was no possibility of speaking to officials to request my passport. "But don't worry," he said, "This is really a very simple matter, and they *will* send me your passport." Then he put his arm around my waist and led me to his desk and showed me a few passports. "See, these were just like yours, but I managed to take them back. Now their owners can come and reclaim them." He patted me on the back, "Now, return to your city and don't wait around here too much. When I receive your passport, I'll call you, and then you can return to Tehran." Sad and heartbroken, I said goodbye: "*Saye shoma kam nashe*; God should not decrease your benevolent shadow over me." I bought a bus ticket and returned to Shiraz.

The political situation in Iran deteriorated as the Iran/Iraq war intensified. Shortages of sugar, beans, and wheat led to rationing of these basic necessities. The face of the city changed. Refugees from Kermanshah and its neighbouring cities doubled Shiraz's population and drained us of our resources. Schools and universities became dormitories. The refugees slept in parks and on every inch of open land around the city, leaving their garbage where the landscaping had been picture-perfect. For bread alone, which was a staple in our diet, we waited in line for hours. Sometimes people slept on the sidewalk outside bakeries all night to buy a few sheets of bread. I had not experienced this kind of misery since the famine of World War II. This time, however, my situation was better than most. Although family members, who had occupied the house when I was gone, had depleted much of the grain, rice, and other necessities that I had stored during the uprising and before leaving for Israel, the poultry farm and the apricot orchard provided enough food to share with the rest of the family.

Despite the Iranian people's collective miseries, the different political and religious parties scrambled for power. The Iraqi bombardment eventually reached Shiraz — intensifying our distress. To protect us from Saddam Hussein's missiles, I hired an engineer to build a bomb shelter in the backyard, a cement-reinforced hole in the ground connected to the house by a tunnel.

Meanwhile, the Revolutionary Guard summoned me to their office and threatened me with arrest and imprisonment if

I didn't produce large quantities of eggs and chickens because people were hungry. The exorbitant price of poultry supplies and the government's inability to import chicks and feed prevented us from running the farm. I dared not tell them that I had imported most materials, including chicks, from Israel. Even if I managed to get supplies, it would take at least three to six months for chicks to mature. I would have to perform a miracle to meet these unrealistic demands. I had to consolidate my assets and leave the country as soon as possible.

## FARIDEH
### October 1980, New Orleans

While the life my father knew was coming to an abrupt end,
Norman and I were expecting our first child. Finishing his
medical residency at Charity Hospital, Norman awaited his
acceptance to a gastroenterology fellowship at Ochsner Clinic.

Farzad graduated from high school that year and, like his
classmates, planned to join the Israeli army. I wrote long letters to him repeatedly, insisting, "Please come to the U.S."
I assumed my young brother, still suffering from the perils of
the Iranian Revolution, needed an education and not a prob-
able war. "Let me apply to college for you here," I begged him.
"You can always go back to serve in the army."

Originally my father had demanded that my brother enrol
in a university in the United States, but before leaving for Iran,
Baba appointed Farzad as the head of the household in Israel
and forbade him to leave our mother and sisters. I felt disloyal

for suggesting that Farzad should ignore Baba's request, think about his own future, his own education. I felt guilty about removing Maman's protection. I remembered, too, the prophecy of the principal at Tikhon Khadash high school. "Why should I take them in? They'll use our resources and leave for the U.S. as soon as they can." But I had to think of my brother alone. Farzad could have perished in the Israel-Lebanon war as many of his contemporaries did. I didn't realize at the time that I had become my father, moving family members around the chessboard of our lives without respect for their wishes. Maybe my brother would have been better off in Israel; maybe he would have been nurtured as a computer scientist in the army; maybe ....

Believing that Farzad deserved a bit of carefree time, I secured a student visa for him from Tulane University. Since our landlord didn't like the idea of having a baby and an extra person living there, we moved to a larger second-floor apartment. I stopped working in my ninth month of pregnancy. Having large blocks of time to myself, in preparation for the baby, I painted the nursery a soft peach colour, had Norman bring up a blue carpet from the basement, and made roman shades of peach and blue fabric with animals and alphabets on it. Before Farzad arrived, I bought sheets to go with the white and yellow quilt in his room and used them to sew draperies and pillowcases by hand. Exhausted by the weight of the baby, I put my feet up on the sectional sofa and started to watch soap operas for the first time. I felt happy.

Lena was born on October 30, 1980, shortly after my father left for Iran. My mother had promised herself that she would not repeat her own mother's sins by not being with her daughters at childbirth. She cried when she heard about the birth of her first grandchild.

Farzad arrived shortly after Lena's birth and enrolled at Tulane for the spring semester. In December of 1981, my two brothers lived in the United States, my two sisters and my mother lived in Israel, and my father had been trapped in Iran for over a year. He called once after Farzad's arrival to check on us. Shocked and disappointed that I had taken the women's male protector away, he expressed his concerns for Maman, Nahid, and Niloufar. "What're they going to do by themselves?" he repeated. "What are they going to do?" Punctuated by the familiar "ach-tof" of bringing up phlegm and spitting, his voice cracked with despair.

"Send your mother and Neli home," he begged. He didn't realize or couldn't believe that we had stopped calling Iran *home*.

"What's Neli going to do there?" I asked. "I can't force them to return."

"Neli is a child. She misses her tricycle. She needs her father."

"How would you feel, Baba, if she started singing Hebrew songs in the marketplace in Shiraz? Are you going to lock her within the walls of the house? "

Baba became quiet. I could hear his laboured breathing. "Baba, are you okay?"

The phone went dead.

WHEN BABA CALLED again a few weeks later, we chatted as if nothing had happened between us. I told him that I craved *kashk*, a pungent Iranian delicacy made of goat's milk. He sent me a large package of *kashk* and Persian herbs and spices. I soaked the dry whey balls, rubbing them against the side of the bowl to dissolve.

Norman asked every day, "When is this concoction going to be ready?"

"Patience. Good things take time," I kept telling him.

In my excitement I made much too much *kashk*. I spent an entire day folding the thick ivory liquid into a variety of

Iranian gourmet food: *kashk* with fried eggplant and onions; *kashk*, rice, and lentils; *kashk* and.... When Norman returned home that night the table was covered with these most ancient of Persian dishes, each beautifully decorated with hot oil, chopped mint, caramelized onions, and accompanied by green onions, flat bread, and a pot of hot mint tea. Farzad and I had a hard time waiting. Anticipating the feast, Norman ate very little that day. I showed him how to tear a piece of flat bread, then put green onion, *kashk* and eggplant on top, fold it and take a bite. Farzad and I stuffed our mouths with the delicacy that we had not eaten since we had left Iran. After his first bite, Norman ran to the kitchen, spat the food in the sink, and washed his mouth, gagging. He claimed it to be the worst food he had ever tasted.

"Good, more for us," I told him.

"It smells like the goats in the Arab villages outside Jerusalem," he said. "It makes me feel sick."

"Leave the room," I added, laughing. Farzad and I ate the dishes for breakfast, lunch, and dinner, and when every morsel was gone, we mourned its passing for months.

THAT YEAR BABA managed to transfer some of his savings out of Iran. He entrusted the sum to a broker who travelled to a neighbouring Arab country, converted the *toman* into dollars, took a percentage for himself, and wired the rest to me. I bought my father Treasury Bills with the money and paid Farzad's and Freydoun's tuitions.

Farzad's presence took away the lonely fear-filled nights when Norman slept at the hospital. My brother's love for Lena brought warmth to our lives. Somehow with his presence we were more of a family. A cautious child, Lena preferred to crawl until Farzad helped her learn how to walk. "*Ta-ti, ta-ti*," Farzad murmured to her, the Persian baby words for taking one step after another. "Say app-le, apple." He taught Lena her first word.

OTHER THAN THE birth of Lena and having Farzad under our roof, the most joyous event of that year was finding Navideh, my childhood friend, whom I had lost touch with after my last trip to Iran in the summer of 1976.

As revolutionary sentiment raged in 1976, I had my own little revolutionary skirmish with my father and the rest of my family. Baba insisted that I return to Shiraz after spending a year in America. He called Uncle Shapour crying and begged him to send me back, as if I were a package. He had found me a suitor that, he thought, I wouldn't be able to refuse. An American-educated engineer, this suitor had a car and had just purchased a four-unit apartment building with his brothers and parents. My father looked upon this communal living situation in a neighborhood within walking distance of my family's house on Hedayat Street as an ideal situation for all of us — living together happily ever after.

I had no choice but to go out with the engineer. Allowing us to go on a date was actually very progressive of my father — he must have known that the Jewish community observed and reported such events. Thinking that I was smitten with the west, my suitor told me how he, too, missed American deli sandwiches with a slice of pickle on the side. I didn't tell him that I actually preferred Iranian food. He also told me that he had originally planned to remain in the United States, but when his mother sent him a tape recording of her voice, begging him to come home, he chose to return. He bragged that our — already his and mine — section of the multifamily compound would be directly across the hall from his parents. That's all I needed — to marry someone I didn't love, prostitute myself for an apartment and a car, and live with his extended family the way my mother had. At the same time, I envied his desire to be close to his family. Why was I the only one running away?

I didn't know how to convince my family to let me be in charge of my own destiny, to let me return to Virginia to continue my education and to marry Norman.

Desperate to talk to someone who would understand me, I walked to Navideh's house the following day. She was the only Jewish friend I could trust with my thoughts. In our younger years, we had raided the black mulberry tree in the backyard of her home; we had studied for the dreaded *konkur*, the college entrance exam, on the floor of a bedroom in my house.

Navideh knew about Norman. She had been one of the first friends I contacted upon returning to Iran.

"His hair is so dark," she said, expecting all Americans to be fair-skinned and blond.

"He is Jewish," I told her. "What do you expect?"

Whereas most my friends and family members found my desire to leave illogical and strange, Navideh was excited and curious about my life in America. The suitor, I realized later, was a distant cousin of hers, and when I finally said NO to marrying him, Navideh found herself in conflict with family members who believed she had said something uncomplimentary to me about him. She assuaged my gloomy mood that summer by introducing me to her friends, by spending time with me and chatting about silly stuff, and by making me laugh. Even now, Norman knows when I'm on the phone with Navideh long before he hears me speak in Farsi; he knows because Navideh makes me laugh freely and deeply. She connects me to the happy, wonderful part of my childhood in Iran. I lost touch with Navideh shortly after returning to the United States.

ONE SUMMER DAY in New Orleans, I returned from grocery shopping, exhausted from the heat, to find Norman with a big smile on his face. "Who is Navideh?" he asked with a gleam in his eyes.

I screamed and jumped up and down like a child. She had found me, my best friend. She ran into a cousin of mine at Montgomery College in Maryland and obtained my married name, which she had forgotten, and discovered that I lived in New Orleans. To this day, she remains my only childhood friend with whom I am in touch. We rarely see each other, but she always knows if I am in trouble or upset. She instinctively calls me when I need her.

I TRIED TO call my father in Iran from time to time. Every time I inquired about why he had not returned to Israel. Instead of answering my question, he asked me to return my mother and Niloufar to him. "You're a married woman. You know how it can be lonely. What should I do here by myself? Get a widow for a wife?" He had a hard time understanding that their return was beyond my wishes or my power.

Too young and naïve to understand that my father couldn't leave, I pressured him to return. I didn't know that Baba felt insecure and vulnerable to blackmail because his wife lived in an enemy country. I didn't pity him even though his anxiety, his frustration, and his anger were palpable over the phone. I couldn't have imagined that his own family members were the ones threatening to report him even though he gave them the fruit of his farm, even though he had protected and supported them.

## BABA
### *1981, Tehran*

I didn't hear back from Mr. Rabizadeh's office. Every time I called, the secretary picked up the phone and promised that she would convey the message. After repeated phone calls, she finally said, "*Aghay-e* Rabizadeh says that you may return to Tehran." I assumed that meant the he had secured my passport. I left for Tehran on the first day of the week and arrived at his office the following day. He entertained me with tea and congenial conversations, but there was no sign of a passport. Every day he said, "Come back tomorrow." And after that day came and left, and the following day and the day after that and I still didn't have my passport, I folded my hands in front of me in a show of humility and respect, and asked him, "Please tell me what to do."

He said, "Go back to Shiraz. I'll be in touch."

Dismayed, I thought that something terrible had happened and that my situation wasn't as easy to resolve as he had promised. Perplexed by the situation, I visited Iraj, the man who had led me to this lawyer, to ask for his advice. I thought maybe he knew something that had escaped me. He listened to my story patiently.

"Did you pay him anything?" he asked.

"No," I said, surprised. "He told me it wasn't necessary."

He shook his head and laughed, "Is it possible, Dayanim, that anyone would do anything for you in this country for free?"

I felt stupid. "I offered. He acted insulted at the mention of payment."

Iraj shook his head again as if he'd seen the most naïve person, "This was *ta'arof*! People in Iran don't just come out and tell you what they want. You know that."

"What should I do?" I asked.

"Go back with two hundred thousand *toman* [around twenty thousand dollars], and discreetly put it in his pocket," Iraj recommended.

"I don't have that kind of money with me," I said.

"Then go back to Shiraz and come back with the money in cash. This time we'll visit him together, give him the money, and reassure him that he'll be paid the rest later."

I returned to Shiraz.

Precious time had expired. During this time of war and unrest, people found ways to escape the country through its various borders. Many flew to Turkey or Austria for vacations and didn't return. Most people sent their children away, especially sons who were in danger of serving in the military. The son of a worker at my farm managed to escape from the front, shaken, half-human with wild eyes. He had witnessed other children buried in a river of tar released by the Iraqis. His fear was so great that he never left his room. Distraught and frightened, he believed that if the government agents found him, they would either kill him for desertion or force him to return to the front line. Hearing these horror stories, many Iranians redoubled their efforts to save their children. Many decided to uproot their entire family and leave Iran for calmer, more secure countries that allowed them entry. To stop this mass exodus, the government closed down passport offices, and no one could leave unless they held passports with at least six months' validity, thereby locking all of us in the larger prison that Iran had become.

Farideh was my only source of information since I could not call my family in Israel, nor could I even mention the country's name, fearing the ears and eyes of a government hostile to Israel. Whenever she called I feared telling her everything especially since I was on the list of the people forbidden to leave the country. With secret words and through metaphors and sometimes Judi (Judeo-Persian) words, which I wasn't quite sure she understood, I tried to convey my impossible condition.

IT TOOK ABOUT two weeks before I could access half of the suggested amount for Mr. Rabizadeh. I returned to Tehran. The consumption and sale of alcohol was forbidden, but Mr. Rabizadeh enjoyed fine, imported alcohol. I took a gallon of American whiskey I had at home for him as well. Fearful of the morality police, I hid the bottle behind the lining of the suitcase. I contacted Iraj and we went to visit Mr. Rabizadeh together. He had not arrived yet. I couldn't help but notice a huge change in his office. Instead of the beautiful secretary, a serious and scary-looking young man with stubble and worry beads sat at the desk. Iraj chatted with him and laughed. It suddenly dawned on me that my so-called friend was a go-between, a *vaseteh*, for the lawyer and was getting a cut of the profit. A woman, who I later realized was Mr. Rabizadeh's wife, sat demurely in another chair, wrapped in a black *chador*. After half an hour, the lawyer arrived dressed simply and without a tie and, ignoring his wife, invited us into his office. The Persian carpets had disappeared. I proffered the whiskey and the money, which again he refused and pretended that he was insulted. I told him that the money was for his expenses to pay off necessary people and that another hundred thousand *toman* would follow soon. With much false reluctance, he accepted the money and hid the bottle quickly underneath his desk. He ordered tea and entertained us for a while, apologizing profusely that my problem was still unresolved, and, again, he promised that by the end of the week it would be done.

I waited in Tehran to the end of the week. I called again and he invited me to his office that Thursday. I had an appointment at 4:00; but I left at 2:00 to give myself enough time. I waited for Rabizadeh at his office, drowned in my own dark thoughts, until 6:00 p.m. The receptionist wouldn't answer my questions. Was he on his way? Should I wait? The deep silence between us was broken by the angry voices of young men on the street, chanting slogans, protesting the government, followed by the pop-pop of guns and the buzz of bullets piercing the air. The members of the *Mojahedin-e-Khalq* were demonstrating against the Islamic government in Takht-e Jamshid Blvd, across the road from the lawyer's office. I jumped, frightened, but the receptionist didn't react and ignored my distress. Then it became quiet again.

I couldn't bear being at the office any longer. As soon as I closed the door behind me and stepped onto the street, two gunmen confronted me, but then let me go. I tried to walk close to the wall, fleeing without running. The blood from a dead body stained the street red, trickling to the drainage sewer. Feeling nauseous, heart pounding, I returned to the office and explained to the secretary what I had seen. Calmly, he played with his worry beads and didn't show any reaction to the horrors I described. I waited for another hour. Mr. Rabizadeh didn't show up, but the streets calmed down. As the sky darkened, I decided to return to my hotel in an area controlled by the *Basij*, their guns ready to fire. No buses, no taxis dared to venture to this battle zone. I counted at least ten other dead bodies on my way before seeing a bus stop. A few women covered in black *chadors* sat, waiting. I decided to join them, but before I could cross the street, two men carrying rifles approached the women. I hid behind a tree. As members of the Basij handcuffed the women, they yelled that they were not demonstrators; they were just waiting for the bus. The angry men shoved them inside a truck and closed the door. I could hear their frightened screams until the truck disappeared from view. Having heard the rumours of the rape and murder of women in detention centres by prison guards, I prayed for them and for myself. I kept walking and praying until I saw the hotel from a distance. Trembling with anxiety and fear, I crawled into bed without having dinner. I remained in Tehran that Friday and Saturday. I called Mr. Rabizadeh on Sunday. He apologized for not coming to the office and asked me to return to Shiraz and await his call. I had no other choice.

Mr. Rabizadeh called me late at night after two weeks and asked me to meet him in Tehran. A year had passed since our first meeting. I had gone to him so very many times, returning disappointed each time, but this was the first time he had initiated a call. I left for Tehran on a bus the following evening.

The Iranian people were restless, hungry, and fed up. Fearing unrest, the government tightened the noose around our necks by introducing further restrictions. Whenever the bus stopped, a few members of the Revolutionary Guard or the *Basij* entered and examined the passengers and questioned everyone, looking for members of the *Mojahedin-e-Khalq* or the Tudeh Party or the sympathizers of the monarchy. If they suspected anyone of antigovernment sentiments, they took them away. They arrested three young men from our bus. They looked inside our suitcases and our carry-on bags of food. Just outside Qom, the city of Ayatollah Khomeini, they stopped us around midnight. The city sat in darkness except for the flash of lights from exploding bombs in the distance. Three planes darted across the sky in the moonlight, followed by repeated explosions. As soon as we thought the bombing was finished, another group of bombers arrived and met with no resistance from the Iranian air force or ground artillery. Helpless in the darkness, Qom crouched in the shadow of Hazrat Fatemeh Masumeh's shrine, praying, asking for her protection. Early in the morning, policemen gave us permission to leave.

In Tehran, Mr. Rabizadeh greeted me warmly, and I could see in his face that he was planning to take care of my problem. Day after day, we went to various government offices. He left me in waiting room after waiting room, entering these various offices, displaying his diligence on my behalf. I remained in Tehran for a week, but nothing happened. He asked me to remain an extra week and kindly insisted that I must have Shabbat dinner with his family. He met me at my hotel and gave me a ride to his house, where his wife, a gracious hostess and a fantastic cook, entertained us with numerous rice dishes and stews.

After a few drinks, Rabizadeh became chatty and spoke about the politics of elections. According to Iranian laws, a Jewish member could be elected to represent his people in the Majles, the Iranian parliament. Mr. Rabizadeh told me that the Jewish community had ignored him during the good times but now, during the dire revolutionary era and amidst a destructive war, they had approached him to represent them. "Although I am not really interested," he asserted, "they are putting much pressure on me to accept running as a member." Having somehow discovered my position as a community leader within the Shirazi Jewish community, Rabizadeh was coercing me to use my connections and my name to secure the community's votes for him. What could I do? He held my future in his hands. I tried to be polite, telling him that I knew of no one else who deserved the job more. He asked me to please spend the night at his house. I bowed out of the invitation and begged his forgiveness. Physically and emotionally exhausted, I wanted to get back to the hotel and crawl into bed. He gave me a ride back to my hotel. Sunday morning he returned and offered to accompany me to the airport to find the whereabouts of my passport. We found the police station at the Mehrabad airport. Mr. Rabizadeh knew the chief of police; as he'd shown before, he knew many government officials. Apparently he'd been supplying the officials with forbidden imported whiskey and wine. After a few minutes he brought up the subject of my passport, but the chief replied that this case belonged to the judiciary system and not the police. They sent these passports to the revolutionary courts or the courts connected with the Evin prison. With much bitterness, I realized that this marked the very first time during this entire year that Rabizadeh had tried to find my passport. A wasted year.

The following day, Rabizadeh picked me up again and took me to the prime minister's office with its many bureaucratic subdivisions. Mohammad-Ali Rajai, the man who had forbidden the Jews to leave the country, held the position of president. We reached the office around eleven o'clock and found a chaotic scene. Ambulances were parked everywhere and policemen ran around in frenzied disorder. A thick cloud of smoke hung over the building. Someone said that a bomb had exploded, killing Mr. Rajai and a few others. The building itself sat in ruins.

At this time, Mr. Rabizadeh looked at me and said, "Sorry!" Sorry for what? That he had given me the runaround for an entire year while my case could have been resolved when the situation had been more favourable? A wolf in a gentleman's attire. From his "sorry" I understood that he was signing off my case, but keeping my money. I returned to Shiraz.

Mr. Rabizadeh didn't win the Jewish votes. The Tehrani Jewish community knew about his repeated misconduct and, in fact, kicked him off the community leadership committee.

## FARIDEH
### *1982–83, Chesapeake*

Another year passed. I was pregnant with a second child. Norman found a position in his hometown of Portsmouth, Virginia. We were moving again. I asked Farzad to switch schools and to enrol at the University of Maryland. I couldn't leave him alone in such a dangerous city, a state university was much cheaper, and Maryland was closer to us.

Tired of rentals, we unwisely bought a small house in a new subdivision of Silverwood in Chesapeake when mortgage rates were at 18 percent. The house was only twenty minutes from Norman's office and Maryview Hospital. We thought we could afford it with the income from Norman's full-time job as a physician but the monthly payments ate up his salary and we barely had enough money for diapers and food at the end of each month. Regular babysitters were out of the question.

Norman spent the first month after our move in post–GI training in Philadelphia.

In that beautiful new development with meticulously kept green lawns, I realized quickly how lonely motherhood could be in American suburbia. My childhood home in Shiraz was surrounded by tall walls but they didn't protect us from our nosy neighbours. I assumed that the openness of my new subdivision, the lack of physical boundaries between homes, would alleviate isolation. My neighbours, mostly new homeowners like us, were hard-working, kind people who spent much of their free time pruning trees, cutting grass, hedging flower borders, planting, cleaning windows, and sweeping sidewalks. We could not keep up. Our grass grew long and ragged; the fallen leaves piled up on our once tidy lawn and blew into the neighbours' raked backyards. The neighbour on our right mowed his lawn to give it that checkered look. I could not understand the purpose of such large green spaces. A neighbour behind our house, who observed my very pregnant status and the child in my arms, asked if I had a husband and sent her son to cut our grass.

Yael was born on June 25, 1982. We did not have any friends in this new city so I spent most of my time at home with the girls. I needed a diversion, but I wasn't interested in escaping into the imaginary world of novels. Instead, in remembrance of my younger years in Iran, I planted a vegetable garden. Soon, long zucchini vines spilled over a neighbour's pistachio-green lawn. He nicely reprimanded me for the sloppy look. I tended the garden, my only source of creativity, while the girls napped. Sometimes I put Yael in her playpen in the backyard and asked Lena to help me with the digging.

The neighbour on our left complained that my trees ruined his beautiful lawn with gumballs and pine needles and asked me to cut them down. I grew up in a desert climate, where trees don't flourish easily. I didn't believe in cutting down trees. Although polite and unobtrusive, my neighbours rarely paid any attention to my children or offered help, as would have happened in Iran. We were never invited over for tea or chitchat. Sometimes we exchanged niceties in the yard, but we rarely crossed over the tall invisible fences that separated our yards.

During those first few years in Virginia, I was preoccupied with the children and Norman was busy with his seemingly never-ending board exams. I, who had resented and rebelled against our collective communal life in Iran, warmly remembered aunts and cousins holding and rocking children and felt even more desolate.

I spent most nights in a rocking chair with Yael, a colicky child, holding her tight, trying unsuccessfully to comfort her. She screamed for hours during the day, wriggling in pain. I ran the vacuum cleaner; the monotonous noise calmed her. We took her for long rides in the car; the motion put her to sleep until we returned home. While I rocked and fed her inconsolable sister, Lena often sat on the sofa alone. Wrapped in her baby blanket, she pulled her legs to her chest and sucked her thumb. Finally, on a doctor's advice, we gave Yael Bentyl with Phenobarbital even though drugging a child was against our philosophy. Norman worked long hours. Even if I had had the money, I feared leaving my screaming daughter alone with a babysitter. If my baby tried my patience, I worried that a young babysitter would hurt her. Whenever I couldn't handle her screams of pain, and my firstborn's hands stretched toward me, wanting to read a book, demanding personal attention that I could no longer give, I locked myself in the bathroom and screamed. And then I was pregnant again.

I had not seen my mother in two years. Nahid called collect from Israel. Something wasn't right. Maman was buckling under the pressure of being alone. She was becoming emotionally unstable without my father there to make decisions for her. Pregnant and with two young children, I couldn't travel to Israel, so I tried very hard to convince my mother to bring Niloufar to Virginia for a short stay. They were denied visas.

Nahid came for a visit. She screamed, "Mazel tov!" when I opened the door, congratulating me on the birth of Yael. Elated about the new baby, she held Yael constantly to the point that I had to wrestle my daughter back from my sister's continuous embrace. My sister cared for Yael, dressed her in ruffled dresses, gathered her curls in a bun on top of her head like Pebbles in *The Flintstones*, and took her for long walks. While I fed Yael, Nahid played games with Lena, made her laugh and took her to the backyard to play. Nahid was a life-saver, giving us room to breathe. No longer overwhelmed by Yael's needs, suddenly we could see what a beautiful child she was. I encouraged my sister to stay, to return to school, and to make a life for herself in the United States, thereby further isolating my mother and Niloufar in Israel.

At the same time, I asked my in-laws, who were travelling to Israel, to petition the American Embassy for visas so that Maman and Niloufar could visit. My mother had tried numerous times to obtain visas and had been rudely refused, at times not even permitted to enter the embassy. Niloufar remembered her returning each time shaken and humiliated, mumbling curses. As American citizens, Norman's parents were allowed entry into the embassy where my mother was turned away.

I knew they were coming when I received a phone call from my maternal grandmother, Touran. My grandmother had never called or written to me. In a state of self-indulgence, I assumed she was going to congratulate me on the birth of my second child or my pregnancy with a third.

"You, ungrateful child! Don't you dare send your mother and the child back to Iran," she screamed in her Hamedani accent.

≈

I STILL TRY to understand my grandmother Touran. She was a woman worthy of fear, a grandmother who showed no love, a mother who sold her daughter into marriage before she reached puberty. In a sale it is customary to receive some monetary benefit. I don't know what Touran gained by giving my mother away other than decreasing her expenses of feeding another mouth and lowering her own anxiety level of having to watch over a vulnerable thirteen-year-old girl.

MY MATERNAL UNCLES' rendition of my grandmother's life, however, is much different from mine and my mother's. Visiting Israel two years after my father's death, Maman, Neli and her family, and I were invited to Tsion's house for dinner. We have become closer to my mother's side of the family since Baba's passing. Over a scrumptious Shabbat dinner of herb and eggplant stews, dill rice and sour cherry rice, the three brothers, Tsion, Shemuel, and Eliahou reminisced about their mother's food. Savouring the grainy texture of *gondi*, a dish made of ground chicken and roasted chickpea flour, I too remembered how Touran's version was infused with the biting taste of cumin.

"The stuffed pumpkin. Do you remember her stuffed pumpkin?" Shemuel asked.

"How did she make it?" I asked, as I ladled more stewed eggplant and tomatoes over basmati rice.

"She used everything that was in season: raisins, carrots, potatoes, turnips. She just chopped them and stuffed them into the carved pumpkin, put the pumpkin in a big pot and took it to the bakery to cook overnight in the *tanoor*. On Shabbat morning, she picked it up from the bakery and put it on a *sofreh* that was laid out on the floor in front of us. It was a scene, five boys seated around the *sofreh*, attacking this piping hot orange beauty, scooping out the stuffing with our spoons, dipping pieces of bread in its juices, cutting chunks out of the pumpkin until we were stuffed pumpkins ourselves. Then she would gather the leftovers and eat."

I HAVE NEVER eaten a giant stuffed pumpkin. I wish I had the recipe, but of course I don't because I rarely saw Touran. She didn't send my mother off to *ghorbat* with her recipes either. If she had, maybe my mother would have had something familiar from home, something to fill in the emptiness and terror of her forced exile. One of my *amus*, who remembered my mother's early years in Shiraz, made fun of her lack of cooking skills. *She was a child*, I thought, but I remained silent. My mother is a wonderful cook now and my daughters always ask for her recipes. "Maman, don't forget to watch Maman-bozorg when she is making stuffed grape leaves." Maybe my mother hadn't remembered the exact recipes for Touran's food, but rather the taste and combination of ingredients for delectable cuisine. My mother, like my *daee*s, remembered how Touran had worked in the kitchen of a Jewish day school, had cleaned homes, baby-sat, washed and ironed clothes for strangers, had done just about any menial job available to a woman of her time to feed her seven children.

Once, on a rare occasion that I visited my grandmother in Tehran, I remember her showing remorse for getting rid of my mother.

"*Che konom*?" replacing some of her "a's" with "o's" in her Hamedani accent, "What could have I done; I had to give Ruhi away before she had her period."

MAYBE GRANDMOTHER TOURAN called me because she was trying to protect her daughter; trying to make up for past mistakes. Maman must have shown Touran how nervous she was at the prospect of being ordered by my father to return to Iran. Having never had control over her own life, my mother must have been convinced that I was being strong-armed by my father.

The day my grandmother called to chastise me, like most other days, I was at home with the girls. Lena was hanging onto my skirt, Yael was in my arms. Exhausted and lonely in this new city, I didn't expect to be reprimanded by my grandmother. I needed kind words; I needed a soothing voice. As she yelled at me, tears rolled down my cheeks; I felt sorry for myself. My grandmother kept screaming through the receiver, "You ungrateful, no-good child. Don't you dare send your mother and the child back to Iran." Across the ocean, from a very faraway place both in time and space, Touran's voice was like the unforgiving thorns of the *sabra* – the cacti outside her home in Kiriat Sharet – it bore under my skin. I slowly put the phone back on its receiver. That was the very last time I heard Maman-bozorg's voice.

MAMAN AND NILOUFAR arrived in America later that month. When my mother saw Norman drinking beer with his *qormeh-sabzi* she predicted, "You'll have a third daughter. Cold foods make baby girls."

In Iran, dairy, fruits, vegetables, fermented drinks such as beer, and just about anything sour were categorized as "cold" foods; "hot" foods were calorie-loaded, things like dates, figs, and red meat.

"You should have asked my advice," she added, "before you got pregnant."

Norman was annoyed at the comments. "Is that true? Did you know this?" he asked. He was hoping for a boy.

"Do you believe this nonsense?" I asked him.

Early on in our marriage Norman had scalded his hand with hot water and, despite his protests, I quickly dunked it in plain yogourt. The relief was immediate. Although Norman is a western-educated physician, he had come to believe that there was more than superstition in Iranian home remedies. I thought this particular belief, which I had heard numerous

147

times from the women of my family, about predicting the gender of a baby by eating "hot and cold" foods to be mere nonsense. I felt a bit manipulated, thinking that Maman was emphasizing her own importance, trying to convince us that we needed her to live close by. Her prediction was correct, though, when we had our third daughter a few weeks later.

Rachel was born on June 18, 1983. I had gained forty pounds while I was pregnant, eating for two, eating for all of us, feeding the strange void inside. Everyone around me was needy: my daughters, my siblings, my mother, and my father. Yet most people who knew me then remember a strong woman who appeared to be in total control. I cooked nutritionally balanced meals every day which I served on china, refusing to use paper plates, made baby food from scratch, kept a very clean house, and had a vegetable garden. But I was insecure in my own foreignness.

Not having been read to as a child, I didn't know much about children's literature. I asked bookstore salespeople and American family members about books they remembered fondly from their childhood. I wanted my daughters to be "American," yet we celebrated all Jewish holidays the Iranian way with Persian foods and Iranian Jewish customs — a Seder with symbolic food for Rosh Hashanah, not just apples and honey, but pomegranate seeds so that our good deeds would surpass the number of seeds in a pomegranate. We ate scallions, squash, dates, black eyed peas, beets and more, each with its symbolic meaning. I taught my extended family and guests to playfully beat one another with spring onions as they sang *dayenu* during our Passover Seders. Remembering the excitement of watching Baba build our Iranian *sukkah* with kilims and palm leaves, I convinced Norman to build a *sukkah* every year. I tried not to complain, to be cheerful and optimistic in public, to be a pillar of strength. I was not going to become my mother.

DEEP DOWN I feared that Maman's visit could be the extra responsibility that would reveal my fragile emotional state. My eight-year-old sister argued with my three-year-old daughter Lena, who was still adjusting to having to share my attention with her two little sisters. In New Orleans, Lena and I had taken long strolls to the Audubon Zoo nearly every day. We read books and cuddled on the sofa, watching "Sesame Street."

Since then, there had been too many separations, too many changes. Lena's familiar peach-coloured bedroom and its blue carpet had disappeared, and Farzad had moved away. In our strange new home there was nothing within walking distance.

I called Baba in Iran, and for the first time in a very long time my parents spoke to each other. I am not sure what they discussed. My father probably asked Maman to return to Iran with Niloufar. My mother was horrified by the thought of returning, and she was so positive that we would send her back that Nahid tore up Maman's Iranian passport to prove that she was safe and to allay her worries and mistrust of her own children.

Norman and I had contemplated adopting Niloufar, since my mother didn't seem capable of taking care of her, always complaining about the hardship of having a young child at an old age. She was thirty-nine years old when Niloufar was born, not so old by today's standards, but she had started early, marrying at thirteen, giving birth to me at fifteen — seven pregnancies altogether, one resulting in a stillbirth and one tubal pregnancy that almost took her life.

We obviously could not take Niloufar away; she was Maman's only companion. The other option was to ask them both to live with us. I had hoped that by coming to the United States I could leave behind Iran, my family, and all of their problems. At age thirty, I lacked the emotional strength, maturity, and courage to ask Maman and Neli to stay, a decision I have often revisited with much regret.

My mother complained nonstop about my father: "What kind of a man leaves his wife and child and disappears for such a long time without even a phone call?" She complained about my sister: "Look at her. She is a big girl, but wants me to carry her in my arms. She is killing my back." She complained about me: "Why is it that you never *dard-o-del*? You never tell me about your problems. Is that natural? A daughter needs a mother. You and your brothers think you don't need anyone, but you all need a mother."

She was right, of course, but with three demanding children under the age of three, suffering quietly from postpartum depression, I couldn't offer up my home, my time, or my space. I ignored the long nights that my mother spent sleeping on the floor by Rachel's crib, getting up to rock and comfort her, giving me a chance to catch up on some much-needed sleep. I preferred the loneliness. My mother returned to Israel with Niloufar, dejected.

HAVING FAILED MY mother and my sister, I decided to help my father. Gone now for three years, Baba had not set eyes upon his grandchildren or kept up with his own little girl. Leaving my three daughters with Nahid, I travelled with Farzad to visit the Iranian interest section of the Algerian embassy in Washington, D.C. Before leaving, Nahid visited an orthopedic surgeon in Portsmouth who wrote a letter on her behalf, indicating that Nahid needed dangerous surgery immediately and her father had to be present.

Farzad and I stayed in a hotel close to the embassy in order to be at the front of the line early the following morning. Still in my maternity clothes, I covered my hair with an old kerchief and tried to look as miserable as possible. Inside the embassy the closed-circuit TV spewed angry anti-American propaganda. When our turn came, I approached the window, and before the grim bearded man behind the glass could attempt to dismiss me, I broke into a loud sob. "Please," I begged. "My sister must have surgery. I left a baby at home to come here. Please, help us." He softened. Two hours later, having secured an exit visa for our father, Farzad and I walked out of the gloomy building into the warm Washington sunshine, exuberant.

## BABA
### 1983, Shiraz

After my experience in Tehran, I lost my belief in human dignity and fairness. How could a presumably reputable man play with my life for such a long time, knowing that I had left my family behind, that I was alone and frightened? If another Jew could betray me so easily, how could I trust anyone else? Away from my family, I suffered, missing my little one especially. Farideh called once in a while to let me know about their wellbeing. The days were long, the nights longer.

Shiraz lacked security. As if the war itself was not enough of a nightmare, members of the Revolutionary Guard and the *Basij* roamed the city, arbitrarily arresting people, executing many without trials. We were not a people of law and order any longer. The government encouraged the citizens to spy on one another. One could not trust one's own child. Suspicion, an ugly inheritance of our centuries of oppression, tightened its grip on our lives. The government's Ministry of Intelligence announced phone numbers on the radio for self-appointed informers to report any suspicious activity: 540934-5 in Shiraz and 333333-9 in Tehran. The Jews especially lived in fear of retaliation by anyone who might have disliked them, who owed them money or who desired their businesses or homes.

Each neighbourhood had its own *roftegar*. They were usually uneducated men in tattered, putrid clothes, who pushed wheelbarrows from house to house every day, collecting rubbish, sorting it, selling some and disposing of the rest by burning it in the vacant lots among people's homes. The fetid odor and dark smoke hovered over courtyards, where women washed clothes, or, on a beautiful day, cleaned herbs and rice, or just visited one another over tea and a smoke of the waterpipe. No one complained. Under the rule of this new government, these *roftegars* became the Revolutionary Guard's eyes and ears, natural collectors not just of rubbish but also of news and gossip. When I was away, the neighbourhood garbage collector had asked my mother about my whereabouts. "He is in Tehran on business," my mother told him. When I returned, I noticed that he was always around. His gaze followed my every movement. He often asked personal questions, something he would have never dared to do before the Revolution. I passed him small sums of money, hush money, under the guise of appreciating his hard work.

I spent most of my days shopping for food, standing in long lines for bread and essentials, or visiting the poultry farm. The city sat in total darkness every night, and I had no diversion from the thoughts of my own uncertain future. The doorbell rang after midnight on one of these sleepless nights. "Who is it?" I asked, heart pounding. No answer. In the morning, I found a handwritten note that had been slipped underneath the door.

PAY US 50,000 TOMAN OR WE WILL TAKE CARE OF YOU.

I tore the letter into pieces and discarded it. The writer had forgotten to specify how and where to give the money, obviously amateurs, maybe the neighbourhood kids. A week later, the doorbell rang again at midnight and I found another letter under the door, threatening me with severe consequences if I disobeyed.

WE'LL GET YOU AND YOUR FAMILY, TOO.

WE ARE WATCHING YOU.

This time, a place and time was named. Who were these people, I wondered. Why did they choose me? Should I call the police? Since I was under investigation, I decided to avoid the authorities. A few days went by. I was awakened one night by the frightening sound of a bullet going through the metal front door. A motorcycle screeched away. The bullet was lodged in the interior wall. Underneath the door, another note in bold letters was waiting for me:

NEXT TIME, THIS BULLET WILL FIND YOUR HEAD.

DO NOT CALL THE POLICE.

BE AT THE VALIAHD CIRCLE, 50 METERS FROM THE GAS STATION. BE THERE AT 1:00 ON FRIDAY.

WE KNOW THAT YOU ARE CAPABLE OF FINDING 50,000 TOMAN.

They knew me well, for they had included the address of the poultry farm and the colour and the make of my car. On Friday, at one o'clock, with the money, I went to the traffic circle and waited. A handsome young man approached me on a motorcycle and very politely said *salam* and asked, "Do you have a package for me, Mr. Dayanim?" I gave him the money. He thanked me and left. Two other motorcyclists followed him at high speed. I never found out who these people were or why they had chosen me.

In a way, I was the lucky one. Other members of the Jewish community were plagued by more terrifying events. Khanom-e

Goel had a haircutting salon for women outside the Jewish ghetto at Sera-he Namazi, serving mostly Jewish women. Married to a man of low income, a mechanic, she worked to help support their three children. Khanom-e Goel had hired a Muslim woman whose fiancé often met her outside the salon to accompany her home. Across the street, one of many government informers sold rice steamers, pressure cookers, kerosene units, and other small kitchen appliances from his little shop. One day, Mohammad-Sadeq Khalkhali, the head of the first Revolutionary court, visited Shiraz to meet with this shopkeeper and the other government informers. The shopkeeper reported that a Jewish hairdresser had hired a Muslim woman and was facilitating her moral corruption by setting up rendezvous between the young woman and men.

Khanom-e Goel closed the shop at the end of the following day as she always did and was heading home to meet her children when she was confronted by the members of the Islamic moral court, arrested, and presented to Mr. Khalkhali, who condemned her to death without trial. She began to scream. They threw her in a burlap bag to stop her from kicking and riddled her body with bullets. Returning home from work, her husband was alarmed that his wife was not home and the children were left alone. He went to the salon, but it was locked. Not wanting to call the police, not knowing what else to do, he returned home. Hours later, a few members of the Revolutionary Guard dropped the bloody sack containing his wife on his doorstep and demanded money for the bullets. The shopkeeper who had reported the supposed crime secured himself a high position in the government, despite the fact that he was illiterate.

This incident, along with the execution of a young man that occurred shortly after, rattled the Jewish community. Mr. Sheeshe-ee, a handsome young man of twenty-five, had moved with his family to the northern part of the city during the Shah's reign. A young Muslim neighbour fell in love with him. They met a few times, but he told her that he had to marry within his faith. The woman later married a Muslim man, and, unwisely, maybe during an argument, maybe wanting to arouse her husband's jealousy, she told him about her crush on the neighbour's son. Because the Islamic laws of the new government prohibited any relationship between a Muslim woman and a man of a different religion (although not the reverse), the husband seized this opportunity for financial gain and requested a large sum of money from this Jewish family in order not to report their son. They refused to give in to the blackmail. He reported a Jewish man's indecent relationship with his wife to the authorities. The police interrogated the wife. She called it a lie. They interrogated Sheeshe-ee. He confessed that he knew the woman, but the relationship hadn't been sexual — just a friendship. The documents were sent to Khalkhali, at the revolutionary courts, who condemned Sheeshe-ee in absentia to execution without a trial, but no one knew about this verdict, including the victim himself.

One night I visited a family member, a leader of the Jewish community, at his fabric shop on Darius Street. As he was about to close the store, a middle-aged man entered and informed us about the verdict, demanding that we, both of us leaders in the community, convince the father of the accused to pay the equivalent of $200,000 to save his son's life.

"If you don't trust me," he said, "keep the money. But after I see the money, I'll give you the young man's passport. Upon release from prison the following day, he must leave the country immediately. Then you can give me the money; otherwise, he will die."

We approached the father with the news, but he didn't believe that his son would be executed for having befriended a Muslim woman years earlier. Plus, who was this man to be entrusted with such tremendous amount of money and how was he supposed to secure that much cash? His son was executed shortly after on charges of raping a Muslim woman.

These events of extortion, random persecutions, and murders added to my anxiety. My blood pressure became so high that, on one sleepless night, I thought my heart would rip through my flesh and fly out of my chest. I was fifty-five years old but looked much older and broken. I had lost weight and had pasty skin. I couldn't trust the authorities and I feared people around me, even my own family. However, one day, after having suffered three years of emotional isolation, I decided to face my worst fears. I sought advice from someone at the passport office in Shiraz who told me to visit the Islamic courts in Tehran, something I hadn't done out of fear. Now it didn't matter. I was dead inside. I told my sister about my plans, requesting that she not share the information with our mother. Someone had to know just in case I disappeared. Frightened, my sister cried, trying to dissuade me, but I had made up my mind. Overhearing us, her son, Vaheed, insisted on accompanying me. I didn't want to endanger his life as well as mine, but he was adamant. I bought two plane tickets to leave for Tehran the following week.

The airport was quiet since, fearing the war with Iraq, international flights had stopped landing at Mehrabad Airport, which housed an office of the revolutionary courts. No one was at the desk. We waited. A solemn, disheveled middle-aged man, with grey stubble and threadbare pants and shirt, house slippers and woolen socks, shuffled to the office. He reminded me of the garbage collector, especially since his beard wasn't long like the mullahs. Along with a few others in the room, I stood up to show respect until he gave us permission to sit. When my turn came, I went in alone, leaving Vaheed in the waiting room. I bowed. He acknowledged the greeting with a slight nod of his head; his penetrating gaze honed in on me. He asked for my name and address and the reason for my visit as he leafed through a large notebook in front of him and sometimes looking in an old metal cabinet behind him. I thought maybe he was looking for my passport, but each time he returned to his desk empty-handed.

"Why did you go to Israel?" he asked. "How long were you there? Who did you meet there?" He didn't pause for my answers.

Cold sweat ran down my back. He stared at me for a few minutes, bowed his head as if he was pondering something, and then stared at me again without uttering a word. I feared for my life. What was going through his mind?

He finally spoke, "Your passport was sent to the revolutionary courts at Evin prison."

Stuttering, I asked, "Why? What should I do now?"

He said, "The matter is in your own hands now," and dismissed me with a harsh tone to his voice, anger dancing in his eyes.

When I returned to the waiting room, wobbly on my legs, my pale look alarmed Vaheed who jumped out of his seat to come to my aid. We decided that the prosecutor had actually taken pity on me by not reporting me to the Revolutionary Guard, who would have arrested me. It was the holy month of Ramadan. Maybe he had decided to be charitable and let me go free. I didn't gain anything from the meeting but I didn't lose anything either, and that was a win. I still could not comprehend why my passport would have been sent to that infamous dungeon, known for its brutal methods of torture and murder of multitudes.

We couldn't find plane tickets back to Shiraz and spent two extra days in Tehran. That Friday, in the month of Ramadan, was called Quds Day, a Palestinian name for Jerusalem Day. People took to the streets, calling for the destruction of the State of Israel and chanting slogans against America. It was also the day of voting for the parliament. We had to go to the polling booths to vote for the predestined Jewish member of the Majles; otherwise, our unstamped identity cards would mark us as disloyal citizens, losing our right to any rationed provisions or to enter government buildings.

Our 707 Boeing to Shiraz that Sunday hovered over the city after the one-hour flight and headed back to Tehran. We feared that maybe we were being hijacked although the stewards told us that everything was fine and not to worry. We circled over Tehran. The wheels opened and then closed. The pilot returned to Shiraz. The red lights illuminating the walkway turned green. We were never told what had actually happened. The tarmac, however, was covered with ambulances and firefighters. The government treated us like children by not disclosing information.

I returned home — *ruz az no'w, ruzi az no'w* — nothing ever changes, it repeats again and again. Farideh called to say that her mother and Niloufar had obtained visas to visit her. I was comforted that my family would be reunited even if without me.

The frightening status of being *mam-nu-ol-khoruj* was not my only problem. From the swamps of hatred and lawlessness, intense anti-Semitism resurfaced like an awakened angry *ejdeha*, the Shahnameh's mythical dragon-like monster. I had good Muslim friends and acquaintances who treated me with kindness and compassion. But there were others who did not. The villagers, who resided in close proximity to a larger farm I had purchased in Zarghan, shouted anti-Semitic slogans and words of anger and hatred at me. These were the same people who had shown me reverence and respect as a major landowner and employer of many young people in the area. Now I feared them.

Moadel-e Zarghani, a landowner in the same village and also an influential member of the local city board, showed interest in buying the farm in Zarghan.

"This farm is of no use to you, Dayanim, and will cause you nothing but trouble."

Alarmed by his comment, I feared that he would take advantage of my vulnerable position. Did he know I was trying to leave the country? In an apologetic voice, I told him that I didn't have permission from the government to sell it. He had been interested in the land before I bought it but was unable to appease the many small farmers who had owned the land. He told me that he *knew* about *everything*. His long soliloquy was pregnant with hidden meanings and although he spoke with a soft voice and gentle words, his words rang like a siren in my head. He was trying to coerce me into relinquishing the farm.

He said, "Just write a letter in your own handwriting to indicate that you have sold me the farm, and I'll take care of the rest. I'll send you the agreed amount when you reach America."

Surely he didn't think I was stupid enough to agree to these terms. Even if I made it to America, what guarantees or legal leverage would I have if he didn't send the money? Plus, he could have taken the letter to the Ministry of Intelligence as proof that I was breaking the law by selling the farm without the government's permission. That would ensure my imprisonment and his ownership of the land as a reward. As a Jew who had visited Israel I was susceptible to intimidation and blackmail. He knew that.

A few months passed. One night I received a phone call around 11:00 p.m. A gruff voice informed me that he was calling from the information branch of the Islamic courts and that I had to present myself to the office of Mr. Jalali, the court prosecutor, Room 12. I wondered if this had to do with my passport situation, and if so, why now, after three years? Had it taken that long for them to reach my files? I didn't know if I had to obediently rush to the courts the following day or to ignore the phone call.

Another two weeks passed. I received another threatening call late at night from the same stern voice, obviously incensed that I had not obeyed his orders. I told him that he forgot to tell me the date and the time of my appointment. "Anytime during the week," he threw the words at me. And if I didn't, he shouted, he would send the Revolutionary Guard to arrest me. He hung up abruptly.

This time I called my nephew Vaheed and told him about my situation just in case I vanished, requesting that he should keep the information private. I couldn't sleep that night, and without having breakfast the following morning, I headed to the Ministry of Intelligence on Zand, the main street in Shiraz which ended at the Felkey-e setad, the roundabout that is named for the army base. There were a few large villas whose owners (Raji-ali Havaee, Dr. Zabihollah Qorban, and Mr. Behbehani) were either in prison or had escaped the country after the Revolution. Their homes were confiscated by the government. The Ministry of Intelligence was located in one of these houses, which, with its expansion, housed a temporary prison and the Islamic courts. Imam Jome-ey-e Shiraz, the Muslim leader of Shiraz, had taken over Dr. Qorban's house. Another house was devoted to the affairs of the martyrs of the war with Iraq.

Passing by that home, I witnessed an unforgettable scene. A large group of young boys sat by a small stream in the shade of nearby trees, waiting to board ten buses that were parked in front of the building. The government had either enticed, coerced, or kidnapped these young boys from the streets, given them each a "key to heaven" — a headband with holy words — and was sending them to the Iran-Iraq border where they would run through mine fields acting as human mine detonators. Their faces showed that they knew the terror of their destiny. Just a few steps away, there were other buses returning from the battlefield. Mothers and fathers were gathered there to retrieve the mutilated bodies of their sons for burial. As the boys watched the mourning parents collecting the bodies of the lifeless child soldiers, they knew their fate.

I found the office of the Ministry down a narrow alleyway, informed the man behind the desk of my purpose — that I was there to see Mr. Jalali — and waited from 9:00 a.m. until noon. After many phone calls, I was told that a man by that name didn't exist at that department and the central office across the street might be able to help. I hurried there and introduced myself once again and was about to state my reasons for being there when someone touched my back. I turned around and felt faint at the sight of a Revolutionary Guard with a tight grip on my shoulder. He smiled and greeted me warmly.

"Don't you remember me, Dayanim?"

Jafar-agha had worked for me at the store where we sold eggs and chicken. Then he opened his own store, where I supplied him with eggs and poultry.

Astonished that I was at this particular office, he asked, "What are you doing here in such a rough neighbourhood?"

I explained everything to him. He went inside and brought back biscuits and tea and asked me to wait as he tried to find out about my situation.

He returned shaking his head, "Dayanim," he said, "You are not the kind of person to ever do something bad. You don't belong here. No one knows about your case. Go home and if the phone rings at night, don't answer it. If we need you, we'll send someone to your house."

Elated, I thanked him and went home. No one called after that. I had a suspicion that Mr. Zarghani was trying to intimidate me.

FARIDEH CALLED ME to let me know that Nahid had seen a surgeon and obtained papers indicating I had to be with her in anticipation of a dangerous surgery. Meanwhile, after years

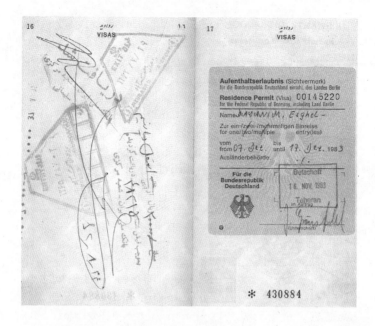

* 430884

A copy of Baba's visa that allowed him to travel to Germany, issued November 17, 1983.

of denying passports to its citizens, the government published a letter in newspapers around the country, asking those who sought passports to complete the attached forms and mail them to the passport agency that would be opening soon. I filled in the forms without indicating my status as *mam-nu-ol-khoruj* since they had not asked the question. The government had been busy labelling its citizens as undesirables and forbidden to leave the country to a point that many people were not even aware of these rulings until they tried to travel. As Iranian citizens we were all constantly under suspicion of misconduct and criminal behavior; our movements, words, and even thoughts were controlled and scrutinized. Thousands lined up to request passports.

The forms would go through the prime minister's office, the censor, and the Ministry of Intelligence before being submitted to the passport office. As a matter of policy, they often refused to grant passports to Jews unless there existed a dire situation. Even then, only one person from each family could leave if he guaranteed his return with large sums of money, landholdings, or a third person's affidavit, someone who would take personal responsibility for his return. Upon returning from his trip, the traveller had to report to courts so that the lien against his own property or his guarantor's life and property could be removed.

I took the papers Farideh had sent me and the surgeon's request for Nahid's imminent surgery to the passport office. After much haggling, I was allowed an audience, but they quickly refused the permission to leave the country. I cried like a frightened child, like a desperate woman, and with no dignity. With immense humility and bowing repeatedly I begged but to no avail. The man in charge advised me to have the papers presented to the Iranian interest office, located at the Algerian Embassy in Washington, D.C.

I told Farideh of this latest stumbling block. She sent me the required forms after visiting the embassy, plus a guarantee from herself and her husband that they would cover the expenses and that I would not need to send money from Iran. I returned to the prime minister's office with the new documents. They asked if I had mailed the newspaper forms. I said, "Yes," and showed them the postal receipt. He said that the foreign affairs ministry in Tehran had to approve the signatures and stamps on these documents. I left for Tehran. After a week of waiting and running from office to office, I managed to get the documents stamped to prove that the previous stamps were indeed authentic and valid. I submitted these forms to the passport office in Shiraz and, once again, requested speedy processing of my passport due to my urgent situation. They complied. I had a new passport valid for one year.

I could not contain my happiness. It was a miracle! I prayed to give my gratitude to God for my good fortune after so many years of hardship and prepared for my trip. I had to obtain a visa to the United States. The American Embassy had closed down after being attacked by the Iranian students, and its workers were kept hostage from November 4, 1979 until January 20, 1981. The only flights to foreign countries were through Iran Air which had a few weekly European flights to Rome, Frankfurt, and Zurich. The war was still raging in the southwestern part of Iran and the flights had to take place when they didn't fear Iraqi bombardments. The planes often veered off course toward the Russian border and then to Europe.

After a few months, I finally managed to secure a visa to Germany. Most European countries didn't want Iranians to linger and ask for asylum. I had to show them my Lufthansa reservations from Frankfurt to the United States to prove that I was not planning a long stay in Germany. A week before the flight, I submitted my passport to Iran Air for inspection as was required of all passengers. I bought small gifts for my wife and children, excited to reunite with them after more than three years of absence.

I LEFT FOR Tehran with Vaheed a day before my overseas flight in mid-November, the early chill of winter already upon us. A snowstorm whipped around the bus as it climbed the winding mountain roads. My luggage was inspected at the airport like everyone else's to see if we carried cash over $20, Persian carpets, jewellery, and, strangely, books. Farideh had asked for a few of her old books, but I had not taken them for fear of being stopped. My luggage passed inspection and I was given a seat number. As the loudspeaker announced our departure, I lined up with other passengers. One by one receiving their stamped passports from a policeman, they exited for the tarmac. Like everyone else, I gave my name, but looking under D, the guard couldn't find mine. He asked my name again and checked the list one more time. Nothing. He went to the back room to double check, but soon returned.

"They're looking for it. Have a seat."

All of the other passengers had boarded, leaving me, waiting. They finally called me to the back office, interrogating me, asking the same questions I had been asked many times before. Informing me that my passport was forged and not valid, they called the plane and ordered my luggage taken off. The world swirled around me. I hit the ground.

When I came around, the policeman gave me water and encouraged me to drink. He was just a regular policeman. Had he been a member of the Revolutionary Guard, I would have probably received a public beating and been sent to prison.

"Pick up your luggage and leave quietly," he advised me. "Go back to the passport office and tell them your story. You know that you are *mam-nu-ol-khoruj*. I don't know how they could have issued you a passport." He then gently patted my back, "Go in peace."

I knew the authorities had actually removed Jews from their seats on the plane, or even turned around planes and forced them to disembark — a cruel game. I didn't know where I fit in this shuffling of cards for amusement. Barely able to walk, I slowly made my way to the waiting room, where Vaheed had waited for the plane to take off even though I had told him to leave. Seeing my pale face and shaking hands, he led me to the airport cafeteria and bought me tea. The loudspeaker screeched throughout the airport waiting area, asking me to retrieve my suitcase. I never discovered the reasoning behind issuing my passport and then calling it a counterfeit.

Desperate, I called a distant relative, Mr. Lalezari, a real estate broker in Tehran, whose job enabled him to know many people including government employees in Tehran. I hoped that he would guide me to an office, to a person in the government, who could solve my complicated problem. I didn't want to linger for too long as I had before. Tired of living in a state of limbo, living a life filled with fears and anxiety among wolves, who could pounce on me for my life and my property, I needed to resolve the situation one way or another.

Mr. Lalezari invited us to dinner at his home and tried to entertain us with good food and backgammon, but my stomach churned with anxiety. Game after game he won, screaming with joy. I couldn't tell him that my heart wasn't in the game. Finally we started talking about the situation at hand. He reassured me that he knew someone who could disentangle my troubles. "Meet me at my real estate office tomorrow at 4:00 p.m. I'll take care of you, Dayanim."

The following day we arrived in his office, located on a second floor of a building in north Tehran. A man at the desk invited us to sit and wait. Mr. Lalezari came in soon after and chatted for about half an hour. Then a scrawny man with ruffled beard and uncombed hair, looking like a drug addict or a beggar, entered. Without uttering a word he crossed the office and disappeared behind a door in the back. After a while Mr. Lalezari told me to go through the same door alone. Surprised, I entered the room where the mysterious man sat behind a metal desk. He offered me a seat.

"Are you ready for me to send you?" he asked.

What was he talking about?

"Don't you want to leave the country?" he asked.

He could arrange for me to leave through the Pakistani border. I could not believe that a disheveled man like that could help anyone. He read my mind. "Don't look at my appearance. I am a millionaire. This is my office and all these people work for me." He gave me a summary of his résumé. He had helped Rabbi Khakham Barukh, a well-known leader of the Jewish community. He told me that I had to take a plane to Zahedan, a northern border town. He would then meet me at the airport and take me to another man who would smuggle me to the refugee camps in Pakistan. "There, you will ask for asylum. They'll send you to Austria." He added, "In the refugee camps in Austria, you'll ask for asylum in America."

Mr. Lalezari had misunderstood me. Knowing that I was forbidden to leave and that my passport was pronounced counterfeit, he had assumed that I wanted to leave the country illegally. I couldn't do that. With my history, if I were caught (and many were), I would be sentenced to death. If I succeeded, I would lose all my property in Iran, and I had little money abroad. I thanked him profusely, "Give me time to see if I can set my affairs in order, and I'll call you." One should not make enemies with such people. I shook hands with the smuggler, thanked Mr. Lalezari, and told him that I would be in touch.

Very early the following day, hoping for some guidance, I went to the passport office, joining a long line snaking around the building to get a date for visiting the ministry. I got an appointment for the following week.

Not knowing what else to do, Vaheed and I wandered around the snow-covered streets of Tehran, looking for something to eat. Doing our best to keep kosher, our diet consisted of flatbread, plain yogourt, and boiled eggs. We were in luck. Before seeing the *laboo* seller and his wooden cart, we both smelled the mouthwatering aroma of the winter delicacy, baked beets. Their delicious sweetness — a diversion from our boring diet — gave us energy and hope and the heat that emanated from the hot coals in the cart warmed us.

The following week, we visited the office of the assistant director of the passport ministry that was nestled in the immense maze of the bureaucratic machinery that controlled Iranian life. They denied us entry since we didn't have a written invitation although we had obtained a reservation number. I haggled and begged my way in to ask for guidance. After greetings and niceties and repeated bowing, I asked an army officer for help. He patiently listened to my story and then apologetically said there was nothing to be done for me in that particular section and kindly advised me to visit the prime minister's office. The temperature outside had dropped rapidly and we exited the building into a heavy snowfall. Shivering and sliding on the sidewalk, we decided it was best to return to the hotel.

The snow stopped the following day. Vaheed and I took a taxi to the prime minister's office, where there were many doors, and at each door another guard refused us entry. I approached a small information window and pleaded for permission to enter. A confused, low-ranking guard didn't have any answers, but finally allowed us entry out of pity. Another guard inside wrote down the address of yet another office close by and told us how to get there. After another hour, and asking many passersby in the slushy snow-covered streets, we finally found the place.

There, in a warm and comfortable room, we encountered a young man dressed impeccably, an anomaly in those days when everyone was trying to look more humble and modest than the rest. Seeing us shivering and wet, he kindly told us to get closer to the space heater. Hearing my story, he shook his head in dismay. It was not something he could tackle, but he picked up the phone, made a few phone calls, and wrote down *Pasteur Street, number 11*. "This is where you need to go," he said and wished us well. Wet, cold, tired, and hungry, I hailed a taxi to take us back to the hotel.

The following day, now our third day of wanderings, we asked another taxi driver to take us to 11 Pasteur Street, but he said the address didn't exist and dropped us off by the prime minister's office once again. Sloshing our way from one street to another, reading street names, we asked passersby, but no one had heard of the street. Finally, we saw a small sign on the wall of a back alleyway, *kouche-ye* Pasteur. Number 11 had no signs indicating that it could be an office building.

There were no other doors in the entire empty narrow side street. So strange! We knocked. The door opened automatically. We climbed the stairs to a room that looked like an iron cage with a small desk and a few metal chairs. In this heavily fortified room, a grim-faced man of around forty with stubble sat behind the desk, talking on the phone. I approached and greeted him with trepidation. He didn't answer. After a few minutes, he finally asked if we had been summoned that day. I said, "No."

He asked, "Then why are you here? Where did you get this address from? Who sent you here?"

I started to explain. He cut me off. "What's your name?"

"Dayanim."

"Sit."

He picked up the phone and spoke to someone he called Agha-haji, then put the phone on its cradle and made himself busy with paperwork. We sat there for two hours on the most uncomfortable cold metal chairs, and I did not dare ask a question. He didn't show any kind of reaction toward us, as if we were invisible. He made phone calls, received calls, thumbed through a ledger in front of him, but didn't look at us. Finally, with a trembling voice, I asked if he had an answer for me. With hateful eyes he stared at me, but didn't say anything and kept doing whatever it was he was doing. I was a ghost. Another two hours passed. I could not tolerate another minute. I pleaded for an answer. He looked at me with narrowed wolf-eyes as if ready to pounce and tear apart his prey. Cursing me with words I am too embarrassed to put on paper, he called me a filthy Jew, an infidel, a spy who schemed to leave the country illegally. I had lived a life of honour and respect, but I had fallen so low. I would have almost welcomed the beating that he threatened me with over the words with which he chose to lash me. Still cursing, he pushed the buzzer to open the cage and told us to get lost. Still apologizing and bowing, I asked in desperation,

"Please, please, what should I do? Where should I go?"

He said, "Go to Evin, that's where."

I begged again.

"Get out," he shouted. "If I need you, I'll call you."

I stood in the freezing weather, shivering and crying, sorry that I had subjected Vaheed to this hellish experience, embarrassed that my nephew had seen me act like a humiliated child.

I returned to Shiraz. I had spun my wheels for three years in this deep mud that the new government had spread over my path. Weary and *darmandeh*, stuck on the threshold of life, not able to cross over, I had returned to my starting line, a prisoner in a city that I had once loved with all my heart and could never have imagined leaving. Was this my punishment for a sin I had committed somewhere? Had I not always been so careful not to break the law, to be just, giving, and compassionate to others? I faced the heavens. "What is my sin?" I howled. Which laws of God or country had I broken? If I were guilty, why wouldn't they just throw me in jail and be done with me? Why had they sent my passport to Evin? If they wanted to lure me to that infamous horrific prison, why wouldn't they just do it? If, like so many other innocent Iranians, I was destined to face the firing squad at Evin, why wouldn't they just arrest me and kill me? Why did they impose this slow torture on me? Why did the man ask me to wait for a phone call? Had they not reached my file after so many years? Life had become an irresolvable riddle. My solutions proved wrong each time because the illogical formulas changed constantly. Was it my fate not ever to see my wife and children again? Could I allow them to live in foreign countries without a source of income? I finally decided that I had to return to Tehran. The key to this stubborn door was there and I had no other choice.

I went to Tehran this time without Vaheed, who had seen enough ugliness. I determinedly marched down the narrow alleyway and rang the doorbell at number 11 Pasteur Street.

The door opened. I went up the same stairs and soon faced the same grim face, who looked at me quizzically, examining me from my shoes to my head as if searching his memory. Suddenly the look on his face changed. He lunged at me, taking me by surprise. Grabbing my collar, he kept me in place and hit me repeatedly on the head. He threw me against the wall, cursing loudly. I fell down hard and curled on the ground. He stood over me, shaking his finger at me, "You damned Jew! Don't you ever come back here. Otherwise," he screamed, "I'll have you arrested and thrown in Evin." He kicked me out of the door and told me to get lost, spitting after me.

I thought of the time when I was around twelve years old, returning from Shabbat services with my father. Because it was raining, we decided to walk outside the tall walls that separated the Jewish quarter from its neighbours in order to avoid the muddy alleyways. I was so proud to be next to him, my father, the gentle, respected Rabbi, *dayan* of the Shirazi community, my father who forever walks beside me even now, even in his death. Suddenly, a few young hoodlums pounced upon us, incensed that we had broken the laws of purity. According to strict Islamic laws, the Jews are *najes*, carriers of spiritual contamination that is easily transmitted through water. Hence, we were forbidden to be outside the walls of the Jewish quarter on rainy days. Standing by, helplessly watching my father's bloody face, his *kippa* on the ground, his *abba* muddied, I felt humiliated for him and for myself. I hated myself for not being able to defend him. Now I wept for myself and for my father, too. Now I knew how he had felt and was thankful that my children could not witness their father's nothingness.

## FARIDEH
### *1983–84, Chesapeake*

Baba received his visa to Germany on November 17, 1983. Lena turned three that October; Yael was not yet two; and Rachel was to celebrate her first birthday the following June. I loved being with my daughters, my constant companions. Sitting on the brown shag carpet, we built houses with blocks. Piling onto the sofa, one on each side, one on my lap, we read *Tikki Tikki Tembo* and *The Cat in the Hat* and listened to Raffi's *Down by the Bay*. We went for long walks on the deserted suburban streets of our neighbourhood — Lena walking slowly by my side, Yael wiggling her feet in the stroller, Rachel, in my arms, clinging to my neck.

There were cars in driveways, sometimes more than one in each. *Where were the people?* Someone to chat with, someone to smile at the beautiful picture we made, someone who would ask us in for a cup of tea?

174

We made challahs on Fridays: Lena sitting on a padded chair, Yael and Rachel in high chairs, watching as I kneaded the dough on the kitchen table. Flour rose in milky clouds in the air. The girls took turns sticking their hands in the dough, laughing, sometimes arguing: *me, me, me, too.*

Braiding the dough, I remembered my Grandmother Khanom-bozorg, squatting in the backyard of our house in the Jewish quarter of Shiraz, her long skirt wrapped tightly around her knees, her white kerchief fastened underneath her chin with a safety pin while she spread a thin layer of dough on the back of an inverted wok-like pan and deposited it on hot coals in a pit she made with stones. The thin crispy lavash she baked filled the backyard with its mouth-watering aroma.

My mother-in-law called from time to time, but when she heard the girls crying or talking in the background, she said, "Oh, I see you are very busy. I won't bother you. I just called to say hello. Goodbye." This respect for personal space marked another unfamiliar representation of my America. An Iranian mother-in-law would have probably lived with her son and daughter-in-law; she would have reached over and comforted a crying baby; for even if she didn't like her daughter-in-law, she would have understood the bonding of women in childcare.

Norman called between patients. The hospital and his office were thirty minutes away, but he was too busy to come home for lunch, the main meal of the day in my tradition, a time the whole family gathered to relax and chat. He grabbed something to eat at the hospital or stopped by his parents' home, who lived just a few blocks away from the hospital.

While the girls napped, I did the laundry, cooked dinner, straightened the house, and looked out over the vast expanse of green lawns and tall majestic trees from the kitchen window as I washed dishes. *Where are my neighbours?*

I enrolled Lena in a daycare at Gomley Chesed Synagogue, the temple Norman's family attended. That gave me a chance to chat with other parents. A few visited me from time to time or invited me to their homes. I had assumed the synagogue would be a centre for Jewish life, where I would meet other young Jewish families. It had once been that way, a friend told me, but it was dying. Norman remembered his childhood and teenage years, when the neighbourhood was vibrant, the Sunday school filled with young people, the sisterhood busy with constant activities. Later, the young people left for other communities and they rarely returned as we had. Some moved to the nearby cities of Norfolk and Virginia Beach with much larger Jewish communities. The synagogue had a minimal role in the lives of the young people who remained in Portsmouth. The daycare centre was a rare place of gathering for those who still lived in the area, mostly well-established families with deep roots in the city, who had little need for new friends.

To meet new people I joined a synagogue in Norfolk. Dressing my daughters in ruffles, bows, and Mary Jane shoes, I dutifully attended services every Shabbat. Beth El's large sanctuary with its tall stained-glass windows stood majestically empty of congregants other than a few, mostly older members, who demanded decorum, and absolute silence from the girls during the long services. This disturbing demand introduced me to another strange and unfamiliar aspect of American culture. I sat away from the complaining congregants, who I had so naïvely thought would welcome and adopt us as new members of their community.

I had never attended religious services on Saturdays in Iran. Schools were closed on Fridays, the Muslim day of rest. Saturdays, the first day of classes, were busy with exams and new lessons. On the rare occasion that I went to Rabizadeh Synagogue in Shiraz during Rosh Hashanah and Yom Kippur, the synagogue had always been noisy and filled with chatter, the hallway covered with street shoes removed before entering the sanctuary as a sign of respect. Children ran around the yard and the sanctuary, where the congregants kindly patted them on the head.

I had not been taught Hebrew in Iran, although my brothers had private lessons at home. Once I had asked my father if I could study as well. At first he agreed; but after just a few lessons, he came home early one day and, startled by the sight of his teenage daughter studying with a young rabbi, he said: "This isn't good. It will give people something to talk about."

I knew a lot about kashering meat, removing the forbidden fat, veins and sinews, salting and washing it three times according to Jewish laws. I knew about the laws of *kashrut*, keeping meat and dairy separate and about the laws for Passover: how to clean the house, how to properly prepare food for the holidays. I also knew about the ceremonial food for Passover, Rosh Hashanah, and Shavuot Seder plates, but I didn't know the story of the Jewish exodus from Egypt because our Haggadahs were in Hebrew. The first time Baba brought home a Haggadah with Persian translations, I read it over and over. *So, this is the story. We were slaves in Egypt.*

Many years later, in Virginia, I used my index finger to locate the words in the *siddur* and tried to follow along with the readings despite my poor Hebrew. I was fascinated by the unfamiliar melodies at Beth El. I listened to the liturgy, and since women were not encouraged to sing in my Iranian household, I sang along in my head, my lips moving without a sound escaping. That year, I attended sisterhood luncheon parties, registered the girls for daycare at the Jewish Community Center (JCC) and signed up for swimming lessons for myself, slowly rejoining a community of people.

## BABA
### 1983–84, Shiraz

I was falling apart. Days gave way to the procession of the war's martyrs to their graves. The blasts of constant bombardment from Iraqi fighters punctured the silence of the nights. An empty shell, unable to tolerate the situation any longer, I decided once again to face my tormentors. You die once, so mourn once.

I returned to number 11, Pasteur Street and rang the doorbell. It buzzed like a hornet and the door opened. At the top of the stairs, in the cage, a different man, a middle-aged man with salt-and-pepper beard, sat at the desk. He had a happy face, a characteristic rarely found in such offices. When I greeted him, he welcomed me and offered the chair. "Where are you from?" he asked, calling me *agha*, sir. He inquired about the weather in Shiraz, the amount of rain, and the situation of agriculture. Sensing his empathy, I spoke of my pressing issues. He phoned someone and then pressed a button. A section of metal bars slid to reveal a passage to the interior of the building, which I had not yet seen. He took me inside and showed me where to go. I thanked him profusely, went down a set of stairs to the courtyard of an abandoned house and wandered around the yard until I found a set of very narrow stairs.

The stairs led me to a closed door. I rang the doorbell and the door opened to a dark and narrow hallway. At the end of the hallway, there was a third door and another bell. When the door opened, my eyes adjusted to the dim light within and a large room came into view. Metal chairs were set up against bare walls. A light bulb swung from the ceiling, its yellow hue revealing the quivering shadows of other men. They waited with downcast eyes in the uncomfortable chairs. I joined them. My body shook from the cold; my chest tightened; my lungs ached. The man sitting next to me asked, "Your first time here?" I said yes. He said that I had to wait until they came for me. When I told him that I was Jewish, he said there were three rooms behind the door we faced. "Pray not to be sent to room 3," he warned, "where a Jew-hater is the interrogator." The man, known as Ali-agha, he told me, had announced that he would proudly drink the blood of a Jew. To calm my soul, I tried to recite *tehillim* in my head, but the words of the psalms I knew so well eluded me.

A young man entered the waiting room and asked me if I was new. I said yes. He gave me a packet of forms to fill out. My teeth chattering from the cold and fear, I read the forms. They wanted to know my reason for being there; about my family members' names: wife, children, father, mother, sisters, brothers and their families; the address of each person's home and business; about my neighbours, their names, their businesses, and their families. Those twenty pages took me over an hour to complete. The young man returned, collected the forms and told me to wait. A few were called in, but none returned. After a few more hours, around noon, they finally called me. Room #1 was windowless, small, and dimly lit. Its only furniture was a strange armchair, facing the wall. A voice from outside the room told me to lift the iron bar that was attached to the right arm of the chair, sit, and then lower it over my lap, trapping myself. I was told to keep my eyes on the wall that was about a metre away. The voice ordered me not to move, a pointless order since I was held in tightly by the chair. The voice told me to answer all his questions without turning my head. There were three doors in the room, the one on my right, where I had entered, a door on my left, and one behind me. I heard the back door open; footsteps approached me. A different voice started to interrogate me.

"Are you a Jew?' was the first question.

"Yes," I answered.

"Do you go to *kanisa* for prayers? Are you religious?"

I took a book of *tehillim* from the pocket of my jacket and raised it overhead to show him. He took it and then returned it me after a few minutes. Then he asked other questions that I had already answered in the forms. I told him again about everyone I knew in the country and those abroad.

"Why did you go to the occupied Palestine?" he asked. "Are you a spy? What business did you have there?"

The questioning went on for hours. I heard him leave the room. Then a voice from outside told me to get out of the chair and exit by the left door. He told me to go back to my own city and wait for a phone call. I raised the bar, moved out of the chair, and left through the third door. I backtracked my way out. The last door closed behind me.

In Shiraz, I waited. No one called. I went back to 11 Pasteur Street three times in the spring and summer of that year. I went through the same routine each time, filling out the same twenty pages, going through the interrogation, and always leaving without results. Four years since my disastrous arrival and a year after my first encounter with the interrogator, during another winter, I rang the doorbell at 11 Pasteur Street. I went through the same procedure, but this time I don't know what happened. Maybe I was angry, maybe I forgot for a second where I was, maybe it was the nature of the question that I no longer remember. Maybe it was the fact that I was in Room #3. I turned my head to answer one of the interrogator's question and saw a man with a hood over his head with two holes for eyes. Then I felt a blow to my head. Stunned, I fell over, and the chair with me stuck in it turned over. On the ground, I absorbed my interrogator's blows, kicks, punches, along with his filthy curses against my family, my ancestors, my wife, children and my religion. On the floor with a concussion, I could not even speak. Cursing me and my Jewish ancestors with unspeakable words, the interrogator told me to get lost. I could barely move. Limping, I exited the room and sat on the stairs, afraid of losing my balance and falling down. I slowly found my way to the street and hailed a taxi to take me back to the hotel. The pain was so excruciating that I assumed I had broken bones. The hotel receptionist helped me to my room and went to the pharmacy to buy painkillers. I called Vaheed and asked him to please come to Tehran. He managed to get to me in two days and took me to see a doctor. I had two broken ribs and a concussion. I looked much older than my years, broken physically and emotionally through these four years of solitude. Vaheed bought us plane tickets and took me back to Shiraz. I had once been his strong uncle, giving him advice and guidance; now I relied on him like a helpless child.

## FARIDEH
*1984, Chesapeake*

Days went by and then months. Seasons changed. Rachel's first tooth broke through the gum; she took her first wobbly steps down the hallway, drooling, showing her one-toothed smile. Yael pulled herself up on my lap with one book after another, "Read, Mommy." Lena, shy, unhappy about her long ride to the Norfolk JCC, often sat by herself at daycare; her teachers had to prod her to mingle. It hurt me to send her when I knew that she preferred being at home, but her half-days at school gave me a much-needed break. Taking two little girls to the grocery store, one sitting in the basket and one in my arms, was manageable. Three posed a challenge. Once in a while I took all of them, two sitting in the basket, leaving little room for groceries. Most people stopped, pointed, and smiled. A few shook their heads.

My father had still never seen my daughters, and sometimes I believed that he didn't care about them. I had seen him holding and loving his siblings' children and grandchildren, but for his own he did not have any words. He rarely asked about my mother, my brothers, my sisters, especially the little one, as if he had deleted them from the list of important things in his life. On the rare occasions that we spoke on the phone, he sounded gruff, even angry. I resented that instead of being a help, my father was a constant source of agony. Baba became one more problem I had to deal with, another long-distance worry. I tried not to let his situation strip me of my energy. I tried to be strong not just for my daughters and my husband but also for my siblings in the United States, ignoring the fact that taking on a parental role in the lives of my sisters and brothers had its own potential for resentment. That's what had happened to Baba. But I followed in his footsteps, mostly because he pressured me to do so. He didn't realize then that by assigning me the role of the elder he would diminish his own power and control.

I couldn't understand why Baba wouldn't leave Iran even though I had arranged for his papers. Angry, I didn't want to phone him. His voice unraveled me. But he was my father, I called.

Baba sounded bitter, his words were laced with a tinge of condemnation as if through some form of intuition I should know about his life. When I probed, he said, "*ta bebeenim che mishe*, let's wait and see what happens," or, *khodet midouni*, you know yourself." Fearing that the government would be eavesdropping on our conversations, Baba would sometimes speak Judi to me, which I did not fully comprehend. He had made sure that his children's lives would be diametrically opposed to the *mahaleh* culture he had endured. Speaking Judi was a big part of the road to that system of oppression that he had masterfully blocked for us.

I did not recognize the sound of depression and hopelessness in Baba. Mentioning his family by name, showing his love for them, would have magnified the lack of love in his own life — his utter loneliness.

In 1984, I was thirty-one years old, my father, an old man to me then, was fifty-eight.

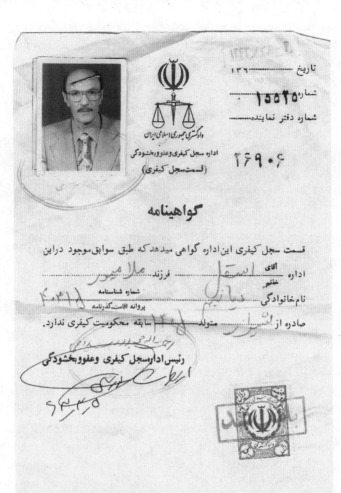

دادگستری جمهوری اسلامی ایران

اداره سجل کیفری وعفووبخشودگی

(قسمت سجل کیفری)

۳۶۹۰۴

# گواهینامه

قسمت سجل کیفری این اداره گواهی میدهدکه طبق سوابق موجود دراین

اداره آقای ........ اسمعیل ........ فرزند ملا میمون ........

نام خانوادگی ........ شماره شناسنامه ........

صادره از ........ متولد ........ پروانه اقامت-گذرنامه ........ سابقه محکومیت کیفری ندارد.

رئیس اداره سجل کیفری وعفووبخشودگی

پس از ابطال، مهر بریال تمبر معتبر است

- An official government document issued in August 1984 certifies that Baba does not have a criminal record.

- An English translation of Baba's criminal background check clearance letter that is required by U.S. Citizenship and Immigration Services of all naturalization applicants.

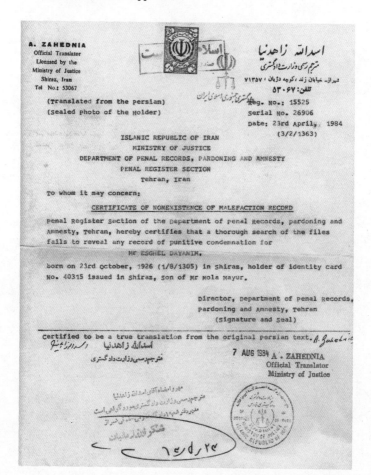

**A. ZAHEDNIA**
Official Translator
Licensed by the
Ministry of Justice
Shiraz, Iran
Tel No.: 53067

اسدالله زاهدنیا
مترجم رسمی وزارت دادگستری
شیراز- خیابان زند ، کوچه دژبان ، ۷۱۳۵۷
تلفن: ۵۳۰۶۷

Reg. No.: 15525
Serial No. 26906
Date: 23rd April, 1984
(3/2/1363)

(Translated from the persian)
(Sealed photo of the Holder)

ISLANIC REPUBLIC OF IRAN
MINISTRY OF JUSTICE
DEPARTMENT OF PENAL RECORDS, PARDONING AND AMNESTY
PENAL REGISTER SECTION
Tehran, Iran

To whom it may concern:

CERTIFICATE OF NONEXISTENCE OF MALEFACTION RECORD

Penal Register Section of the Department of Penal Records, pardoning and Amnesty, Tehran, hereby certifies that a thorough search of the files fails to reveal any record of punitive condemnation for
MF ESGHEL DAYANIM,

born on 23rd October, 1926 (1/8/1305) in Shiraz, holder of identity card No. 40315 issued in Shiraz, son of Mr Mola Mayur.

Director, Department of Penal Records,
pardoning and Amnesty, Tehran
(signature and Seal)

Certified to be a true translation from the original persian text. A. Zahednia

مترجم رسمی وزارت دادگستری اسدالله زاهدنیا

7 AUG 1984 A. ZAHEDNIA
Official Translator
Ministry of Justice

مهر و امضاء آقای اسدالله زاهدنیا
مترجم رسمی وزارت دادگستری و عهم دو گای الهی است
علیرغم دفتر شماره ۱ وزارت ... تهران ... شیراز
تشکر فرائد ... خیابان

## BABA
*1984, Tehran*

Two months later, still suffering from bruises on my chest, I received a late-night phone call from a familiar voice: Ali-agha, my tormentor from 11 Pasteur street was phoning from the prime minister's office. He told me that my documents had been presented in court, which had demanded a payment of one million toman, ($150,000 at that time) to lift my status as *mam-nu-ol-khoruj*. I told him that I didn't have access to that kind of money. Then, there was nothing else he could do for me, he replied. He gave me the address of the place to which I had to submit the cashier's cheque. My ribs still aching from Ali-agha's beatings, I returned to Tehran to the address he had given me. A stern young man sat at the desk. A sign behind him read: "*To agar be jebheh namiri az che roo tavaqofe komak dari?* If you have not fought in the war, how dare you ask for help?" I greeted the man and told him about the phone call. He thought I was there to pay and gave me a form for the bank. I told him that I did not have that much money and requested to meet with the secretary of the court. There, my tormentor, Ali-agha, sat behind a desk, obviously having more than one job. He took me to another man whose position was unknown to me and reiterated that without the money there would be no passport. I offered them my farm, my house, and my business as collateral. No, cash only. I cried. No pity. Still sobbing, defeated, I returned to Shiraz.

A month went by and the phone rang again late at night. Ali-agha said that the papers were resubmitted to the courts and the sum was cut in half. "Take it or leave it," he said.

I emptied all my accounts, sold a few things, and carried the cash to the minister's office in Tehran. The stern secretary told me to take the money to Bank Bazargani on Enqelab Street, deposit it to a certain account, and bring back the receipt. The bank clerk by mistake forgot to seal the document, enabling me to make a copy of it on my way back to the ministry. The secretary called the bank to make sure it was deposited and screamed at them for not having sealed the envelope. Then, he gave me another envelope, sealed and stamped, to take to the passport office.

I ran into Ali-agha outside the building, he had planted himself in my path on purpose. My ribs still bruised from his blows, I took off my hat, put my right hand on my heart, bowed and thanked him profusely. He asked me to bring him back an expensive camera from the United States. That was what it was always about. The shabby clothing, the house slippers, the stubble on the face, and the disheveled look were all a show of humility and vow of penury until it came to real money — my cheque and now a camera. I shook his hand, bowed again, and told him that it would be my pleasure and honour.

To bypass the alarmingly long line outside the passport office, I approached the guard and told him about my urgent case and showed him the letter from the prime minister's office. Going directly to the head of the courts, I gave him the letter, which was passed to another officer who opened a box and pulled out a file containing both passports and a letter. He read the note and apologetically said that I had been sentenced twice as *mam-nu-ol-khoruj*, once at the Turkish border and a second time at the airport. The letter cancelled only one. He suggested that I return to the prime minister's office and request another letter to cancel the second sentence.

I picked up my passport two days later. Since my exit visa, valid for just one year, had expired, I went to the passport office in Shiraz. The man in charge of the office, who had been reprimanded by the ministry in Tehran for granting me a new passport, recognized me immediately. "Did you manage to take care of your *forged* passport?" He said mockingly "How much did you have to pay?" Shaking his head, he extended my exit visa.

This time I requested a visa to Italy in order to have my American visa processed. My brother, Shapour, an American citizen, had left for the U.S. in July of 1961 for his medical residency, married an American woman, and did not visit Iran for fear of having to serve in the army. He had applied for a green card on my behalf years ago. When I applied for the visa to Italy, my brother's previous paperwork was forwarded to the American consulate in Naples.

Outside the Italian Embassy in Tehran, more than four hundred people waited for thirty or forty available visas. I left, returning very early the following day but couldn't get inside. The third day, I left for the embassy the night before at 10:00 p.m. Only a few sat against the wall, waiting. Another huge crowd was gathered outside by 9:00 a.m. An Italian man and his translator left the embassy around 11:00 a.m. to collect information and documents, returning mine around 2:00 p.m. I was denied visa because I could carry only $300, the maximum allotted amount by the Iranian government at the time. They wanted a guarantee from someone outside the country that I wouldn't be a financial burden on the Italian government. I returned to Shiraz to retrieve a letter of support Farideh had sent plus the medical documents. Nevertheless, I was rejected for a second time. Farideh called to see what was going on. A month later she called and asked me to return to the Italian embassy, assuring me that this time things would be okay.

I left for Tehran again and spent the night by the embassy. I was the first to be called even though I stood a few rows back. The embassy personnel treated me with utmost respect. The translator asked me about my connections in the United States. They had received a letter from the office of the foreign affairs in Italy, asking why they had delayed my case. After stamping my passport, we shook hands. Later I discovered that Farideh had contacted her congressman in Virginia, and he had interceded on my behalf.

# 12

**FARIDEH**
*1984, Chesapeake*

"What kind of a man would leave his family for such a long time?" Maman complained repeatedly whenever I called her. "Where is your father? Call him and ask him what we are supposed to do here by ourselves." Then there came a time of total silence that allowed me to forget about her problems and to shed the burden of responsibility placed on me as the eldest of five children. Later, I would learn from Neli that during those silent months my mother took antidepressants to cope with her despair, but the medication made her into a robotic zombie, and Neli was forced to become a mother to our mother at age nine.

The nagging voice of accountability and responsibility accompanied me everywhere. I worried about Niloufar living with an emotionally unstable mother. Naïvely, I had assumed that Maman's close proximity to her own mother would be

190

comforting to her. She had spoken so longingly about Israel during my childhood that I had presumed living in Israel would solve many of her problems — her loneliness, her oppression at the hands of her in-laws. I did not realize then that she had idealized Israel the way I had revered America. To us, these faraway lands promised new beginnings. We had disregarded the complexities associated with these distant spaces. Suddenly my mother found herself away from the source of her unhappiness, isolation, and anxiety. Leaving Iran meant that Maman had escaped her mother-in-law, sisters-in-law, and brothers-in-law, the people she had so feared, and yet she felt no relief. The sudden absence of emotional abuse didn't necessarily create happiness and stability; rather it left a deep emotional void that if not dealt with caved in like an excavated mountain, leaving a heap of rubble. Maman fell apart.

Niloufar told me years later that our mother, who had never worked outside the home, found a job in a factory, doing menial repetitive work. She had never had control over more than 100 toman (about $10 in Iran at that time) at any one time. Now she had to calculate their expenses: rent, food, medicine, and clothing for unspecified amounts of time. Financially strained, Maman worried that the bit of money Baba had left would run out, but she never told me about this; she never asked for financial help. I didn't know; I didn't offer.

During Baba's captivity in Iran, Freydoun switched from Queens College to Rutgers on recommendations from Norman's sister and brother-in-law, both of whom were Rutgers alumni. Having visited my brother's lonely basement apartment in Queens, I hoped that living on campus would help him out of his closed shell. He went to his graduation from Rutgers by himself. He asked me to come but I couldn't travel with small children.

Farzad did well at the University of Maryland. I managed to attend his graduation, leaving the children with two different babysitters so that Norman didn't have to take time off from work. My daughters adored my brothers, who often came for short visits, brightening our lives. Freydoun and Farzad, too, felt distant and estranged from our father, who was emotionally and physically absent. They scarcely spoke with Baba, but when they did, the young men felt Baba's anger, not his love. Baba didn't know the meaning of love as it was defined in the west. He knew only of duty and family loyalty, which he fulfilled by sending his sons the scant money he had managed to save to help them pay for college in America. In return, he expected blind loyalty, something he had given to his mother and siblings.

In the fall of 1984, I received a phone call from my father. Finally, free to leave Iran, Baba had to make a stop in Italy to have his papers processed by the American embassy. I called the Hebrew Immigrant Aid Society (HIAS), asking them to facilitate his stay, especially since he kept kosher. "Why doesn't he go to Israel?" they asked. Had my father done so, he would have had an impossible task obtaining a green card later. The gateway to Iran would have closed, forcing him to relinquish all his assets to his brother and to the government. HIAS finally agreed to help Baba by providing him with an inexpensive place to stay while he awaited his immigration number.

To facilitate Baba's paperwork, Norman and I had contacted Virginia Congressman Norman Sisisky. He kindly wrote a letter on our behalf, first to expedite Baba's green card and then to help him obtain a visa to Italy. Suspicious of all figures of authority in Iran, Sisisky's kindness and his office's efficiency and willingness to help us surprised me.

My family had taught me to avoid anything government-related and to fear anyone in uniform. Norman often teased me, "I bet you tremble and perspire when you see the tunnel toll collector because he wears a government-issued uniform." It was these fears that almost resulted in me refusing to accept the invitation to meet Congressman Sisisky as I dropped off a few forms at his office. Gracious, he asked about my father's well-being, giving me a chance to thank him.

Baba asked me to meet him in Italy. He was afraid that he wouldn't be able to find his way around a strange land with an unfamiliar language and customs. "You speak English," he pleaded, "You'll be able to communicate better." I declined, although I felt guilty. He expected me to act in a manner opposed to his own views of femininity.

A TRULY OLD-FASHIONED patriarch, Baba had monitored most aspects of my life in Iran. When I filled out my application form for the national college exam, *konkur*, he grabbed it from me, scanned it, and said, "Look what you've done. You've ruined it." My dream was to study journalism at Tehran University's School of Journalism. My local university did not offer that major, which was fine with me because I desperately wanted to get away from my family. My second choice was English literature. My father thought that since I had stubbornly selected mathematics in high school — I had envisioned that mathematics would free me from the rote memorization that the natural sciences required — I had to continue my education in a related field. He carefully scratched out every single entry with the sharp tip of a razor and selected the three most competitive majors in engineering: electric, civil, and mechanic — none of which was of any interest to me.

I had performed poorly in high school. I had hoped that by enrolling, against my father's wishes, in the new elite, co-ed Pahlavi University High School I would receive a better education, a fair education with no discrimination against women, but the gender discrimination I had experienced in a regular school continued in this elite environment.

To my father's and my own great personal humiliation, I wasn't accepted into college. The results were printed in our local paper, and the entire community knew that Farideh Dayanim wasn't so smart after all. I felt that my life had unraveled, but the clueless women of my family, most of whom had had little education, didn't offer me any sympathy. Life went on as usual. As I mourned my uncertain future, my grandmother said, "My legs hurt. Give me a ride." My mother, lost in her own world, was frying fish in the kitchen. She lifted her head long enough to say, "Run to the bakery. Buy four sheets of *naan* for lunch." Ignoring it all, I went outside and sat on the stairs to the backyard, pondering my future with a sinking feeling. I was ruined.

Baba came home for lunch and threw the newspaper at me. "Now we just have to marry you off. Go, help your mother in the kitchen."

I shuffled to the bakery, wrapped in my mother's white calico *chador* to avoid the baker's derogatory comments about my immodesty. So what if my westernized classmates saw me looking like a maid. Hopefully they wouldn't recognize me.

I was lucky that year. The university decided to open an evening program for math teachers who worked during the day. Entry to the school was determined by an aptitude test rather than the onerous knowledge-based exam. Upon being accepted into the math program, my immediate excitement was quickly replaced with apprehension when I realized that the same misogynist math teacher I had had in high school also taught Calculus I and II at the university. In class, I raised my hand to ask a question. "Such a stupid question!" he said. His long moustache dancing over his lips, he always laughed and shook his head as he refused to answer questions posed by me or any other female students. "Come here and put one *toman* in the box for wasting my time." He pointed to a punishment box that women filled with money and was later used to pay for ice cream given to male students as they went over problems after school.

I'd had enough of the abuse. Acknowledging defeat in my fight against the system, I switched my major to English Literature without informing my father.

It was just about impossible to change majors in those days. The chair of the English department told me, "We don't like accepting rejects from other departments." My friend Shohreh, who was also majoring in math and trying to escape the oppressive classroom situation, asked her uncle, a university administrator, to intervene on her behalf. Learning from Shohreh, I asked an uncle, a well-known dentist, to give the chair of the English department a call. Baba, surprised and disappointed, eventually accepted the decision. Liberal arts wouldn't be a bad major for a woman, he reasoned to save face. He bragged, "My daughter has a gift for languages; she is fluent in English." I wasn't.

It always made Baba uncomfortable when I diverted from the traditional path for a good Iranian Jewish woman. Fearing the judgement of his community, Baba resisted new ideas. Driving a car? "What are people going to say about a young woman behind the wheel? What if you got into an accident?" Guitar lessons? "You are going to be called *raqas, motreb,* a dancer, a cheap entertainer," all inappropriate occupations for a woman. Tennis? "Do you know of another Jewish woman playing that stupid game? No!"

When I chose to marry an American man, Baba was devastated at first. He knew that people were talking. *Why a foreigner? Are there no good Iranian men*? It was Baba's job to find me a good husband. A foreign man did not fit into that notion. Plus, my father had never imagined that his daughter could live in a faraway land. He had plans of his own for me, living close by where we could visit, have holidays and Shabbat together. Sadly, it was not meant to be. Even if I had remained and married an Iranian man, the brewing Revolution would have scattered us, destroying all these hopes and dreams.

≈

MAYBE BECAUSE I had broken so many of the rules of feminine conduct, Baba began expecting things from me that did not fit into his own definition of a woman's responsibilities. By arranging for Congressman Sisisky, a figure of American authority, to be involved in his visa procedures, I further solidified Baba's belief that I possessed unusual qualities. I didn't.

The notion that I could leave three young children and my husband to help him in Italy was so absolutely against anything he had believed a woman could and should do that at first I was speechless.

I tried to explain to Baba that none of his children living in the United States could help him. Freydoun had refugee status and didn't have a passport to leave the country. Farzad and Nahid would have to miss school and reapply for student visas in order to return. Of course there would be no guarantee of a return for them since the United States was not fond of Iranians at the time.

Baba was on his own. Again, his children were a source of disappointment.

"How have I raised my kids?" he said with a tinge of despair in his voice. Once again, comparing me and my siblings to other unknown children of Iranian refugees, who were better, more responsible. "Other people's children meet them in Europe with love and respect."

My father, my omnipotent father, was scared. My heart sank at the realization.

# BABA
### *1984, Rome*

After being away from my family for four years, and having had so many ups and downs, I was afraid to be joyous even with my passport and exit visa in hand. I decided to visit Mehrabad Airport before returning to Shiraz, determined to find the same policeman, show him my passport, and make sure that everything was going to go right. *Ma'ar gazideh az risman-e siah o-safeed meetarseh.* Once bitten by a snake, a person fears even a black and white rope.

At first the airport security wouldn't let me in, forcing me to lie, telling them that I was a passenger in order to gain entry. After finding the kind policeman, I begged him to check my files. Even though it was illegal for him to interfere, he finally agreed to check my files on the condition that he would confiscate the passport if there were any discrepancies. I agreed. I had to know before packing my bag.

After thirty minutes, which felt like eternity, the police-man returned with his hands behind his back. "Dayanim, I am sorry," he said.

I didn't know why he was smiling. Was he happy for my misfortune? I lost my colour and swayed like a drunk.

Seeing me in distress, he quickly retrieved the passport from his back pocket and put it in my hand. "Everything's okay," he said, patting me on my shoulder. "I was just joking. Sorry if I scared you. Do you hear me, Dayanim? Everything is okay."

Recognizing the burgundy colour of my passport, I bent over to kiss his hand but he refused.

I returned to Shiraz.

FARIDEH CALLED AGAIN inquiring about my departure date. Giving me a name and a phone number in Rome, she said an HIAS representative would meet me at the airport, find me a place to stay, and expedite my immigration paperwork.

I bought $300 from the bank and $200 from illegal money-lenders on the streets and, since taking that much money out of the country was illegal, I hid them well in the lining of my suitcase. On a Sunday in October of 1984, with my stomach churning, heart pounding, chest burning, I made it through the line at Mehrabad Airport and boarded an Iran-Air flight for Italy with a fifteen-day Italian visa.

After exiting customs in Rome, I looked for a sign with my name, as Farideh had promised, but didn't see anyone. After waiting for over two hours, I asked the clerk at the information desk in my broken English and sign language to call the number for HIAS. When no one answered, the clerk found me a cheap hotel with a room to share with another person for $35 in cash, but the taxi ride to the far away hotel cost me $30. At this rate the $500 could disappear very quickly.

I didn't speak Italian and knew few English words but sign language saved me many times. Obtaining a map from the hotel, I ventured outside and came to a beautiful boulevard with a small pool in the middle and statues of naked men peeing into the fountain. What a strange and funny country! How could they display private body parts in the land of the Christian Pope? Most shops were closed, and keeping kosher limited the food choice, but I found a small cafe and bought an egg sandwich for dinner and returned to my hotel before it was too dark.

Dialing HIAS in the morning, I explained my situation in broken English. A man told me to wait, then came back apologizing, telling me to wait at the hotel to be picked up, and spoke to the hotel clerk for directions. Around noon a man showed up introducing himself as a member of HIAS. Although we couldn't communicate well, I followed him to his car. As we drove south through narrow streets, I suddenly felt afraid. Where was I going? Who was this man? We finally stopped after an hour of driving, and he motioned for me to follow him to a very old and rundown building. The driver left me with a very big, tall, and heavy-set man, like a warrior in the Persian epic, *The Shahnameh*. A cage elevator, barely accommodating his huge body, took us to a large room where about thirty others sat on metal chairs around an old black-and-white TV. For a minute I felt as if I were back in that cold waiting room on Pasteur Street, waiting to know my fate. Lightheaded, I looked around for a water fountain. I asked, *Water*? But no one understood my English. Finally a young teenage girl approached me and said, "A moment." She came back with a glass of water, held my hand and led me to a small kitchen where a young woman was preparing dinner.

I became friendly with the girl's parents who had left the Soviet Union, awaiting their refugee visas to the United States. The other travellers helped set the table and prepare dinner, which consisted of a bowl of consommé, mashed potatoes, and one apple, nothing to fill anyone's stomach.

An hour later, Mario, the owner of the pensione, brought my suitcase in and helped me settle in a bedroom with a key for privacy. A deep, dreamless sleep overtook me. I woke up to a breakfast of hot milk, bread, cheese, and tea.

There were two pensiones in the same neighbourhood, both owned by Mario, who used the first for Jewish refugees and the second for poor travellers. The train station and the main street, lined with shops and restaurants, were not too far away.

Two days went by. On the third day someone gave me a ride to a large building that housed the HIAS headquarters to meet a man in charge of applying for refugee visas to the United States. Once the forms were submitted to the American Embassy, refugees would be transferred to a special camp in Rome to wait the six months it often took to process their visas.

Not knowing much about HIAS then, I thought that they could help me obtain my green card. Instead, they wanted me to bring my wife and daughter to Rome so that we could be processed as a family. They dialed my wife's number in Israel for me. Niloufar picked up the phone. I had not seen or spoken to her for over four years. She was almost nine years old now. My little one who had needed a father's love the most during her childhood had not heard my voice for all these years, an eternity for a child. She must have thought that I had completely abandoned them. I said, "Neli. Neli *joon*." I don't know what emotions she must have felt. "Call your mother." She recognized my voice. "Is that you, Baba? Maman isn't at home." She started sobbing and the phone went dead. I couldn't stop my own sobs. People gathered around me to comfort me.

My chest heavy, I started running a fever that night. I asked the HIAS representative to take me to a doctor, but he said that I had to take care of it myself. Meanwhile they insisted on obtaining refugee visas for us as a family and would not help me with my green card. If I had wanted refugee status, I would have left with smugglers through Pakistan. I had to have the option of returning to Iran to sell my property.

After the first week, I heard Persian spoken, and followed the complaining voices about the inadequacy of the pensione. They sounded frightened, the way I had been on the first day. I introduced myself and welcomed them. The young Jewish couple had escaped from Tehran through Austria. The man hugged me and kissed me on both cheeks, so happy to see a *hamvatan*. The Boostani family and I spent some time together. The wife suffered from arthritis in her legs and limped. I gave them a few Valium pills I had brought from Iran. I complained to Mr. Boostani about the little shower that served so many people and the water was often cold. We went around the city chatting. He spoke French fluently but didn't know a word of English. If the Italians didn't understand his French, I jumped in with a few words in English. Visiting the Vatican one day, we encountered huge crowds. It must have been a special day since we managed to get a glimpse of the Pope himself. Naked statues stood shamelessly around the church in this holy place. What a strange land! What a contrast to a synagogue where image and statues were forbidden. A policeman approached me, saying things I didn't understand. Did I do something wrong? Finally, he took my hat off. Then I understood that it was disrespectful to cover one's head in a church.

I suffered from a runny nose and persistent coughs that week. Finally feeling better and my head clearing, I decided that HIAS wasn't for me. I needed to help myself. I contacted Israel again from HIAS headquarters and this time I spoke to my wife. We tried to catch up with events in our lives after such a long separation. I explained what HIAS wanted to do and asked her opinion. She said the decision was up to me. The American Embassy was located in Naples. That Wednesday, I asked Mario to keep my suitcase and gave him the key to the room, said goodbye to the Boostani family since they were heading for the camp, and took the train to Naples, arriving around 9:00 a.m. on Thursday. I had only my raincoat, a briefcase with my documents, my leftover money from the $300, clean underwear and a shirt. The taxi driver took me to a street facing the well-guarded American consulate and told me that I had to walk the rest of the way. The entry door was made of bulletproof glass, and one had to converse with those inside through a device on the door like something one might see in a penitentiary. I found it a bit unnerving. The guard kept asking questions in Italian which I could not comprehend. Finally I understood that I couldn't take my briefcase inside. I opened it and poured the stuff out. He took a few steps back frightened, screaming at me. He might have thought that I was a terrorist. I don't know. We finally understood each other, and I was allowed entry.

I showed the guard an English letter Farideh had written, stating that I was there for my green card. He sent me to the fourth floor, room number five. I gave them my documents. The woman in charge returned after about an hour and told me that they had been waiting for me. "Why didn't you come earlier?" she asked. I tried to tell her about my troubles. I don't remember the woman's name, but I will never forget her kindness and compassion. She asked me if I had a phone number in America. I gave her Farideh's number. She asked me to wait outside. After an hour she called me in and gave me the phone. Farideh was on the line and explained to me that each embassy was given a certain number of visas to be granted for permanent residency. The Italian embassy had run out of numbers for that year. I had to wait until the next calendar year, a few months away. They were going to make a few phone calls to see if they could pull one from the following year's numbers. Farideh said that I had to wait until it was daytime in America and the offices opened. Meanwhile, in order to expedite the process, a secretary asked me questions in simple English and typed my answers into a long form. I struggled to understand each question and to answer them in my broken English. With each answer she paused, puzzled, then figured out my answer and giggled. Finally, we were done. The first lady returned and asked me to have lunch with her in the cafeteria beneath the building, which was reserved for the workers in the consulate.

She contacted the offices in America after lunch and her request was granted. They would give me a number. She told me that I needed a physical first. She added that it usually cost about $100 and asked me if I had enough money with me. I said yes. She told me that unfortunately it was already too late, and I had to see the doctor the following day. She asked me if I had a place to stay in Naples. I said no. She said that if I left for Rome, I might not get back in time the following day, Friday, and then there would be the weekend and everything would have to be postponed. She made a few phone calls and found me a cheap hotel, around $20, close to the consulate. "Make sure to come back early tomorrow," she said. She was obviously worried about me and repeated the directions to the hotel a few times, making sure that I wouldn't get lost.

I headed toward the hotel, taking a seaside road. Although I was still feverish, had a terrible headache, and my chest hurt, I enjoyed watching the sunset over the water. When I entered the hotel, I found a huge black dog, slumbering on the floor, staring at me, I thought, in an attack mode. I was startled. A young man at the desk told me not to be afraid and took my passport and guided me to my room. Starved, I didn't have the energy to go out in search of food; my fever spiked; my ribs ached from persistent coughing. I woke up at 5:00 a.m. soaked in sweat but I felt better; the fever had finally broken after two weeks. Afraid of not waking up in time, I showered, dressed, and had breakfast at the hotel. I paid the clerk, retrieved my passport from him, and was tempted to wave goodbye to the dog but he eyed me with a fierce look.

At the consulate I met the doctor for my physical. The rest of the procedures took hours. This time the nice lady approached me and told me that she couldn't take me to the staff cafeteria. Someone must have given her a hard time. She gave me directions to a small cafe close by and told me to return by 2:00 p.m. On the oceanfront I found a small restaurant that had loaves of bread larger than I could ever have imagined, each one probably weighing two to three kilos. The owner cut slices of these gigantic loaves for sandwiches for his customers. I decided to take a table instead of walking away with my food in a bag like the rest of the customers. The owner asked me what I wanted. Not knowing any other words, I said, "Spaghetti and beer." He gave me the beer with some bread and something that looked like cooked spinach and went back to the kitchen to cook. I filled up with these tasty morsels and thought of leaving since it was already close to 2:00 p.m., when the owner brought me a huge bowl of noodles, enough to feed a family, with different kinds of forbidden shellfish, most of which I had never seen before. I paid him for the food but didn't touch it. Trying hard to convey his message through hand signals and a few English words, I think he kept asking if it wasn't good; if he should wrap it for me to take. I said, "No, thank you," and rushed back.

BY 4:00 P.M. that Friday, I had all my documents in a sealed envelope to submit to immigration officials at Kennedy Airport. The nice lady asked me about my plans. I told her that I had to return to Rome. She phoned the train station and told me the last train for the day would leave at 5:00 p.m. She called a taxi.

There are always those who go beyond the call of duty.

I showed my ticket at the information desk, hoping to be guided to the right train. The attendant said something in Italian, which I didn't understand, but he kept repeating the same words, each time louder. I, in return, kept saying in English, *Don't understand*, and he shouted in Italian whatever it was he was saying. I looked at my watch. I didn't have much time left. I screamed back at him saying that I would be late. He finally just pointed to the stairs and I hurriedly climbed them only to realize that there were numerous trains leaving from that point. I asked a policeman for help but he ignored me. It was hard for me to believe a policeman did not know a word of English, especially since I kept saying, *Rome*, and I was showing him my ticket. I ran around showing my ticket and asking people, but they just shook their heads. I was getting frightened. What would happen to me if I missed my train? I saw a family with children between ages five and twelve. I asked the oldest, hoping that she had learned a few English words. Maybe she would be as nice as the young girl at the pensione. I had guessed right. She spoke with her mother and pointed to a sign and told me that the train was delayed until 5:30. I was grateful. Two young people standing under the sign spoke to each other in English. I asked them if this was the right train just to make sure. They said yes, 5:30. They told me that they, too, were going to Rome, and I could follow them to the right train. We boarded and they headed to the back, but I was tired and sat down in the first empty chair and didn't see them afterward.

I looked at my surroundings and was amazed at the luxury of the cabin. I could recline my seat and nap. I thought that the man shouting at me must have been saying that this was a luxury train, and I had just a regular ticket. If that was the case, it was a good thing I didn't understand him. I had to return to Rome and didn't have any money left for luxury accommodations. Now I worried again. What if the comptroller asked for my ticket and said I was not supposed to be on this luxury train? When he finally came, I showed him my ticket and when he started yelling, I pushed the ticket back at him. What else could I have done? He finally left and brought back two people, one in uniform. They spoke to me in English. I shrugged my shoulders. They spoke French to me. I shrugged my shoulders. I gave them my ticket. "Rome," I said. They finally took my ticket and left me alone. What a nice ride! I had now been in Italy for fourteen days and I had $10 left of my $300. The rest of the money I had left in the lining of my suitcase at the *pensione*. The *pensione* itself was very cheap, $8 for me and free for others who were seeking asylum, but their food never filled me up. I bought food to supplement my diet.

I arrived in Rome around 8:00 p.m. and walked to the *pensione*, arriving in time for dinner. My Iranian friends had already left. For the first time in four years, I slept well. I went to HIAS on Monday and explained to them that I had my green card and asked them to help me to reserve my plane ticket for America. They looked at me with unbelieving eyes, not taking me seriously. They asked me to return with the documents to prove my words. I said fine but went looking for a travel agency. I found the office of Lufthansa. They would accept my ticket, but I had to make a stop in Germany first. Then I spotted the office of Iran Air. Of course I knew that they didn't fly to the U.S, but I was sure they could help me. After all they were my *hamvatan*s, my countrymen. They spoke my language; they possessed the warmth of the people of my country. They secured a direct flight with Alitalia for the following Sunday, November 5 at noon. I had to be there at least two hours earlier, and if I missed my flight, they warned me, it wasn't redeemable.

The following day I went back to HIAS and showed them my sealed documents which, of course, they could not open. They nevertheless gave me their congratulations. The woman in charge said that I should allow the HIAS bus to take me to the airport for the same price as a taxi. Their driver would take me inside and make sure that I was safe. I gladly accepted and prepaid $30 to be picked up by 9:00 a.m. on Sunday.

I had five days left. I wandered around the city, spending most of my time around the train station. I found a branch of the telephone company and asked if I could call America collect and gave Farideh my flight information.

I HAD NOTICED a solitary man from Bulgaria at the *pensione* who kept to himself. He didn't speak Italian, English, or any other language that anyone could understand. It seemed that he had been there much longer than anyone else, around four months, which was quite unusual. A strange man with his own idiosyncrasies, he had chosen a glass cup as his own. In the morning, he transferred the warm milk, at lunch his soup, at night his water to this cup. One day as I left the pensione for a regular outing to the train station, he left too and we ended up walking together. We sat on the same bench — he was still holding his cup in his hand like a security blanket. I sensed his extreme loneliness and pointed to the telephone office, trying to find out if he had anyone to call. He took an address book out of his wallet and showed me a number. His daughter, I understood, lived in Canada, but he didn't have any money to contact her. I took him to the telephone office and helped him make a collect call. Luckily, the daughter was at home and accepted the call. He cried with joy. Such a moving scene! Afterwards, he gave me the phone and his daughter kept saying, "Thank you." Not knowing of his fate, she had been worried about him.

I PAID MARIO $160 for my accommodations and thanked him for his services. I had $20 left and was afraid to spend any money. I dared to treat myself to a boiled corn on the cob, but nothing else. On Sunday, as arranged, I waited with my suitcase at the door at 8:30 a.m. By 9:00 a.m., the bus had not arrived. I went inside and told Mario that I was afraid I wouldn't make my flight. He called HIAS, but the office was closed. By 10:00 a.m., heart pounding with anxiety, I went back inside, "Mario, please help me, please." He kept telling me to calm down. By 11:00 a.m. the bus was still not there. I didn't have enough money for a taxi. Like a madman, I yelled, "Mario, PLEASE!" He brought his car around, put the luggage in the trunk, and drove me to the airport. He kept telling me to be calm, that everything would be okay, that the flights never took off on time in Italy. I was lucky, the flight was delayed until 1:00 p.m. Mario helped me check in and took me to the gate. I was the only one not on board. He shook my hand and wished me well. He was my guardian angel that day, and I will never forget him. I put my last bit of money, $19, in his hand.

He smiled and put the money back in my pocket. "Goodbye," he said.

"Goodbye, my friend."

## FARIDEH
### *December 1984, Norfolk*

I had last seen Baba in Israel in January 1980 when I was pregnant with Lena. Four years later and in the midst of another winter I stood among travellers at the arrivals gate of Norfolk airport, eager to see Baba and anxious that I might be late to pick up my daughters from daycare.

Baba emerged from the dark mouth of the jet bridge with blank eyes. He was hunched over, skin and bones. Squinting his eyes, he didn't recognize me at first. I waved, took a few steps toward him. Without loosening his grip on a black briefcase, Baba tried to hug me with his free hand as I walked along the rail that separated us until airport security asked me to move along.

Tears glistening in his eyes, lips moving without uttering a word, he finally wrapped an arm around me and kissed my forehead as soon as he left the secure area.

"Baba, *safar khoob bood*? Did you have a good trip?" I patted
him on the back and for an awkward moment we didn't know
what else to do, what else to say.

In the car, his tiny suitcase in the trunk, his briefcase beside
him, he finally broke the silence, "*Shekasteh shodeed!*" Using the
formal plural "you," he said that I looked *broken*.

I imagined him seeing me like a crackle vase with fine lines
embedded in the glass. I could be useless as a broken vase;
I could be artwork. The fancy, untranslatable phrase meant
that I looked as if I had suffered. I think that's what Baba had
hoped I would tell him.

"I am okay, Baba, and happy you're here."

"I'm embarrassed by my looks. People are staring at me,
thinking that I suffer from malnutrition."

"No one is looking at you, Baba."

"I'm ashamed. What will Norman say when he sees me?"

Self-loathing and self-pity, I remembered from my life
in Iran, often carried a certain satisfaction. Whenever my
grandmother, her daughters, or friends saw each other, they
greeted one another with a litany of unhappy tales, stories
of sickness and misery in their lives. No one was "just great;
just fine." Maybe they believed that by enumerating their
sufferings they fooled the *jinn* and averted the evil eye, or
maybe it denoted their need for love, sympathy, comforting
words, and hugs.

Undeniably my father had suffered; he was the "broken"
one; he had the right to feel sorry for himself. I didn't respond
because I didn't know how to react or what to say. Instead,
I worried about the traffic on I-64.

211

I TOOK BABA directly to the JCC to pick up the girls. We were early after all, so we sat in the hallway for about a half an hour, waiting for my daughters. Between intermittent coughs, Baba told me the story of his crossing to Iran from Turkey.

"They took my hand suddenly," Baba reenacted the scene by grabbing mine, "and led me to a room that looked like a dungeon."

I didn't understand the sequence of events he was describing, his words were out of context, not making sense to me.

"Baba, you are here now. Just forget all that." Hadn't I begged him not to return to Iran?

Picking up Baba at the airport had interrupted my regular schedule. I kept thinking of that day's undone chores, the unpaid bills, the dirty laundry, the empty refrigerator. *What would we eat for dinner?* The girls must be hungry; I had forgotten to bring snacks with me.

"I can't believe I am a grandfather," Baba broke the string of my worry beads with his words. I was touched.

Waving that day's artwork, the girls came running toward us laughing loudly, wearing their colourful leggings and tops. My father, who was accustomed to seeing little unsmiling girls in black *chadors*, taking little steps out of modesty, looked surprised and even disenchanted.

"This is your other grandpa, Baba-bozorg. Give him a hug." I told the girls. They became quiet and hid behind me.

"Leave them alone," my father said. "They don't know who I am. Later, later."

But I insisted and my daughters reluctantly allowed the stranger's embrace.

Excited about that day's events, a longer stay at the pool, a birthday party, a new song, the little happenings that always brightened their day, the girls chatted and laughed. Clutching his black briefcase, my father didn't try to communicate with his little foreign granddaughters who didn't speak Farsi.

I wanted to say to him what he had always said to me, *Sit up straight, Baba*.

And then my father said, "I miss Jahangir's daughters. Their faces dance in front of me like a movie."

After so many years, I didn't want to hear about my father's love for his brother's children, especially when he was in the presence of his own granddaughters for the first time. Then it dawned on me that he had not mentioned his own little girl either, little Niloufar, the water lily who had floated on her own smarts for so many terrible years, taking care of her own affairs and Maman's, too. *Nothing has changed*, I thought. *Baba loves others more than his own.*

With no joy in our reunion, we quickly fell back into our established patterns of misunderstandings, disappointments, family loyalty, and responsibility. I asked the girls about that day's events, about their friends and camp counsellors, and I didn't bother to translate the conversation. Baba remained silent, staring straight on the long ride to Chesapeake.

Every day, after dropping the girls off at the JCC, I took care of Baba's affairs. We visited a doctor because Baba was suffering from constant stomach cramps and a persistent cough. When the doctor, a middle-aged man with red cheeks and a perpetual smile, asked Baba to take off his shirt in order to listen to his chest, Baba, who was sitting hunched over on the edge of the table, turned red and said, "*khejalat meekesham*." He was embarrassed. I thought he felt uncomfortable about being shirtless in front of me. I was about to turn around, but before I could say, *Baba, please forgive my back toward you*, an impolite gesture toward an elder, he added, "I'm so embarrassed that I look like a cadaver, skin and bones. I've lost so much weight. Tell him that I am not a pauper, that I've just gone through a hard time." Body fat is a sign of riches; I had forgotten that. Feeling sorry for himself, Baba was trying to engage the doctor in a conversation about his misfortunes.

I had managed Baba's finances during his absence. Together, we went to the bank to open an account in Baba's name and to re-examine his financial situation. He sat quietly to the side as I communicated with the bank officer, turning to Baba once in a while to translate. Baba took some cash out of his account, looked at the balance, and shook his head in disbelief.

He unlocked the black briefcase, peeked in, deposited his ID, and locked it again. I assumed that the mysterious black relic held only random papers and I was annoyed by his secretive behaviour. I wondered if the attaché case gave him a sense of dignity and purpose, especially now that he felt so helpless and ashamed, now that a woman had taken control of his affairs.

After we left the bank, Baba asked, "Do you remember when we went to the bank in New York?"

Norman and I had taken my father to the bank after our wedding in 1977. We had tried to open a savings account for him and transfer some of the small fortune he had amassed in Iran. The bank refused Baba because he didn't have a social security number.

"I remember, Baba."

What a difference it would have made in his life if he had secured that money in an American bank. Maybe he would have not poured it back into his farm.

The following day, I took Baba, briefcase in hand, to the immigration office in Norfolk to follow up on his residency status. He said something like, "Tell the officer not to mention Israel in my files." He was already thinking about his return to Iran.

"Baba, I can't do that."

"Why not?"

"Because! I am afraid."

"This is America. You don't have to be afraid. Do it for my sake."

I stumbled over my words as I asked the officer to grant my father's request. I must have jumbled the words badly since he kept asking me to repeat myself. Maybe he couldn't believe what he was hearing. He opened the half door to the office and motioned for me to enter the secure area. Slamming the door shut behind me, he shook his index finger at me. "You are asking me to lie — an officer of the United States government — to lie? I can throw you in jail for this."

Pale and teary, I replied with a shaky voice, "I know, officer. He is my father. He left all his assets in Iran. If he returns with that information on his file, they'll kill him. Don't lie; just don't include it, please."

"Get back to the waiting room and consider yourself lucky if I don't report you."

I nodded, returned to the waiting room, and sat next to my father. When I told him in a muted voice what had happened, Baba replied, "Naaa. What do you say? This is America. They understand."

Covered in cold sweat, I wondered, *What have I done?*

The officer appeared at the desk an hour later, he motioned with his hand for me to approach, and, without looking at me, left my father's papers on the counter.

"Thank you," I mumbled, still teary.

He turned his back and disappeared behind the partition wall. He took pity on both of us, but I felt guilty for having insisted on deleting the name of a country that had helped my family on their initial exodus.

Opening his black briefcase just enough to put away the papers, Baba smiled, "I told you he would do it."

THAT NIGHT, the girls climbed up on the sofa to sit with me, as they did every night, to listen to their favourite stories, *Green Eggs and Ham* and *Alexander and the Terrible, Horrible, No Good Very Bad Day*. Baba sat silently on the elevated brick hearth of the fireplace, which was a novelty to him. Staring at the fire, he smoked pensively, his eyes betraying a deep sadness and the strange wildness of someone who had returned from a close encounter with a beast. He didn't tell me then the story of his perilous journey. The details of his emotional imprisonment in Iran would be revealed slowly, over several decades, and finally more fully in his memoir.

After the girls were asleep, I knelt by the fireplace and reached to the back of the firebox to collect the cigarette butts my father had discarded. "Don't throw them in the there, Baba. They don't burn." I was too embarrassed to ask him to smoke outside in the cold weather.

"I had heard of this thing here from someone who'd been in America, but I couldn't visualize it."

"It's like the *tanoor* in the kitchen, Baba."

"No, the one in the kitchen we used for cooking spewed smoke and blackened the walls. Such genius! How did they come up with such a system where no smoke escapes? You don't even have a window open. American ingenuity!"

So, that's the reason he stared into the fireplace. He was trying to figure out its structural magic.

"You know," he said, "the same guy who told me about the fireplace, you remember him, Chamani. He had a fabric shop and left for America long ago — he said that everything good comes from here."

He pointed to the bag of Indian basmati rice in the open pantry. "See that? It says India on the burlap, but it's really misspelled."

"Baba, what are you saying? Don't believe everything you hear."

"*Naaa.* Let me show you." He went to the pantry and brought back the burlap bag of basmati rice. "See this word, India? This is really Indiana, misspelled."

My sophisticated father, who recited classical Persian

poetry by heart, incorporating it into his everyday speech, my curious father who had spent weeks poring over engineering manuals for chicken incubators, who had studied books on poultry diseases and their cures, my father who had figured out how the fireplace worked, had allowed himself to believe the words of a boasting, manipulative friend because Baba so venerated America.

NORMAN OFTEN CAME home late after making his rounds at the hospital. My father was disturbed by Norman's absence. "You two work too hard," he kept saying. "You are so busy with the children. They run your life. And Norman is busy all day and some nights at work."

"Did you forget how late you used to come home, Baba?"

"That was different. You are home alone with the kids. In Iran everyone was around. And here," he pointed to the dark woods outside, "nobody is around. Aren't you afraid at night? At home, alone with three children?" He shook his head.

He had forgotten how hard my mother had worked. While my father hammered away at gold and silver in his store late into the night, Maman took care of the children, her mother-in-law, and her brothers-in-law. There was no point reminding my father of past events.

BABA ALWAYS CHEERED up when Norman came home. The two men would sit at the kitchen table and play backgammon, sipping Scotch. My father would offer Norman a cigarette, but Norman had already quit smoking. After the girls were asleep, I would clean up the kitchen and crawl into bed, often too tired to sit around and translate.

Sometimes I woke up in the middle of night and saw the burning light of my father's cigarette moving back and forth in the screened-in porch. Often, early in the morning, when

I followed the girls into the kitchen to get breakfast ready, I saw Baba, hunched over, pacing in the yard, hands locked behind his back, his gaze fixed on the ground as if in search of a diamond lost in the long blades of grass.

Baba called my mother a few times to explain why it had taken him so long to return to Israel. When I got on the phone, my mother sounded subdued and didn't want to talk. She answered every question with "humm, ok, *bashe*." I worried about my parents' reunion after all these years of separation.

NEARLY ONE YEAR after leaving Iran for the U.S., Baba left for Israel with his American travel documents and his temporary passport in hand. The morning of his departure, Norman tried to shake hands with Baba before leaving for work, but Baba pulled Norman to him, hugging and kissing him on both cheeks. Before leaving for the airport, Baba took out a worn out book of *tehillim* from his pocket, recited a few psalms, and kissed the *mezuzah* on the entry door. The girls watched him with curiosity. With Baba seated next to me in the car, his briefcase on his lap, I dropped off my daughters at the JCC. They waved to Baba, another temporary visitor, and ran off to join their friends.

"Take care of yourself," Baba said at the airport. "You're too busy."

I gave him a hug. "Okay, Baba. Have a safe flight."

I missed his silent presence on the ride home. At the same time the air in the car felt fresher; it was easier to breathe.

## BABA
### *1985–86, Tel Aviv*

I arrived at Tel Aviv's Ben Gurion airport around 5:00 p.m. —
five years after leaving for Istanbul on my fateful journey to
Iran. Niloufar had been a child of five and now I could barely
recognize her from the image burned in my memory. She threw
herself at me, her hands around my neck, kissing me. Had I
been reborn? Was this a new life? The joy of holding my little
one is a precious memory I'll never forget. On that glorious day
I tried not to think of my uncertain future or the bad omen
that had followed me all those lost years.

Neli approached me the following day as I sat on the floor
drinking tea, drowned in my own thoughts. She had skipped
school that first day after my return and had a favour to ask.
Speaking Hebrew to her mother during my absence, she spoke
to me in broken Farsi with a thick Israeli accent and Hebrew
syntax. I couldn't understand my own child and her mother

219

had to translate the words. During those five years her class-mates had wondered if she indeed had a father. Would I go with her to Bialek school for show and tell?

We went first to the principal's office, who told me that my daughter had had a hard time concentrating during my absence. Then they led me to Neli's class and introduced me to her friends. I taught them about the long history of Jewish life in Iran

I had always been a smoker, but during the lonely years in Iran I had become a chain smoker. I bought two cartons of cigarettes at Kennedy airport on my way to Israel. Deep in my thoughts, I smoked non-stop. One day Neli brought the packages to me and begged me to discard them. "Please, Baba. It's going to kill you. You cough all the time." I couldn't refuse her. She destroyed the cigarettes and I quit cold turkey, forever indebted to her for saving me from my addiction.

Lacking mental energy, I did little other than visit the market and an elderly cousin in the old section of Tel Aviv. I spent most days at home, watching Iranian TV. My wife tried to get me out, signing me up for Hebrew classes, but my mind wandered. The initial joy of seeing my family was clouded by dark thoughts of our poverty and betrayal. No longer able to work to provide for my wife and children, I feared destitution and an eventual dependence on my children for sustenance. Returning to Iran to reclaim all I had worked for and left in my brother's care became an unavoidable reality.

## BABA
### *1987, Philadelphia*

I had never imagined a day that my family would be dispersed.
My wife and I suffered away from our four children who lived
in the United States. Our sons wanted us to move closer to
them, but Niloufar refused to leave Israel. At age fifty-nine, I
didn't know how to control this child, almost a teenager now,
who had grown up without my supervision in the runaway
culture of the west. She needed her brothers' protection as
well as mine. My sons, both of whom lived in the Philadelphia
area, rented an apartment for us in Cherry Hill, New Jersey,
and arranged for Niloufar's enrolment at the local school. We
packed everything, locked the door to the dilapidated apartment my wife had bought unwisely when I was in Iran, and
flew to Philadelphia to start a new life.

Once again, I explored the option of returning to Iran to
sell my assets at any cost. The exit visa had given me six

months to return to Iran, but two years had gone by as I had waited for my visa processing in Italy, then for my travel documents in the United States, and finally for the healing process with my daughter and wife in Israel. My Iranian passport had expired as well, necessitating a visit to the Interest Section of the Islamic Republic of Iran in Washington, D.C. to renew it. From the Iranians, I received a five-year permit to travel to Iran as many times as I wished because I had a green card, but I could not stay longer than four months each time — not enough time to take care of my assets. Fortunately, I did not need an exit visa, but they warned me that if I overstayed the four-month limit, my passport would be confiscated.

Feeling reassured that my sons would take care of their mother and Niloufar in the United States, I bought a round trip ticket from New York to Hamburg with a connecting flight to Tehran. Surprised, my children opposed my decision, but how could I have left a lifetime of labour and dreams in Iran to live in penury in my old age? They were young; they did not understand.

## FARIDEH
### *1987, Portsmouth*

Both of my brothers were living in the suburbs of Philadelphia when my parents moved to America with Niloufar. We decided as a family that it would be best if my parents settled in the Philadelphia area with my brothers. My parents didn't own a car and we knew that without one they would have found themselves very isolated in Portsmouth. Even though my brothers had previously decided never to live together — assuming that their very different personalities would make it too difficult — they chose to rent a large apartment in Cherry Hill in the bordering state of New Jersey. They would all live together.

After my parents and Niloufar moved to Cherry Hill, my brothers drove them to Portsmouth for a short visit. Baba repeatedly told us that we had moved to the wrong shore.

"Most Iranian Jews live in Los Angeles, and here you are away from all Iranians and from one another," he said with a sigh.

He was right. It would have been much easier for them had we lived on the west coast, where so many Iranian Jewish immigrants had settled, where our parents could have listened to Iranian radio, watched Iranian television programs, shopped at Iranian grocery stores that lined the streets of Santa Monica and Pico, and lived within a cluster of Iranian culture. Baba asked if we would consider relocating. "No." I said. "It's too late."

I tried to explain that our jobs, our routine, our financial complications prevented us from moving even if we desired to do so. We had just moved, this time to the Glenshella neighbourhood of Portsmouth, a short drive to Maryview and Portsmouth General hospitals for Norman and much closer to the tunnel to Norfolk. Norman had left his job and started his own practice. His parents, the only grandparents our daughters knew well and could communicate with, lived around the corner from our new house. We were not moving to California to be among other Iranian Jews. Baba looked down at his folded hands in disappointment and controlled anger.

The financial burden of my family's new living arrangements fell on Freydoun, who paid for most of the expenses since Farzad was still a student. He didn't ask for my help and I didn't think about offering assistance. None of us knew at the time that Baba had planned to return to Iran soon after arriving.

My father and brothers visited me in Virginia a second time after stopping in Washington to renew Baba's passport. That day as we sat down for lunch, Jahangir, my father's brother, called from California.

"Tell your father not to return. News is circulating here that things in Iran are bad right now. Don't tell him that I told you this."

"Baba, don't go back." I begged.

"Who was that?" Baba questioned.

"Iranians in LA say that things are bad in Iran."

"Who said that? You're making it up."

"*Amu* said, okay!"

He called Jahangir back, but my uncle denied his words. Iranians don't like direct speech. "She misunderstood me," he told my father, not wanting to upset his brother.

"You *tow'te'eh chini mikoni*, you conspire against me," Baba said. "You know how afraid I am, and instead of giving me emotional support, you pour more fear into my heart. You aren't my daughter. Who set you up to do this to your own father?"

My brothers looked on silently.

Norman asked, "What's going on?"

"I don't know," I said, truly incapable of comprehending what had happened to make my father so furious with me.

Pensive and hunched, Baba didn't touch his lunch. The rest of us ate silently.

I didn't know what had happened to Baba in Iran, but since his return he was afraid and suspicious of everyone, including his own children. I didn't realize that his own family members, whom he had trusted, had threatened to report him as a Zionist if he didn't turn over the deed to the farm to his brother, Morad.

I tried to hug my father goodbye before he climbed into Freydoun's car, but Baba pushed me away and turned his back.

My parents and brothers had invested precious money in the misadventure of bringing the family together. Soon after my father left for Iran, it became clear that neither Niloufar nor Maman were adjusting well to the lonely life of the suburbs. The sidewalks were devoid of pedestrians; the neighbors wanted to be left alone. Once when my mother lost her key to the apartment on a stormy day, the neighbour wouldn't allow Maman inside to wait for my brothers. The bus schedule was unfamiliar and infrequent. Used to walking and taking buses, suddenly Maman and Neli became dependent on my brothers for the smallest things. The young men would return home after long days at work and school to find Maman waiting for them impatiently. Niloufar, who struggled to learn yet another new language, needed my brothers' help with homework. She missed her friends, her school, and her independence. A popular girl in Israel, her American classmates shunned her, making her feel like an outcast in her new school. Feeling lost, Maman spent unending lonely hours at the apartment.

They came for another visit. Freydoun said, "I don't know how to be a parent to our sister. Teach me how to do it."

"Are you overwhelmed?" I asked.

"Yes," he said teary. "I don't know how to take care of them. I am concerned about their safety."

"Maybe they need to be back in their own environment," I said, "where they can speak the language, go to the store and school on their own; where they won't have to wait for you all day long."

Maman and Niloufar returned to Israel the following week.

# 18

## BABA
### *1987, Shiraz*

My heart pounded as the plane approached Mehrabad Airport. I trembled with anxiety, but nothing happened. After spending the night in Tehran, I flew to Shiraz the following day.

I was elated to see my dear mother. I visited my siblings who seemed happy to see me, but my partner in business, my brother Morad, received me with a false smile and robotic words, without making eye contact and avoiding physical touch, even a polite handshake. Fearing that he could sabotage my efforts to settle our financial assets, I decided not to tell him about my limited time in Iran. We had not managed to sell and divide our assets during the five years in Iran partly because I lived in fear and did not have leverage against my brother, who knew time was on his side. After two days, he had still not asked me to go to the farm with him, and my own car, which had been parked in the back of the courtyard under the grapevines, was missing.

I called him and asked for a ride to the farm, which he did grudg-ingly, avoiding small talk. I chatted with my workers, a few of whom were from Afghanistan. As I toured the farm, I realized that the place was empty: no chicks, no grain, no eggs. I once again asked my brother about our shared assets. He shrugged. Since he had been going to the farm by himself, he had assumed that everything belonged to him alone, the farm, the house, my car. I irritated him like a desert thorn lodged underneath the skin. He resented my questions and once again, saying that he had not kept records, he refused to show me the papers.

My brother had moved my car to the farm. I drove it back. The following day, we argued again over the accounts with no results. I didn't know what to do anymore. My mother, who knew her wicked son only too well, begged me not to tangle with him.

Because my mother suffered from extreme muscle pain, my sisters had hired a woman to take care of her. Although Morad lived in the unit above her, he had completely avoided her despite her condition, ignoring her as if she had not given birth to him.

Two months went by without a resolution. My sister's husband, who was the community leader, tried to mediate, but Morad wouldn't compromise. I solicited the elders of the community to intercede, hoping they could resolve this issue without involving the Islamic courts. Still Morad resisted, refusing to answer any of my questions, insisting that he had kept no records, and that he owed me nothing.

I had tried to keep a low profile even in the Jewish commun-ity, but now suspicion kept me awake at night and I worried that Morad or one of his supporters could report to the govern-ment that I was trying to liquidate my assets. My four months came to an end, forcing me to leave for a short time. I told my sisters that I had some unfinished business in Tehran and I quietly left the country.

## FARIDEH

### *1987, Portsmouth*

When Baba returned to the United States after four months in Iran without any success, he was shocked to find out that Maman and Niloufar had returned to Israel. He assumed that I was the mastermind behind their failed attempt to adjust to America.

"You jeopardized my situation in Iran," he told my brothers. "You took your orders from your gang leader, your master," he spoke about me without mentioning my name.

Believing that I had usurped his position as the elder of the family, that I had manipulated my brothers, convincing them to return our mother and sister to Israel. He refused to speak to me for two years and forbade Maman and Niloufar to mention my name in the house. I was dead to him.

BABA'S FINANCIAL DEVASTATION was even more drastic because he had also lost his position in society. He was the son of Mola Meir Moshe Dayanim, a well-known, well-respected chief rabbi of the Shirazi Jewish community. Baba could trace back eight generations of such community leaders in his forefathers: Mola Shalom, Mola Darvish, Mola Pinas, Mola Rahim, Mola Asher, Mola Yousef, Mola Sholomo, and then his father. The Jewish community did not trust the government, so they took their everyday judicial as well as religious affairs to revered rabbis, calling them Molas, in the tradition of the land they had inhabited for centuries. When Reza Shah ordered all citizens to take a surname, my grandfather, Mola Meir Moshe, naturally chose the name Dayanim, meaning "judges" in Hebrew. As the eldest son of his father's second marriage, Baba was the beneficiary of much respect, conducting similar mediations, sharing the position with his oldest half-brother.

Even under the reign of a friendly king, most Shirazi Jews kept away from the courts. After the Revolution, they feared the Islamic courts even more and avoided them as much as possible.

Baba gathered elders from his family and community to mediate on his behalf. He would do so directly in personal meetings in Iran and later indirectly through mail and phone calls when in the United States. While in Israel, Baba would send his sealed letters to me in a large envelopes with a short note. I would remove them from the envelope marked with Israeli stamps and mail them to Iran using American stamps. We hoped this would safeguard Baba from the Islamic government who opposed Israel. I am not sure how he contacted Iran after he stopped communicating with me.

According to the old system of record-keeping in Iran, whoever had the deed of the land, house, or car in hand was technically capable of manipulating its ownership. Since it was illegal to take documents out of the country, Baba had entrusted the deeds to the house and the farm to family

The Elders of the Jewish community of Shiraz, ca. 1885. Baba's grandfather, Mola Sholomo, stands third from the right in a turban and Baba's father, Mola Meir Moshe Dayanim, sits in front of his father, second to the right.

members when he left Iran in the winter of 1984. At the time, it was just about impossible to sell property in Iran, especially for Jews.

Throughout the years that my father was away from Iran, he kept in touch with these family members, often begging them to resist Morad's appeals. Baba knew that his property would be lost with no hope of ever recovering a penny from his shared assets if Morad got ahold of the documents. Morad also knew this, and he used intimidation, coercion, and even kindness alternately in an attempt to acquire the deeds to the house and farm. I often wonder how my grandfather, the *dayan*, would have resolved the hostilities between his own two sons. How would he have righted the wrongs in a country whose laws granted no protection?

A YEAR AFTER he returned to the U.S. from his fruitless trip, Baba decided to go to Iran once again. Baba still refused to speak to me so I heard about the decision from my siblings. My mother, my sisters, and my brothers tried their best to dissuade Baba. They promised to do whatever possible to help him financially, but our father was a proud man who had once been the patriarch of his large family. For years he had been the one who had provided for others, for family members in need. He was the one who had helped to set up a house for his widowed sister, Behjat, furnishing the house with appliances we did not even own ourselves.

Baba refused his sons' handouts. The thought of counting on his children for financial support was damning, especially since wealth that was rightfully his was held up in Iran, in the hands of a cunning brother who was going to devour it shamelessly.

Baba returned to Iran again and again over those years, locking his old horns with the sharper ones of his younger brother at the same time, searching for a place to belong, a country to call his own.

Since he was absent and vulnerable, his property and possessions became free to all. His brother-in-law took a silver tea set that had been a wedding gift to Maman. When my father demanded that he return it, he was barred from visiting their house. The Persian carpets, kitchen utensils, bedding, even the books I had left behind disappeared from the house.

Whatever the government did not take away, the family, especially the man Baba had raised and supported all his life, eventually would.

Meanwhile, the hostility took Baba away from his wife and young daughter. Neli grew up without a father. Four years in Iran, six months in Italy, almost a year in the United States waiting for his papers, and the subsequent returns to Iran left an emotional void that Niloufar filled with friends, Maman with dark thoughts. They both insist that Baba was absent for a decade.

## FARIDEH
### *1989, Nags Head*

Norman's parents bought a condo on the Currituck Sound. In the summer of 1989, we spent a weekend there with friends. Sitting on a beach chair by the pool, I tried to ignore my other life, the one that connected me to Iran.

Baba and I had made a cold peace. I rarely heard from him, my mother, or Neli. I had last seen them when they came to Virginia for Nahid's wedding in 1988. The chasm between Baba and I grew wider and became more obvious because Baba still believed that I had tried to seize his position as the leader of the family. Being in charge of the arrangements for Nahid's wedding made matters worse. As I kept busy with the caterer, the florist, and the synagogue, Baba carried his locked black briefcase everywhere — never letting it out of his sight. He reminded me constantly that I had to help him renew his green card.

"Later, Baba," I kept saying.

Maman and Neli had arrived with only a small suitcase of necessities, counting on me to take them shopping. "Let them wear whatever they have," Baba said. Pointing to the briefcase again, he emphasized, "This is more important."

I didn't find the time to take him to the immigration office on that trip, which meant he would have to renew his green card in Philadelphia. Disappointed, he left without saying goodbye.

Staring into the blue-brown water of the Currituck Sound, I tried to reassure myself that everything was okay. It was normal for parents and children not to keep in touch. I needed a break from my parents after all. It was just fine that Baba mistrusted me. I didn't need him; he didn't need me.

I kept an eye on the girls in the pool. They swam better than their mother. The first time I saw a pool was in my last year of high school. I had had to sneak out of the house on the days the public pool opened for women. I never became a good swimmer, but I made sure that my daughters had started swimming lessons by age two.

My friend Susan, her hair bleached from the sun, finished her book, rolled over and gave it to me. "You've got to read this book."

I took a quick look: *A Time to Kill* by John Grisham.

"The first scene is hard to read. Such a beautiful book," her husband said.

"I don't need to read sad books," I said and pushed it aside.

"You never read," Norman said. "Just take the book and give it a try."

"I don't know if my English is good enough. It's been a long time. I don't have the patience for reading with a dictionary next to me."

"I'll translate the words you don't know," Norman said.

"Ask us," our friends said.

"Ok. Later. Got to watch the girls."

"I'll watch them," Norman said. Putting the book on my lap, he jumped into the pool to play with the girls.

I HAD FORGOTTEN. After so many years of not reading, I had forgotten about my connection to the world of fiction; I had forgotten about my obsession with the written word. After discovering novels in high school, I had read nonstop. They had saved me from despair and loneliness; they had been my best friends, my saviours. Yet I had not read a novel, or even a short story, since quitting my education in 1977.

On that summer afternoon, lounging on a beach chair by the pool, inhaling the cool breeze of the Currituck Sound, I fell in love with literature again. I finished the book by nightfall. I hadn't needed a dictionary. Not bad.

When we returned home, I felt restless. A void that had been hidden underneath worries and responsibilities began to widen inside me. I had been a good writer in Persian; my high school classmates were always eager to hear my essays, but I had not read or written anything in Persian since leaving Iran, and I felt that I was no longer fluent in my mother tongue. Yet I had not nurtured my English either. I was a woman without a language.

I had often blamed my father for my lack of achievements. I was a terrible swimmer, I never learned to play the guitar, and I had to stop playing tennis because Baba found these things to be inappropriate for a young woman.

Norman, tired of hearing my sad stories over and over, said, "But your father isn't here. Who's keeping you from playing now?" He was right. I signed up for tennis lessons and tried to improve my swimming. Guitar lessons didn't excite me anymore.

To make up for the fact that I had not been allowed to study journalism, I took a class in journalism at Old Dominion

University in the fall of 1988 and dropped it the very first week after the teacher told us that he would deduct five points for each misplaced comma. I still didn't know when to use or not to use *the*.

I gave up college that year and drowned myself in community work, finding friends who were not intimidated by or mistrustful of my foreignness. I served on boards of various Jewish organizations, becoming the president of the PTA at the Hebrew Academy (a Jewish school my daughters attended), the co-chair of various women's events in the community, including the education committee of the Women's Division of the Jewish Federation. My busy schedule kept my mind off the problems of my extended family.

AFTER WE RETURNED from Nags Head, it was clear to me that my busy life had only masked my problems. I visited Old Dominion University again and found out that the Humanities program allowed me to select courses and choose my own path. I was a student again, taking one class at a time. One day I would graduate, but for now the joy of being in the classroom was enough. After years of talking about diapers and children's homework with friends, after years of helping with food preparation for various community functions, in the fall of 1989 I sat in Douglas Green's course, Humanities on Trial, and allowed his words to replenish my mind like raindrops on wilted flowers.

He was curious about Zoroastrianism in Iran, so to make my teacher happy I wrote my paper on the burial rites in Zoroastrianism, reconnecting with my own culture through my research. The following semester I wrote another paper for him on Iranian Jewish life. With an Arabic dictionary by my side, I read Khomeini's *Velayat-e faqih* (Islamic Government: Governance of the Jurist) for my research, fascinated to discover unbelievable similarities between his book and Hitler's *Mein*

*Kampf.* As I studied the history of Iranian Jews — of pogroms, poverty, and discrimination among short bursts of enlightenment and growth — I understood, for the very first time, the stories passed down to me by my grandmother and father. I understood their shock and disbelief when I chose to mingle with Muslim friends and their families. I had lived with my parents and extended family in the same house for twenty-three years, yet this was the first time I had an inkling about the lives they had lived, the origins of their fears, and the insulated Jewish lives in a Muslim neighbourhood. Slowly the Iranian life that I had tried so hard to sever from my new American reality pulled me back, inviting me to take another look at it, to examine it, to try to understand it.

For my graduate degree, I had to choose two areas of concentration. A classmate suggested Women's Studies. I laughed, "I didn't know women had to be studied." Not amused, she narrowed her eyes and after a long silence said, "This shows that you need to be in the program." I met the director, Anita Fellman, at a Jewish Family Services meeting, where we were planning a new community program. I asked. "What *is* women's studies?" Anita was teaching the history of women in America, an undergraduate class. I begged her to allow me to take the class as a graduate student, doing extra work. She hesitated. "I don't know anything about this topic and have to start from the beginning," I said. Anita gave the class a questionnaire on the first day to measure our knowledge.

"Who is Rosa Parks?" I asked. My classmates laughed, but not mockingly.

"It's okay," a student with long curly hair and a wide smile said. "It isn't your culture."

*I am ignorant*, I thought. *What have I done to myself?*

To show my competence and diligence, I memorized every lesson prior to our midterm exam and regurgitated pages of information on the exam paper.

On my corrected exam Anita wrote, "Wow! So much information and yet I don't think you've understood the questions."

My Iranian teachers had insisted on rote memorization – not a word out of place on exam papers. What was my American teacher talking about? I had given her all the information. Word for word.

My term paper had to be better. Maybe Norman's grandmother, Fannie, would be a good topic for research. We were both immigrant women who left our birth countries for a better life in America. Fannie left Russia alone in steerage at age fifteen in the hopes of earning enough money in America to save her sister from pogroms. I met her at the end of her life, sitting in a wheelchair in the waiting room of a Jewish nursing home in Richmond. She sat like a man with her legs apart, revealing her thick stockings. A hair dresser at the old age home had set Fannie's white hair in stiff curls that were intact in the front and crushed in the back and on the right side. She spoke with a thick unfamiliar Yiddish accent.

As I wrote about her amazing adventures and her courage, I was sorry I hadn't taken the opportunity to ask her about Jewish life in Russia. I interviewed her children, pored over history books and books about Jewish life in Kiev and Odessa.

Anita returned it with numerous markings. She had given me permission to write a creative essay instead of a research paper, maybe hoping that I would write about my life in Iran. "It's interesting that you wrote a paper about your husband's heritage and not your own," she commented. "I wonder why."

It was a good paper; I had worked very hard on it. *What did she want from me?*

## FARIDEH
### *1991, Portsmouth*

In January 1991, Saddam Hussein's scud missiles poured down on Tel Aviv and Haifa. American reporters endangered their lives on Tel Aviv rooftops to report on the location of the strikes. Crying and screaming, I threw a loaf of bread at the television set. These journalists were unwittingly helping Saddam Hussein, who didn't need spies in Israel as long as these reporters provided him with these internationally broadcasted videos.

I called Israel. My parents and sister had locked themselves in the safe room without a telephone. Niloufar ran outside to answer the phone.

"Allo?"

I saw an explosion on the TV screen and heard it through the telephone. The line went dead.

I kept calling.

Niloufar picked up the phone again, "Don't call," she screamed. "Don't you know we are under attack?"

The phone rang a few minutes later. I grabbed it immediately. It wasn't Niloufar as I had hoped. Sniffling, I told my friend, "I am a mess."

She said, "I'm having a bad day myself. David has a cold. I was hoping you could take care of him. I have to go to work."

"No," I said. *Seriously*? One person's life-and-death issues are another's headline news.

I WAS THE co-chair of Jewish Education for the Women's Cabinet of the United Jewish Federation of Tidewater that year. To release my anger and frustration over the recent war, I decided to prepare a speech about the exodus of Iraqi Jews to Israel via Iran in the 1950s. Reba Karp, the editor of *Tidewater Jewish News*, asked me to send her a copy for publication. It would be my first published essay. Over the next five years I wrote other articles for the paper, including the story of my family's exodus from Iran. I had originally read this story at a dinner that celebrated Israel Independence Day in honour of Israeli friends who had temporarily moved to the Virginia Beach area to help the U.S. military. First there was a deep silence. *They hated it*, I thought. Then the entire audience rose. I looked behind me to see who had arrived, thinking that the applause was for someone else.

The speeches and their publication gave me confidence in my English skills as a speaker and a writer. My father had tried very hard to instill in me the importance of elocution. One summer, he demanded that I write a speech a week and perform it for him right before Shabbat. Having never been able to obey orders, I didn't have a speech ready for him that week or any of weeks that followed. Every Friday afternoon, I would stand in front of Baba on the stairs to the backyard in total silence, not able to think of anything to say. Disappointed,

Baba stopped asking me to prepare speeches for him. Now that I had finally found my voice, Baba had gone silent, absent from my life, rarely communicating.

IN 1991, as I searched the course catalogue for classes in Women's Studies, I discovered another professor, Nancy Bazin, a well-known feminist who taught a course on women writers and post-colonial literature. I had found my other area of concentration for my degree in the humanities. Reading the work of women writers from around the world — Anita Desai, Tsitsi Dangarembga, and Margaret Laurence. I was obsessed with literature written by non-western women, and for the first time I truly understood these stories because, in a strange way, they were my stories too. I took every class that Nancy taught. On my journal and papers she repeatedly wrote, "You must publish these." As a child I had always dreamed of becoming a writer, a real writer. Would it really be possible? Would it be possible in a language that was not my own?

## BABA
*1992, Shiraz*

I floated in the fog of time for years, indecisive, drained of all
energy. In May of 1992, I cleared my head and decided to return
to Iran once again to claim my property before my passport
expired. Facing strong resistance from my wife and children
who feared for my life, I remained resolute. Not being able to
let go of a lifetime of hard work to live in *ghorbat*, dependent
on handouts from others, I left for the United States. Even
though Israel was a short flight from Tehran, there were no
longer direct flights from Israel to Iran which forced me to
make the long trip to the States to keep the pretense of living
there. Otherwise Israel would be a liability for me, endanger-
ing my life and exposing me to blackmail as had happened on
my previous trips. Once there, I bought an open ticket from
Swiss Air and left for Europe from Philadelphia, where my
sons lived. There were only forty or fifty passengers travelling

on the Boeing 707 to Boston, where the rest of the passengers joined us for our flight to Zurich after a ten-hour layover. A small rundown plane with little leg room and uncomfortable seats took off from Zurich for Tehran, where the inexperienced pilot landed by mistake on a bumpy runway under construction, causing the passengers to think we had crashed. Not a good omen.

I returned to my usual lodging, Hotel Shiraz in Tehran, and spent Shabbat there. I arrived in Shiraz that Sunday night to find my mother still awake. I kissed her hands and her forehead, my heart aching for having abandoned her. The following day, I contacted my sister Monir and her husband, Khaled, who invited me to lunch in their newly built home in a fashionable neighbourhood.

Arriving around 10:00 a.m., I found my family gathered at the house which was empty of its furnishings. What followed would make an indelible mark on my life.

Khaled held my hand and asked me to sit down next to him. "We are leaving," he said, "to join our three children in America." They would leave on Wednesday for Tehran and fly to Turkey three days later, where they would apply for American visas. The government had refused exit visas to Jews and had refused issuing passports to most people. How had they managed it? It was especially unbelievable that the government had issued passports to both of them without asking one to remain behind to ensure the return of the other. Aghast at their brazen act of selling their belongings so openly and allowing others to know of their imminent departure, I worried for all of them.

Monir said that it was a great omen that she had a chance to see me before leaving. The whole year had been auspicious. "A miracle," she added, "a miracle I can never forget." Khaled picked up the thread of her words and helped weave their tale. Their children had been persuading them to leave the country to be closer to them. At the passport office, they were told that only one could leave, but they insisted that they would like to visit their children together. They were refused, but months later they received a call. "Your passports have been ready for a while. Why haven't you picked them up?" a government official inquired. "Both passports," Monir said. "Wasn't that a miracle?"

The news went through my body like an electric jolt. How could that be possible? My brother-in-law had many influential Muslim friends. I asked if someone had helped them. "No," he said. "*That* was the miracle." Now truly apprehensive, I didn't dare to destroy their joy. Maybe my cynical views stemmed from my own traumatizing experiences.

Their son Ben, young and strong, capable of walking through the mountainous region of the Iranian border with Turkey, would leave with smugglers the following day. Another son, an American citizen, awaited both parents and Ben in Turkey and would arrange for their American visas.

"Stay a bit longer," Monir said, to meet the middleman who had arranged the transfer over the border. With a heavy heart, I had lunch with them but the food tasted bitter in my mouth. I had hoped to discuss my own situation, to ask for their advice and help, but now I remained silent. We had barely finished lunch when the doorbell rang; the middle-man for the smuggler entered to take my nephew and two other Jews from Shiraz to Ardabil, closer to the border with Turkey.

After the men left, Khaled said that he had sold the house but had not received the entire amount yet. The buyer would pay $200,000 to my other brother-in-law, Zamani, whom he had given power of attorney to sign the documents and trans-fer the money to the United States. He asked me to accompany him on some errands but I refused in order to keep my arrival as quiet as possible. Giving my nephew a hug and a kiss, I wished him a successful journey, trying to hide my own anxieties and fears.

The following day, Zamani called and invited me to accompany them to the airport to say goodbye to Monir and her family, as it was customary for all family members to escort the travellers. Trying to keep a low profile, I found an excuse to decline the invitation. Not hearing anything about the flight, I assumed that my fears had been baseless. Around 8:00 p.m., I called Zamani's house. The phone rang repeatedly, but went unanswered. I called again every half hour until 10:30 that night. Finally my nephew Fard picked up the phone and with uneasiness told me to speak to his mother. Ferdos' sobs frightened me. Since she couldn't utter a word, her husband finally picked up the phone and told me what had happened. Around 3:00 p.m., the whole family had gathered at the airport. Monir went through security and boarded the plane. Her husband followed but was asked to wait for a few more minutes. After all passengers boarded, the security guard escorted Khaled to the office of the Revolutionary Guard, where he was told that they had to ask a few more questions and, in the interest of time, it would be best to take his luggage off the plane and to ask his wife to disembark. They would reserve spots for both of them on the following flight. After an hour, they were escorted to an official car waiting outside to be taken to the Ministry of Information for further questioning. Their suitcases would be safe at the airport, waiting for their return.

The family entourage waited at the airport. Hours went by and no news arrived. At 9:00 p.m. a member of the Revolutionary Guard told them to leave. When they asked about the whereabouts of the couple, someone told them to visit the Ministry of Information. Khaled's brother took the suitcases home, and the rest departed for the Ministry of Information, where, after much waiting, they returned to their homes without obtaining any news.

Worried about my sister and her husband, my stomach churned as I remembered my own nightmarish experiences with repeated interrogations and beatings. Tasting the bitter bile on my dry tongue, I wondered if they would come for me as well.

On Thursday, Mr. Zamani and his son Fard went to Mr. Khalid's brother's house to review the situation. They wondered what the charges were and how they could obtain information. The doorbell rang. A few members of the Revolutionary Guard marched in and demanded to have the suitcases, which were in the room untouched, still locked and secured. Questioning everyone in the room, they went through the house, examining its contents. Fard protested. Why have they arrested the couple? Why were they roaming around the house? A guard silenced him quickly with a hard blow on the head. They took Fard along with the suitcases. Now there was another prisoner.

Khaled was the head of the Jewish community and, like many other Shirazi Jews, he owned a store, selling fabric on Dariush Street, one of the main shopping areas in the city. The news of his arrest spread through the Jewish community like a virus and infected our lives with fear and uncertainty. In meekness, the Shirazi Jews tried to become even more invisible.

That Thursday marked the fourth day of my return to Shiraz. I thought that it would be best to leave as soon as possible. I asked Ferdos, my sister, to withhold the news of the arrests from our sick mother who could not withstand such a shock. Let her think that they were all in America. Friday morning, kissing my mother, I told her not to wait for me since I would be with friends. Looking sad, sensing that I was leaving her, she said, "My son, why do you leave your wife and children in *ghorbat* and come here?" I told her that I would discuss it with her later. Meanwhile since Friday was the Muslim Sabbath, I hoped that nothing would happen until Sunday when I would be on my way to America. I left by bus for Tehran around

4:00 p.m., arriving around 6:00 a.m. Fearing that I would be discovered, I decided not to go to a hotel. After picking up my ticket from Swiss Air, I wandered around a public park all day until dark. I took a taxi to the airport, resting there until my midnight flight. My son in Philadelphia picked me up, shocked that I had returned so quickly. I had returned with a heavy heart and empty pockets.

I called Ferdos in Shiraz, who, not surprised that I had left, said a few members of the Revolutionary Guard had stopped by the house asking for me. My mother told them that I would be back the following day.

My sister explained that Monir and Khaled's passports had been originally denied, but then someone discovered that he was the head of the Jewish community and decided to test him. Maybe they thought he could have been an Israeli spy; maybe they just wanted to warn the Jewish community and scare them into total submission as if they were not already meek enough.

They released Fard and told him that he would be contacted soon. Dazed and disoriented, he wouldn't share what had happened to him other than saying that he had seen his cousin Ben, who had been arrested in Ardabil, in the interrogation room. Soon after, Khaled's brother was arrested as well. They were not allowed visitations.

Shortly after the arrests, a member of the Ministry of Information called on shopkeepers on Dariush street and spread the gossip that Khaled was very sick and would be hospitalized soon. Then threatening rumours were spread promising other arrests, frightening the Jewish community to a point that they became suspicious of one another, not trusting even family members.

To make matters worse, the Revolutionary Guard arrested Rabbi Ba'alaness, the only spiritual leader of the Shirazi Jewish community. Although they kept him for just one day, he was treated like a common criminal and interrogated with the utmost disrespect. The Guard claimed that the Rabbi and the lay leaders of the community had conspired with outsiders against the government.

A few more months went by without any news. Then a man, who said he spoke for the Ministry of Information, approached Yousef, a Jewish man, and asked him to deliver a message to my brother-in-law Zamani. If the equivalent of $200,000 (the exact amount of the money he was holding for Khaled from the sale of the house), was donated to the ministry, my imprisoned family members would be allowed one visitor. Zamani refused the blackmail. A second message was delivered saying that their lives would be in jeopardy unless the money was transferred, but a visitation was granted. Zamani met each of them separately and discovered that they were unaware of each other's imprisonment. Khaled and Monir did not know that their son had not made it across the border and that he too had been arrested. Khaled and Monir were afraid of talking about any matters, including the money. To increase the pressure on Zamani to take the bribe, the government officials arrested Khaled's two younger brothers.

Six months went by. Another message was sent. This time Yousef actually visited Zamani at his home and told him that the government knew about the sale of the house. If he didn't give them the money, his own son would be arrested. Since Zamani did not have the money, Fard was arrested that day. Two days after his son's imprisonment, Zamani cashed the check and visited the revolutionary court, where he was told the money would be sent to Hezbollah in Lebanon to kill Israelis. They released all the prisoners a few days later. Having lost everything, they would never speak of their months in prison.

Frightened, Rabbi Ba'alaness left Shiraz and lived quietly in Tehran for a few years until he managed to escape with his family to Los Angeles. The terror continued. In 1999, thirteen Shirazi Jews, including one teenager, were arrested on charges of spying for Israel. To remind the Jews of their vulnerability and the relentless pursuit of those who resisted the government's demands, the Islamic court issued an international warrant for the Rabbi's arrest.

I HAVE MUCH respect for the democratic way of life in Israel, a country that gave us refuge. Yet human nature is the same around the world, a few need to feel superior to others. At the Ministry of Interior in Holon, Misrad Hapnim a young female secretary, whose job was to extend visas, treated me with disrespect and contempt. My wife and daughter had accepted Israeli citizenship, but because I had left all my assets in Iran, I had to be able to return to Iran in order to salvage as much as possible. An Israeli citizenship meant torture and death for me. Explaining my situation, I asked the secretary to extend my visa. Showing disgust, she illegally denied me the extension. This time, upon returning to the United States, I asked Freydoun to take me to Washington to renew my Israeli visa in order to avoid this woman. I had to return to Israel, to my wife and daughter in embarrassment since I had not accomplished what I had promised them. Instead I had wasted little resources we had on travel expenses.

Fearing blackmail by those who could have benefited from my leaving and abandoning my property, I had led everyone to believe that I resided in the United States. Freydoun called me to let me know that Khaled, thinking that I lived in America, had called to let me know that my mother was sick and that I should return to see her. Fearing trouble for the family and myself, I could not call my mother from Israel since calls were monitored by the Iranian government. I left again for the United States and called my mother upon arriving. My mother refused to eat and lost consciousness from time to time, but whenever she came around, she called my name. I had to go back to Shiraz to be with her. Visiting the Algerian Embassy in Washington to renew my Iranian passport, I was told that they were waiting for a new batch of passports with different formatting. Days went by. I kept calling my mother and spoke to my sisters who were at my mother's deathbed. Every time I called, my mother didn't have the strength to speak. I kept calling the embassy to no avail. There was no time to waste. Then my mother passed away without me seeing her; she passed away calling my name. I had failed her. I sat *shiva* for her in Philadelphia, feeling abandoned, desperate, lost.

# FARIDEH
## *1992, Norfolk*

I had so hoped for my daughters to become "true" Americans
that I didn't teach them Persian. Sometimes when I spoke
with my parents, they said, *"vaay! che lahjehi daree!* What an
accent!" They were surprised to hear me speak Persian with an
American accent, the way Norman was amused by my Persian
accent when I spoke English. Baba chastised me for this isolation from Iranian culture.

Rachel's speech therapist, too, laughed upon meeting me.
"Your daughter doesn't have a speech impediment," she said.
"She mimics her mother's accent."

When my daughters were young, they were surprised that
their classmates told them their mother spoke "funny." They
started to listen to me more carefully, discovering my foreignness and its impact on their own language skills. When Rachel,
the mischievous one, had a bad cold, she asked Norman with

a gleam in her eyes, "Dad, why does Mom ask if I can 'breed'? I am too young." Norman's laughter prompted the girls to look for other fun phrases worthy of repeating. When I complained that he encouraged them, Norman promised he would never ever do it again – and of course he did.

One Saturday, Norman offered to be a true gentleman and bring the car around as we left the synagogue after a bat-mitzvah. With his umbrella for protection from the downpour, Norman escorted each one of us to the car. Others waiting under the awning smiled with approval of his gallantry. I wore a new pomegranate-coloured suit, matching hat, and high heels. Norman held my arm as we descended the stone stairs so that I wouldn't slip. None of us realized that the sunroof of his car had been damaged and collected water. As soon as he turned on the car, I felt what seemed to be a bucket of cold water dump on my head. My hat wilted, my silk skirt shriveled. Panicky, I screamed, "The leak is roofing – the leak is roofing!" The sound of Norman and the girls' screams was replaced very quickly with unstoppable laughter. Shivering inside my wet clothes, I started to cry, still not knowing why they laughed at my misery. They stopped.

"I'm sorry, Mom." Rachel said.

"Are you okay?" Yael and Lena asked.

"Sorry, honey," Norman added.

They found a roll of paper towels in the car and helped me dry off my face and hands, and the chair.

Then Rachel started to laugh again, "The leak is roofing!" she screamed, and that's when I understood.

"I said that?" and I joined in their laughter.

24

## BABA
### *1992, Shiraz*

Zamani called me again, encouraging me to return to Iran, telling me that this time things would be easier for me. My wife said that I could go but for the very last time and made me promise that after this trip we would spend the rest of our lives in Israel, for better or for worse, even if in poverty.

Before flying from Tehran to Shiraz, I called Zamani, who invited me to go directly to his house and stay with them. On the plane, we were given unkosher meat sandwiches, which I couldn't eat. I offered mine to the young man sitting next to me. He devoured it quickly and became friendly. His friends sat in front of us with a man in the long garb of an Islamic scholar and an *amameh*, a white turban. I listened in on their conversation.

One of the young men said that he had heard that although prostitution was less visible since the introduction of harsher penalties by new Islamic law, pimps could lead interested men to the prostitutes who were now in hiding. I was quite surprised to hear this kind of open conversation about prostitution with a religious authority, but I soon discovered that the mullah himself had initiated the discussion with the other young men. The mullah pulled a photo album out of his briefcase and presented photographs of beautiful women to these salivating men. He then gave each of the men a business card to contact him for temporary marriages of an hour, a night, a day, as they wished. What had happened to my country? One kind of prostitution had replaced another. One kind warranted severe punishment by the authorities, even stoning to death. The other kind was accepted, even promoted by some mullahs, who benefited by women' s destitution and helplessness. To me, this represented a new kind of lawlessness, a new kind of injustice. And this was the country to which I was returning to demand my rights.

In Shiraz, Zamani told me that Monir, who was trying to recuperate from her ordeal in prison and the death of our mother, had finally obtained permission to visit her children in America. Khaled was not given an exit visa as it was the policy of the government to keep at least one family member as collateral for the return of the other.

My brothers-in-law invited Morad to accompany us to my mother's grave in an attempt to avoid Morad's overt hostility, abuse and physical violence. Before leaving for the cemetery, I asked Zamani for the deeds to the farm that I had entrusted to him before leaving Iran since it was illegal to take documents out of the country. He told me that the key to the safe wasn't at home, but he would give me the documents later.

After paying our respects at the cemetery, lacking the required ten men to say *kaddish*, we stopped by Rabizadeh Synagogue to pray. Morad walked to his Paykan, ready to drive away, when Zamani ran toward him, screaming. They exchanged a few heated words and then Zamani grabbed Morad by the collar, pulled him out of the car, and the two tangled in rage. Morad tore Zamani's jacket off him as we watched in amazement, fearing that the police might see us. Exchanging terrible words outside this holy place, they scratched and punched one another. Khaled finally separated the two and told Zamani that he would resolve the problem. Morad peeled himself off the road, jumped in his Paykan, and sped off in anger.

Returning to Zamani's home, he explained that my brother had visited numerous times, bringing gifts from the farm, *katooni*, apples, cherries, eggs, and chickens. Then he showed up one day, asking for the documents, promising that he would return them that afternoon. Surprised that he knew about their whereabouts, but indebted to Morad for the gifts, my brother-in-law agreed, and soon forgot that they had not been returned. When I asked him for the papers, he realized that Morad still held them and asked for their return after leaving the synagogue, but Morad refused. Zamani promised that even if it cost him his life, he would retrieve the papers, the only legal documents that proved my ownership of the land.

I visited Khaled that night, begging him to intervene. "Why has my brother taken my papers? Is he using them for unlawful purposes? Why did you tell me that this was a good time to return? What do you know about all these betrayals?"

He remained silent.

I went to my house the following day for the last time. I could feel my dear mother's presence everywhere, a memory I could not bear. Since they could not return to Iran, my children had asked for pictures of their childhood home so I took a few photos for them. I took a final glance at the house I had built with much hope, the house that had brought me no happiness, then I locked the door and left.

Khaled arranged for a meeting with my brother. It was revealed that Morad had sold the house and the retail store where we had sold eggs and chicken. He had signed my name to all documents and deposited the money in his own account. I didn't know what to do anymore. Why had I been asked to return?

Soon after, I discovered that Morad had illegally taken the farm documents as well and a sale was in progress with my forged signature. I visited the office of land management and inquired about the documents. "Whose name is registered as the real landowner?" I asked. The officer turned pale. Not expecting my return, he had collaborated with my brother, probably for a cut from the sale. Throwing the papers at me, he asked me to leave. When I hesitated, he held my arm firmly and led me out, fearing for his job if I made a scene.

As the familiar *zarbolmasal* says "A man was walking home with an earthen bowl of yogourt for his hungry family when he stumbled and fell. Vagrants swarmed over the broken pieces and licked off the yogourt that was the man's sustenance." There was a Revolution; the government fell apart; the wicked and the cheaters swarmed over the broken pieces of my country, my life.

A week later, I visited Khaled at his request. He told me that my brother had given him the original farm documents and he could return them to me. I asked him to keep them in trust, but he wouldn't accept. With Khaled's help I would receive half the price of the house later, when I had returned to America. That day, however, I wondered what his role was. How could he have convinced Morad to return the documents? Outside Khaled's house, Morad was hiding, waiting for me. As soon as I turned the corner, he rushed toward me and grabbed me by the collar. How had he known I was there? Other than the guard who had arrested me at the Turkish border, I have never seen so much hatred in someone's eyes. His fist came toward my face. We locked eyes. How could he do this to me? Had I not raised him? Given him his livelihood with my own resourcefulness?

He had taken everything that was mine. What else did he want? My life? His fist was suspended in mid-air. But then he pulled it back, turned around, and walked away — the very last time I saw him.

Once a man of distinction pitied a baby wolf and adopted him, fed him, and kept him alive, not realizing that the grown beast would one day devour him.

## FARIDEH
### *1966, Shiraz*

My father and mother complained about Morad consistently, insistently, repeatedly for decades. My siblings and I have not been able to forgive them for exposing us to that unhappiness and abuse. We have never understood the nature of the bond that held the two brothers together, an interdependence that was equal parts love and hate.

≈

IN 1966, during the spring of my thirteenth year, even the desert bloomed in Shiraz. We had had an unusually rainy month. Hailstorms swept through every afternoon with pistachio-sized ice balls dancing on the grass. My grandmother told us stories of hailstorms from her past; how one storm caught her, my aunt, and a female cousin off guard as they shopped outside the vaulted bazaar. A hailstone the size of a walnut hit my cousin in the head and she was rushed to the hospital. My grandmother reminded us that a day that had begun with the joy of shopping in the colourful bazaar ended in the local hospital with blood on the women's hands and *chador*s.

When the storms finally ended that spring, we resumed our life outside in the walled-in yard, spreading a red and blue Persian carpet on the veranda, preparing late afternoon tea, enjoying the green of the grass and the scent of roses. Morad had spotted one in particular, a white long-stemmed rose whose fragrance was intoxicating. He told us to keep away from it; this one was his alone to enjoy. He watched it grow each day, perfect; its closed fleshy pursed lips ready to open; a rose straight out of Persian poetry.

My grandmother, my sister, my brothers, and my aunts were all sitting on the porch steps in the yard the day Morad spoke about the beauty of that rose.

"I've never smelt a flower with the fragrance of rosewater like this before," he said.

Seeing the glimmer in his brother's eyes, Baba walked slowly to the flower.

"Is this it?" he asked. Then he swiftly reached down with a paring knife in his hand and cut the flower bud from its source of nourishment.

"Don't," screamed Morad too late.

Baba brought the flower to his nose, and deeply inhaled its scent, "You're right. What a special flower this is!"

We all went silent. I had never seen Morad so distraught, almost in tears, angry like a wounded beast.

My father narrowed his eyes, "Such insolence. You are telling me that I can't cut a flower from my own garden?" My father was ready for combat. The children braced for the next round of skirmishes.

Morad stomped past us toward the covered well.

My grandmother yelled after him, "Don't bring your blood to a boil; you'll just hurt yourself."

Then Morad screamed and disappeared.

It happened so fast that we didn't realize what was happening. The only person who ran toward the well without hesitation – dropping the flower on the ground – was Baba. He dove headfirst toward the wide open mouth of the well and reached out for his brother's hand. My father screamed for help as Morad's weight pulled him down. But he did not let go. My other uncle ran to them and together they pulled Morad out of the well, whose brick and stone walls had caved in because of the rainy spring. We could hear the bricks hitting the water at the bottom of the well, splashing. The well was full.

Under the feet of all of those who had run to Morad's aid lay the white rose, crushed into the brick pavement – a white slippery pulp.

## BABA
### *1992, Shiraz*

I had lost everything to my brother's treachery and a lawless
government. There was nothing left to be done and nothing
that could undo the injustice. I walked around the city saying
goodbye to familiar places. The shrines of the poets Saadi
and Hafez and the beautiful gardens that had made my city
famous were all ornaments that could not hide the miserable
state of Shiraz. Once a centre of tourism, the city was devoid
of any visitors. It had once been known as the city of poets,
beautiful women, and extraordinary wine. The Revolution had
killed the poets, transformed desperate women into prostitutes, and made the wine, like all other pleasures, a forbidden,
ugly thing.

I visited the bazaar for the last time to buy gifts for my
granddaughters. At my daughter's request, I searched for the
distinctive clothing of the Ghashghai people, a nomadic tribe.

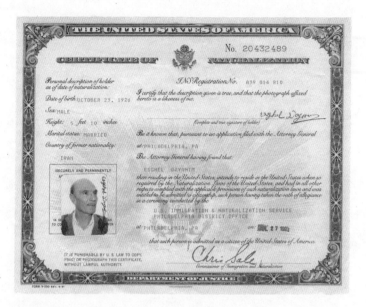

Baba's naturalization papers. I assumed that Baba would move to the U.S. once he received his citizenship.

Passing the stalls selling Persian carpets, someone called my name. I recognized the merchant who invited me into his shop. Both he and his brother were called *haji*. Trying to keep a low profile, I was apprehensive about this invitation. What did he want? Was this a trap? Having felt my trepidation, he first sent his young apprentice, Ahmad, to get us tea before chatting amicably. When the tea came he offered me one, took one for himself, and sent the boy on another errand.

"Dayanim," he said. "I am about to explode but don't have anyone to talk to about the ache in my heart. You are a Jew and I can trust you." He told me how he and his brother had participated in anti-Shah processions in support of the Revolution, thinking that it would make people's lives better. "Not only did we not get anything better," he added, "we lost all we had. I tell you what I cannot tell even to my own wife," he added. "Khomeini put his legs on either side of Iran and had diarrhea on top of us all."

I listened without expressing any ideas. Then we bid each other farewell.

I had to pack my bags. Since Khaled had not agreed to keep the documents, I asked Zamani, who refused to help me as well, forcing me to ask his son-in-law, begging him to have pity on me, to keep the documents that were the proof of decades of hard work, in trust. Maybe one day the situation would improve and I could return to claim what was rightfully mine. He agreed. I returned to Israel and became a citizen.

## FARIDEH
### *1993, Norfolk*

Baba received his naturalization papers in the summer of 1993 when he and my mother came to Virginia to attend Lena's bat-mitzvah. We had moved to Norfolk by then, and it seemed that with each move, we displaced something, lost something precious. On my first trip to the United States, I had forgotten to bring my two notebooks filled with my handwritten essays. When we were robbed in New Orleans, we lost other things: a silver cuff inscribed with Hebrew words (a wedding gift), spices my father had sent from Iran, and a Persian carpet (another wedding gift). I lost a gold bracelet during the move to Chesapeake. Moving to Portsmouth, I had ruined my wedding and engagement rings by carrying them in my handbag with a thermometer — one of the girls had been running a fever. I had not had the courage to tell Norman that the slippery mercury ate the gold, turning it black as it glided across the surface of the rings.

> An official document issued on October 25, 1983, that proves that Baba is the owner of a poultry farm with a capacity of 30,000 chickens on the Pole Fassa road in Shiraz.

There was nothing to be done, no miracle to reverse the chemical interaction between gold and mercury, as one jeweller after another told me. It was nature at work. During our last move to Norfolk, I dropped a crystal bowl, shattering it to pieces.

Baba and I had made peace, we never did discuss our past estrangement. We moved on as if nothing had happened, as if we had not lost precious time together to heal the wounds we had inflicted on each other. When he finally decided not to return to Iran, when he let go of his losses and was no longer battle-ready, Baba looked happy. He asked to make an announcement during Lena's bat-mitzvah party.

"There was a time maybe that I was resistant to Farideh marrying an American," he said. "I just want to say that I love Norman as my own son. Mazel tov!"

THE CLASSES I took that year were instrumental to my writing career. I read *Of Woman Born* by Adrienne Rich, whose idea of motherhood as an institution was a novelty to me. I was looking forward to reading the chapter on mothers and daughters, thinking of myself as the mother of three daughters — I didn't realize that its content would force me to look at myself as a daughter who had not been mothered, that it would make me confront my fear of becoming my mother. It took me more than a week to read the few pages because I had to put down the book many times. Rich's words hit a raw nerve, giving me a clearer view of my mother. I had to accept that my mother's experiences as a daughter, deprived of emotional support and nurturing, as an unwanted child-bride, had been so painful to me that I had tried to put as much distance as possible between myself and the woman from whose body I had emerged.

266

A. ZAHEDNIA
Official Translator
Licensed by the
Ministry of Justice
Shiraz, Iran
Tel. No.: 53067

اسدالله زاهدنیا
مترجم رسمی وزارت دادگستری

شیراز ــ خیابان زند ، کوچه دژبان ، ۷۱۳۵۷
تلفن: ۵۳۰۶۷

(Translated from the persian)

No.: 6601/$\frac{8}{9}$

Date: 25th october, 1983
(3/8/1362)

ISLAMIC REPUBLIC OF IRAN
MINISTRY OF AGRICULTURE AND RURAL DEVELOPMENT
DEPARTMENT OF ANIMAL HUSBANDRY OF FARS PROVINCE
Shiraz, Iran

To whom it may concern:

This is hereby certified that Mr ESGHEL DAYANIM, holder of identity card
No. 40315 issued in shiraz, possesses a poultry husbandry unit with a
capacity of 30,000 hens, located on pole passa/shiraz Road. He is personally
performing the management of his poultry husbandry.

This certification is released at his own request dated 25th october, 1983.

saied soltani
Director of Department of Animal Husbandry
of Fars province

(signature and seal)

Certified to be a true translation from the original persian text. A. Zahednia

25 OCT 1983

A. ZAHEDNIA
Official Translator
Ministry of Justice

اسدالله زاهدنیا
مترجم رسمی وزارت دادگستری

MY "ALIEN" VIEW of American life, the unusual twist I put on its language, the cultural miscues, often made me question myself. I questioned every decision I made, every hostility or disagreement I encountered. If someone screamed at me, told me off, made derogatory or hateful comments, I didn't respond. *What did I do wrong?* I asked myself. *Did I miscommunicate? Maybe I misread the cultural cues.* If so, the fault was all mine.

I applied the same principle to childrearing, reading continuously about the "best" way, the "American" way to raise my daughters so that they would grow up to be my friends; so that they would want to be with me and to love me forever unconditionally — so that they wouldn't treat me the way I had treated my own mother. So when Lena, my creative daughter, became a teenager and distanced herself from me in order to explore her independence and individuality, I was astonished. Horrified, I turned against myself. I had now come full circle; my daughter was me as a young woman and I had become my mother: a clueless, helpless, even pitiful person. Lessons from Adrienne Rich came back to me. *What had I done to my mother?* I had been my daughter's teacher, showing her that mothers were not needed; mothers should be pushed aside so that their daughters can blossom.

Confused and uncertain about my parenting skills, I craved being back in my own culture for the first time since leaving Iran. I felt as if cutting myself off from everything Iranian had been akin to cutting off my right hand — my writing hand.

## BABA
### *1994, Tel Aviv*

Years went by. Every time I visited my children in America, I called my family in Iran. During one of these phone calls, family members told me that the Ministry of Intelligence had stormed my niece's house, ransacked every room and confiscated the deed to the farm. How would they have known that my niece's husband had hidden the documents for me? What was the use of these papers for anyone in the government? If they had wanted the land, they could have simply possessed it without the paperwork. My niece, her husband and children, and Morad and his family left for the United States shortly after the incident. My brother settled in an expensive neighbourhood in New York.

I heard that the farm was sold to Mr. Haji Safaee Yazdi, who used to supply us with feed for the poultry farm. Feeling a sharp pain in my heart, I wondered who sold the farm. I will never know for certain.

## FARIDEH
### *1994, Baltimore*

In the summer of 1994, my paternal male cousin invited us to his daughter's bat-mitzvah in Maryland. They were Orthodox Jews and the celebration was held on a Sunday night rather than at the usual Saturday services for young men. Norman couldn't go; he had to work the following day. Although I hated to drive alone, especially to an unfamiliar place, I forced myself to make the four-hour trip with my daughters. I needed to reconnect with my culture and my extended family. When I arrived with my daughters, brothers, and sister, the aroma of *gondi* greeted me. My aunt and uncle, the bat-mitzvah girl's grandparents, who had recently arrived from Iran, welcomed us with their comforting Shirazi Jewish accent. Feeling at home, I could remove my invisible mask and not be on guard about my accent and my words that often felt strung upside down in Persian syntax. With a glass of Champagne in hand and the taste of cumin deliciously lodged between my teeth, I saw my uncle, my father's brother-in-law, Zamani, the same man who had gone to Hamedan with Baba to find my mother. After examining each of us, my siblings, me and my daughters, he said, "You're all here because of me." He went on to recount his adventures with Baba, how the two men had seen my mother at someone's house, how they had knocked on my grandmother's door and asked her to give them her thirteen-year-old daughter to take to Shiraz, a day's drive from Hamedan. I had heard the story as my mother told it many times, always ignoring her, always telling her to leave me alone, but Zamani's words were difficult to dismiss. Lena, at fourteen, was older than my mother had been at the time of her marriage.

I felt paralyzed after returning from Baltimore the following day. I woke up, made breakfast for the girls, prepared their lunch, escorted them to their school bus, and crawled back into bed until it was time to cook dinner. After a few weeks of empty days, I saw a pad of paper that was left on the counter. Instinctively, I did what I had done as a girl when I couldn't trust anyone with my frightening thoughts — I wrote. I wrote down Zamani's retelling of my mother's story and hid the pad underneath the cleaning supplies in the garage, the same way I had hidden my diary in a secret space at the bottom of an armoire in Shiraz years ago.

I was embarrassed by my mother's story and ashamed of myself partly because I had to admit that I, too, had embraced my family's attitude. I had accepted that my mother was less of a human being. I didn't want to be associated with her, to become her, and I feared that by retelling my mother's story I would jeopardize not only my own place in society as the wife of a respected physician but also the future of my daughters who would be associated with my parents' "primitive" history. I was betraying my Iranian family by retelling a story that was supposed to remain private, a story that was to be our unspoken secret. At the same time, I felt a sense of relief for the first time in years; I felt as if I had unloaded an unbearably heavy weight. Another week went by before I dug the story out again. I had burned the diary I kept while I was a teenager, fearful that it would be discovered. *Should I destroy this record too?* I took the yellow pad upstairs, sat at my computer, and typed out the words. *What am I doing? Shame — shame!* I thought, but then I gently pushed away my doubts and spilled my uncle's words onto the screen.

"I am like Eliezer in the Torah. I went to find a wife for your father the way Eliezer found Rebecca for Isaac."

In his eyes, Zamani had done holy work. But the Rebecca of the Bible had been asked by her parents and had consented to leave for an unfamiliar land to marry a man she didn't know. No one had consulted my mother. I repeatedly tapped return on the keyboard until there was a wide white space in the middle of Zamani's story, where I inserted my mother's words in italics.

*I begged them not to send me. Please, please, I told my mother. I'll be your servant. Don't send me away.*

I was finally hearing Maman's words. I had feared that getting close to my mother, loving her, could bring about a curse, condemning me to a life similar to hers.

The writing of my mother's story freed me from a deep depression, but the fear lingered. What would my siblings say if they knew that I had exposed us all, betraying a family secret? And Norman? Would he think less of me, think of me as primitive, as his friend had called me? And our daughters? Would they grow up to judge me, their grandmother, and their grandfather? Or would they realize that Baba had been a victim too?

Weeks later, I gave a copy of the story to Norman.

"This shows that you have to write," he said.

I was surprised that he didn't tell me to hide such a hideous story of abuse; I was surprised that he didn't tell me to keep the story secret so as not to stain our family name.

When my sister and brothers visited a few weeks later during Thanksgiving, I gathered all my courage, gave them and each of their spouses a copy, and left the room. Twenty minutes later Norman ran upstairs. "What did you do? Just half an hour ago they were all sitting around, joking and laughing; now everyone's crying."

I went to the dining room expecting to find furious siblings. Instead, they asked if I had other stories. Their spouses especially wanted to know more. I had not been the only one keeping secrets. None of our American spouses knew much about our upbringing, about moments and events that affected us seemingly without a cause. Once I was freed from my darkest story, I could not stop writing.

## BABA
### 2003, Holon

Farideh, my dear daughter, I kiss you from afar. I hope you are
doing well and are in good health. How is the doctor? Please
give him my warm regards. And the children? How are they?
Please kiss them for me and tell them that we miss them. And
your in-laws? How are they? Please give them our best wishes.

I hope you'll forgive me for interfering in your life, but I
am a father and concerned about your safety and well-being.
First, I want to tell you that we are very proud of you for being
a public speaker and a writer. But a word of advice: Be careful
talking or writing about private matters. Your grandmother
is deceased and one has to respect the dead. Please don't talk
or write about her. I had a letter from my sister — a copy is
enclosed — complaining about you. Of course I can't read
the story you wrote since it is in English, but your aunt said
that you lied about your grandmother. Of course, I know you

wouldn't do such a thing, but family can misinterpret your words. Why write anything that might upset people? Just write fiction. See, I am old and talk with the voice of a man who has experienced many things and seen a lot. It's always best not to upset people, especially family.

I really don't know how to tell you this. I don't want to upset you, but you know America is a litigious country. You know better than me since you live there. I hear that Americans sue one another for the most trivial issues. Please be careful. It isn't worth it. Your aunt is upset that you wrote this article and is threatening a lawsuit. What good does it serve to put yourself in jeopardy? You don't want her to sue you and to get you involved in a long and costly legal battle.

Again, I apologize for interfering in your private life. I want what is best for you. Please give the doctor our best and kiss the girls.

Your loving father.

### FARIDEH
*2002–03, Norfolk*

Somehow my *ameh* in New York had seen a copy of "Feathers and Hair," an essay of mine that was published in *ORT Magazine* as a promotional piece for the anthology *The Flying Camel*. She sent a copy to my father. After translating a short section for my father, she indicated that the rest was garbage, too vulgar, too embarrassing to even read. She told Baba that she would sue me if I wrote or spoke about her mother, my grandmother. She had also heard about a conversation I had had with a young cousin and my uncle during Shabbat dinner, telling her that our grandmother had been married off at age nine. My aunt had demanded that *amou*, an elder of the family, stop me from talking. She was now making the same demands of Baba, telling him to stop me from writing. Frightened, Baba begged me to stop.

"You are getting yourself into trouble," he said. "You'll be taken to court; you'll go to prison."

"This is America, Baba. Do you remember your own words? I don't live in Iran." I said angrily, "Let her sue me."

"She is your elder," said my father, ever the voice of conciliation, always asking us to back down from confrontation.

"It's okay, Baba," I said. "She stopped speaking to me decades ago. I have no obligation toward her."

"But ... I want what is best for you. Be discreet."

"Okay, Baba. Don't worry. I'll be okay."

Although I was trying to comfort Baba, I was frightened and had a hard time sleeping through the night. I consulted a lawyer.

"What are you afraid of?" Norman asked, "That she won't be your friend? That she won't speak to you? Let her sue you. How can anyone sue someone over writing about her own dead grandmother?"

When I got over my fears, I was angry, tired of being scrutinized and intimidated by my extended family. I had to write about everything that had happened to us. At the same time I worried about my father's reaction to the stories that spilled onto the page. *What would he do if he knew I had written about him as well?*

In 2003, *Wedding Song*, a compilation of most of the stories I had written, was published. I sent a copy to Niloufar, asking her to explain the story to our parents before they heard about it from other family members. My father was furious that I had written about his marriage to my mother before she reached puberty. He asked Niloufar, "What are my grandchildren going to think of me now?"

I called Israel. Maman picked up the phone. Baba refused to speak to me but his words poured out of my mother's mouth.

"What good is it to write about such private matters?"

The tone of her voice betrayed a certain calm. I had written and published these stories to let her know that I had finally heard her voice. Even though she couldn't read the book,

I had hoped the pictures alone would give her the sense that she was not "nothing," not just another forgotten child-bride. Although my father refused to speak to me for months, my mother's voice was conciliatory, comforting.

I heard indirectly from other relatives in the months that followed. Even distant relatives called my uncle to complain, to explain that the book was comprised of lies that dishonoured not just the family but the entire Shirazi Jewish community. My sister received a call from another *ameh* who demanded that my sister write a letter to a Jewish publication in Los Angeles, denouncing me as a lunatic. I received phone calls and e-mails from others asking me to make revisions to the book and to delete anything that could be remotely related to them. "I fear my children might read this book and believe what you have written," said a cousin I had not spoken to in thirty years. Another cousin called and asked, "Who gave you permission to write about these things?" I tried to ignore the criticism, but it was taking a toll on my body. The anxiety and tension froze my shoulders, a problem I grappled with for over a year. The pain was excruciating, radiating down my arm to my hand, making it impossible to write.

As I was going through physical therapy, rumors circulated in Los Angeles that the book was being translated into Persian. There was another series of uproars, letters to male elders asking them to stop me, an announcement from an aunt that she was going to have a book-burning party in the middle of Santa Monica Boulevard.

Norman laughed. "I love it! I'll make sure that the media shows up. What a great publicity for your book."

Maybe that's the reason I married him. He is my opposite. I need an optimist when I struggle with my demons.

## FARIDEH
### *2005, Tel Aviv*

I went to Israel for a three-day conference at Tel Aviv University in 2005. Baba insisted on accompanying me to the hotel, checking my room, and making sure that I was safe.

"I'm proud of you," he said. "My daughter's expenses are paid to come to Israel to speak at a university. It's an honour for me, too." Then he took the bus back to Holon.

I extended my trip for an extra week to visit family and friends. I told Baba that I was going to Jerusalem on my last day to buy a *talit*, a prayer shawl, for Rachel's fiancé, my son-in-law-to-be.

"You can't go by yourself. I'll go with you."

I wanted to tell him, *Baba, I am fifty-two years old,* but I didn't. Instead, I told him that Menashe Amir, an Iranian radio celebrity, the main broadcaster for the Voice of Israel in Persian, had asked me for an interview while I was in Jerusalem.

"Menashe Amir asked *you* for an interview?" I wasn't sure if he was puzzled, proud, or concerned.

"Farideh," he said after a long pause. "You wrote a book about our lives in Iran and now the entire family is upset. You spoke in Israel; I didn't ask what you were going to talk about." He chewed on a pencil, a habit of his when he is nervous. "Farideh, I can't tell you what to do, but people in Shiraz don't need to know about our family affairs."

I was hesitant about the interview as well. I wasn't sure if I had a scholar's command of Persian. Even though I had finished four years of college in Iran, I have never given a talk in Persian. Not unlike other Iranians who have lived abroad since the Revolution and have not been able to return, English has become my intellectual language.

ON THAT TRIP to Israel, I had hoped to find a dress for Rachel's wedding in August. I asked an Israeli friend, Shanit, to go shopping with me. I invited Niloufar to join us as well. "I can't," she said. "We're designing a new software program. I'm behind schedule as it is."

I didn't ask my mother because she buys cheap dresses from small shops and kiosks in Holon. I didn't want to embarrass her by spending more money than she would on herself; I didn't want to embarrass myself by walking into a nice shop with her dressed in mismatched, poorly fitting pants and tops, dragging her heavy shoes on the marble floors, touching expensive dresses with her calloused hands, asking inappropriate questions in poor Hebrew.

After looking at a few shops, we were strolling down Dizengof with Shanit, searching for a cozy café to have a leisurely lunch of Israeli salads and limeade with fresh mint when Niloufar called.

"Baba's in the hospital. He was having heart palpitations when shopping for groceries. He took a taxi to the hospital."

*Oh, my God*. I thought. He was nervous about the interview. *Is it my fault*? "Did he have a heart attack?" I asked.

"I don't know. I don't think so. Where are you? I'll pick you up."

Fifteen minutes later, Neli double-parked her green Renault on the busy street and got out of the car, her long soft curls pulled back in a ponytail. In her casual work environment, Neli wore jeans and a white tank top.

Oblivious to the blasting horns of impatient Israelis on the congested street, she screamed, "Farideh," rolling the "r" in my name as Israelis do, "Hurry up!"

Dodging mopeds and bicycles, I ran toward her, turning to wave to Shanit, who had taken the day off to be with me. I raised my voice over the crowd, "*Shalom, Lehitraot*, see you later, sorry." She stood on the sidewalk, dressed impeccably in khaki capri pants, a black tank top, and dark sunglasses. She ran her hand through her short blond highlighted hair.

"Let me know," she said.


I HAD ALWAYS assumed that Israeli medical care was superb. But Wolfson Hospital reminded me of an old institution where my great-uncle was kept before his death some forty years earlier in Shiraz. Niloufar and I took rapid steps to reach our father's bedside on the upper floor. In the narrow hallway we had to stop for an unshaven patient in a wheelchair to pass. Wearing his light blue hospital gown, his IV and oxygen tank hooked up to his chair, he puffed on a cigarette, blatantly disregarding a large sign that forbade smoking in the hospital hallways. Nurses passed by him without comment.

We found Baba in a large room along with six other men. They were resting on old-fashioned metal beds. The bare walls intersected with dingy colourless floors. This was not the Hadassah Hospital — whose glossy colour photographs were displayed at high-profile conventions — that dealt with the most complicated medical cases, that catered to Arabs and Jews alike. I recognized immediately that this hospital catered to poor immigrants, and inadequately trained doctors practiced on obedient *Mizrakhim*, Eastern Jews.

I wasn't sure how to behave in the presence of these other men in the room, there were no curtains, no privacy. The pajamas worn by the patients reminded me of the blue prison uniforms given to the thirteen Iranian Jews from Shiraz who had been arrested on charges of spying for Israel in 1999. My father had taped a propaganda piece from Iranian TV on the subject. I remember the prisoners marching into a large room to consult with their lawyers, supposedly to show the fairness of the Iranian justice system.

Maman, who had taken a taxi to the hospital, stood awkwardly by the wall. Niloufar sat on the bed next to Baba. Their eyes were identical, almond-shaped, the deep colour of well-steeped tea. I didn't know what to do. I didn't speak Hebrew so I left Neli in charge of communicating with the hospital staff.

There were no doctors in sight; the nurses smiled but they didn't know much about my father's condition.

Baba told us about each patient. "Are you going to Jerusalem tomorrow?" he asked me.

"Yes, but I don't think I'll have time for the interview."

He nodded. "You shouldn't go alone. Ask your uncle Shemuel to take you."

"It's okay, Baba. I'll take a taxi."

"A taxi? All by yourself? You'll get lost."

"Don't worry, Baba."

"So expensive! I would've taken you by bus."

"It's fifty dollars. It's worth it for me since I have so little time left here."

"What if they don't take dollars? Do you have any *shekalim*?"

"I do, Baba. Most of them take dollars, too."

"How will you get home?"

"Another taxi."

"What if no taxi agrees to bring you back to Holon? What if they don't know how to get to Holon from Jerusalem?"

"I'll be okay. I've got a phone. I'll call you."

"Be careful which taxi you get into. Don't take an Arab taxi. Terrible things have happened."

"I promise I'll be careful."

Maman broke off the discussion. Wearing a pair of black cotton pants that she had sewn by hand, the elastic waistband stretching over her protruding belly, grease stains on one knee. She had rushed to the hospital from the kitchen, where she left half-cooked okra stew and steaming basmati rice on the stove. Like me, she doesn't like to wear aprons; our shirts, skirts, and pants often carry the flavours and colours of our kitchens, especially the orange of turmeric.

"I'll bring you dinner," my mother told Baba. "What should I cook for you?" As always, she used "*shoma*," the formal plural "you," to address him.

"*Khoob paziraee mikonan*," Baba refused her offer. "The food here is great."

"I can braise a young chicken without the skin for you."

"There is no need."

"What about a few boiled eggs and potatoes?"

"No, *lazem nist*." It isn't necessary, he said.

I didn't know if Baba was refusing the food in the customary Iranian way but expecting it nonetheless. Iranians love indirectness and deference. Maybe Baba enjoyed being served in bed by the hospital's friendly staff, their kindness and smiles compensating for the ward's lack of modern medical supplies and expertise.

Later in the car, Maman said, "Maybe I should make the chicken and take it to him anyway."

"Maman, there is no need. He said, No."

"Maybe he doesn't mean it. He'll be mad at me later."

Niloufar whispered in my ear that during a previous visit Baba told her that he loved the hospital's sweet hot cereal, cooked with whole milk, something he would have never included in his stringent diet of no fat and no sugar. Maybe he loved it too because like the colourless, scratchy, threadbare towels he had brought with him from Iran, the hospital reminded him of something soothingly familiar, of the country that he had left behind physically but not emotionally.

Maman, Niloufar, and I returned to my parents' ghetto-like apartment compound for a lunch of pita and *mast-o-khiar*, plain yogourt mixed with grated cucumbers and mint. Maman made tea. I was too restless to sip tea, to munch on roasted almonds and pistachios. In a few weeks my parents would finally move to a newly built apartment. It was a good time to discard old stuff.

I am good at breaking away from the past, the old. I attacked Baba's closet first. I gathered up torn shirts, stained pants, and worn-out socks that Baba had brought from Iran decades earlier and kept close to his skin because they still carried the scent and the feel of Iran. I threw the old scratchy towels on top of the heap and placed them on a faded sheet — another Iranian relic — crossed the opposite corners, the way my grandmother and so many other women had done in Iran, and tied them together. I put the bundle in the hallway to be taken to the dumpster — I needed to cleanse this place of our Iranian past.

Maman kept saying, "Oh, he'll be so upset. Your father won't like this. What I am going to tell him?"

My mother has never uttered our father's name, Esghel, an Iranian version of an old-fashioned Hebrew name, Yehezkel, Ezekiel.

"Tell Baba it was me. Tell him Farideh did it. Tell him you couldn't stop me."

I wiped and restocked the drawers with the unopened packages I had brought from America years ago: socks, undershirts, pants with the price tag still attached, and soft fluffy towels. To the trash pile I added two rickety counter chairs on wheels, their once white synthetic stuffing poking through the rips in the faded brown vinyl. The first time I saw Baba pulling himself up on one to reach the storage area high above the kitchen cabinets, I screamed at him. "Are you crazy? You're an old man. You'll fall and break your neck."

He had smiled and said, "Don't worry, dear. I do this all the time. I have fallen, too — not a big deal."

I DRAGGED THOSE chairs, bumping against each stair, to the first floor and across the street, but recuperating from frozen shoulders, I couldn't lift the stools high enough to throw them into the dumpster.

Baba returned home from the hospital while I was in Jerusalem, but he didn't mention the missing items. I left for the United States two days later, and as I was loading my luggage into Niloufar's car I noticed one of the chairs peeking out from behind the shrubs where I had hidden them. Such trash, even the poor had not taken them.

## FARIDEH
### *2006, Norfolk*

My parents visited the United States in August of 2006 for Rachel's wedding. Baba and I had reached a comfortable place in our turbulent relationship. I visited my parents once a year in Israel and I tried to be respectful of my father and kind to my mother.

Before the wedding I asked Navideh, whose father was well-versed in Persian poetry, to suggest a poem to read to my father during the reception, something that acknowledged his pain and suffering, something indirect, beautiful, the way he liked it. The poem brought tears to Baba's eyes.

The day after the wedding I stood beside my brother's car waiting for Baba to get in the car to drive back to Philadelphia. My brother's children were getting restless. Baba didn't want to say goodbye. I hugged him.

"Baba, go. You know that I'll come to Israel to see you." Baba gave me his memoir. "I'll take care of it. I'll translate it," I reassured him. "Go in peace, Baba."

I SKYPED MY parents shortly after their return to Israel.

"You wouldn't believe what happened," my mother said, "Your father stood on a stool to put the suitcases away and fell over the computer desk, *khoda kheili rahmesh kard*, God was merciful to him. He could have broken his head."

"Stool? Which stool?" I asked.

"Don't you know your father? He brought back the stools — the ones you threw away. I told you it wouldn't work."

AGGRAVATED BY MY housekeeping, Baba had rolled the stools back to the apartment and, unable to carry them up to the fourth floor himself, he had hidden them underneath the stairway, next to the opening of the apartment's bomb shelter. When they moved to the new place, he had the stools moved as well. I was furious.

"Let me talk to Baba."

I watched my father on the computer monitor, limping, hugging a wall, then holding onto the corner of the table. He probably expected sympathy and loving words from me.

"Baba, why? Didn't I tell you not to? I can't believe you took that piece of trash to your new apartment."

I was breaking a promise I had made to myself to avoid being outspoken with my father in order to improve our relationship.

The two men in my life pulled me in opposite directions.

Norman chastised me for speaking too softly. "I can't hear you. Speak up." He teased me when I used my own indirect ways, "Norman, would you like tea?" he would answer, "Oh, you mean can *I* make you tea? Why don't you just ask the question directly? You and your Iranian ways." Living with Norman,

I had adopted some of his habits. I had become more assertive.

Baba, in contrast, stopped in his tracks whenever I acted "American." He looked down and bit his lower lip, controlling his disappointment and anger. To keep the peace with my father I learned to defer to him, "Baba, you are my elder. You have more experience. You are a better judge of these issues."

But I hadn't been able to control my reaction this time. Sitting in front of the computer camcorder, my father, surprised at my outburst, paused for a few minutes and then chose to ignore my indiscretion, "Don't worry, dear," he said. "I'll be okay."

Even more infuriated, I raised my voice even more. "I'm not so worried about *you*," I tried to convey the consequences of his stubbornness. "I'm worried about Maman."

I felt his disappointment and puzzlement through the fuzzy computer screen.

"Do you ever think of your wife? She isn't so young either. Now she has to take care of you with her own bad back."

My father turned his back to me without uttering a word. His image faded as he walked away, disappearing from the computer screen. That was our last conversation.

THE FALL FROM the stool marked the beginning of the end for Baba. Health-conscious, he took daily brisk walks from Holon to Kiriat Sharet or even Jaffa. On bed rest to recuperate from his back injury, he found it difficult to cough up the phlegm from his scarred lungs — lungs damaged by the gold dust that had floated in the air of his jewellery workshop, by the chemicals from the silo at the poultry farm, and from years of smoking.

A few days later, I Skyped my parents again at 2:00 in the afternoon. Maman usually spent her afternoons at the *moadon*, the senior's recreation centre, where she learned to crochet and to speak better Hebrew, though really just to get out of the apartment. I expected to catch Baba alone and to force him to talk to me. Instead, my mother's face appeared on the screen. Her eyes looked puffy, her curly hair unkempt. I wasn't sure if the transmission was poor or if I had just woken her up. She had a habit of nodding off on the sofa.

"Your father isn't feeling good," she said. "He coughs a lot." Another bout of pneumonia, I thought.

"Let me talk to him."

Maman turned the camcorder. From the farthest reach of the screen the camera transmitted the image of Baba's emaciated body curled up on the bed. I heard Maman ask. "It's Farideh. Do you want to talk?"

Maman turned the camera around. "No, he doesn't."

I assumed that he was punishing me with his silence, a tactic of mine as well. I knew that he thought I had abandoned him, that I had been callous and disrespectful when he was hurting.

"Do you want me to come to Israel?" I asked Maman.

I heard her repeat the question to my father.

"No," a muffled voice whimpered in the background.

"It's old age," Maman said. "This is the way it is. You don't need to come."

Their Skype connection, often left on continuously, went dead after that conversation and remained that way.

FOUR MONTHS LATER Niloufar called me. "Baba *mord*," she said in her halting Farsi.

"What do you mean?" I responded. "What do you mean? I repeated.

She had to say it again in Farsi, and one more time in English, and that's when I believed her.

## BABA

*December 2006, Holon*

In closing, *kha'am budam, pokhteh shodam, sukhtam*. I was raw; I cooked; I burned.

I WAS ONCE young, hard-working, and selfless. In my old age, as I hear my father's voice calling me from the grave, I look back on my life and I wonder. Why did I make myself responsible for the lives and the well-being of the entire family? Why didn't I go out on my own? Why didn't I make my own fortune, taking care of my own wife and children? What was the good? I am trying not to be bitter. I do love my siblings whom I raised and their children, but what do I receive now in my old age from them? Maybe a phone call once or twice a year — maybe not even that. What did I receive from sheltering a young brother, keeping him off the streets, sharing with him my ideas, my livelihood, my business? He stole from me — from my children's mouths. I don't know. I don't know.

TO MY CHILDREN, I love you. I pray to God that you and your families might be granted good lives, happy lives — that you may never experience my sufferings or my sorrows.